N.B.

Second edition, April 2016

Copyright © 2015 by Charlotte Shane.
All rights reserved.

ISBN: 978-0-9970444-3-0

For more information visit www.charlotteshane.com

N.B.

WRITING FROM 2008 - 2013

CHARLOTTE SHANE

Nightmare Brunette was the URL chosen on a whim for the blog I started in 2008. It ran through May of 2013. Later that year, I deleted it.

Much of the writing saved from that time is included in these pages. I was lonely and isolated, so I wrote a lot.

The first section is taken from my text-only blog, and the second is comprised of shorter pieces posted on my tumblr. One reads more like a journal and the other like a notebook. I included both here because it felt untrue to choose one over the other.

I didn't save my tumblr writing with dates, but it's ordered chronologically. When dates weren't available for a blog post, I tried to estimate where it most likely fell among the other entries.

CONTENTS

Volume I

2008	*3*
2009	*13*
2010	*141*
2011	*205*
2012	*233*
2013	*255*

Volume II	*265*

VOLUME
I

2008

VOLUME I

One Good Story
March 28, 2008

I walked to his window at a red light and asked if he would take me to the Clift. I was wearing a cardigan, jeans, a big deal designer bag, sunglasses to soften the unfamiliar city.

"Working or staying?" He asked. He had white hair and an air of relaxation about him that suggested we were familiar to one another.

"Staying," I replied.

He asked where I was from, kept pressing me for what I did. I was obtuse, bratty, stubborn in insisting that I did nothing, was visiting for no reason. He told me I needed to fall in love with something and then everything else would be easy. But I knew that already, and what's left to say about middle aged men trying to impart wisdom to younger women? We talked about Lacan because when not driving taxis, he was a professor. He saw who was waiting for me when we pulled up at the front doors, and that made me uncomfortable, like what he saw explained everything.

Later that night, the DJ played Daft Punk and Khia, A Ha and vintage Snoop, to a pack of inexplicably pleasant, dancing people. My breasts pushed up to the edge of my square neckline with lace and boning and the need to always be leaning forward, to speak, to hear, to avoid a stranger's drink. I changed my pantyhose in the beer closet with Maddie after a small man tried to keep me out by holding his hand against the door as I pulled the knob. The ease with which it opened after he took his hand away seemed miraculous to me at the time. It was unbelievable so little effort could keep me from doing what I want. Of course, I had a considerable amount of alcohol in me by then.

In the girl's bathroom after the bar closed, the man who'd spent at least fifteen minutes telling me about his fabulous wife guided two keyfuls, one after the other, to my nose, wiped the excess off tenderly with his thumb, and asked, "Can we just stay here and make out for a minute?"

Without a hint of self-consciousness: "Can I just respect your beauty?"

I said, "Hmm . . . How about we just hug?"

I threw my body against his, he was taller than me, which is so rare, and I was happy. Maddie came in and the man left, and the bartender who invited us to stay late moved to smell my neck, but I fell away laughing and embarrassed that I was so wholly unable to control my body's reactions. He looked like he had come to life after someone fashioned him as a talisman, sprung into being with all his power intact and concentrated behind his eyes, which would have once been flecks of onyx, or coal, or something black and from the earth.

His room was full of long coats and taxidermied small animals. He fed Maddie and I tea, and the next night we saw his band play. They were very good and he kissed me on the cheek when they were done.

It May Be Another False Start
July 13, 2008

So here's the dilemma: you're a sex worker, current or former, and you're being honest about your life, which is as complex and flawed and rich as every other human being's. Within this context, your honesty becomes a weapon to be used against you and against women who are friends of yours, other women you respect, even women you don't know but who are laboring under enough stigma that they don't need to be burdened with more.

You snort coke for the first time in three years and you're a drug addict. You have bad sex with your boyfriend and it's a sign that you're permanently ruined for relationships. You wish your hips were narrower and it's proof you learned to hate yourself because you use your body to make money.

I wasn't sure I wanted to do this again, but here I am. Let's see what comes of it.

"I'm Red Riding Hood And You're The Big Bad Wolf"
August 10 2008

Last Tango In Paris is not a sexy movie. The sex is aggressively anti-erotic. It's born of frustration, energetic but devoid of chemistry. Paul is passionate only in grief, not lust for Jeanne's body or for the pleasure it might give him. He has sex to obliterate the moment.

There's an intimacy that sex can facilitate but which sex itself may not always—may never—replicate. My first real sex was with a man twice my age. He was my first regular partner, the first man I orgasmed with, the first etc., etc. The first person with whom I built a sex life. What you're suspecting is true; I did not have a strong father figure in my life as a child. I wanted a father figure, and I wanted him to fuck me. I still want it. I may never stop.

Jeanne says, "I feel like a child here," and it's not because Paul cares for her in any practical way. He doesn't. But he welcomes her childishness and he answers it with his own, which is the greatest proof of acceptance. This is not childishness in the sense of pettiness or selfishness, of course, but childishness as in lack of ego, exuberance, innocence. When she gives a loud, mangled, animal sound as her name, he asks her to repeat it and then he repeats it, until they've dissolved into howling and barking in one another's arms. In my older lover's presence, I made noises to express everything, in bed and out, whimpers and mews and growls. I think it came from a desire to be preverbal. Preverbal but still understood, and loved.

Sex is often idle and it can be ugly. It can be pointedly cruel, and I do not mean forced but rather used as a weapon within a partner's consent. Jeanne never turns down Paul. Even during the infamous anal scene, when she says, "No," it's as much to what he is telling her as to what he is physically doing. She doesn't have the conviction to deny him, even if she intuits she ought to protest. The intimacy forged is larger than either of them. It's a dynamic she could never control and can't escape, which is why the movie ends as it does. What happens when someone has seen you at your most unselfconscious, not merely opened, but with layers and layers of yourself peeled down and curled back around themselves? It's debasement in its purest form. You're reduced to the truth of who you are.

Even if they forget what they saw, you never will forget you showed it to them. And you will never be the same.

Return
December 2, 2008

He said, "X is going to the Taj tomorrow. He's going to have the military bring him our things."

I said, "You're bribing them."

"Yes." He coughed. He didn't want to talk about it.

"They're keeping the cash in the room?"

"No. Something else. Don't worry about it."

"But I want to know." I couldn't think of what one would bribe with besides money. "Are you giving them women?"

He laughed obligatorily. "Yes, it's women."

It's probably best I stop thinking about it.

We left late for the party. If we had left on time, we would have been in the lobby when the gunmen came in. If we had stayed later, we might have left and encountered the terrorists, or realized what was happening and not left, and tried to wait it out in the room. A CEO of an Indian bank, among others, was found dead on the 19th floor. That was where we were. There were no blasts in our tower but I keep asking myself, "If the room was on fire, could I have jumped?" It's easy to imagine all the ways you could have died and far more difficult to imagine any other ways to have stayed alive.

In my dreams, the people I love are in more danger than I am, although I'm always the one being shot at. In reality I was not shot at and in reality, the people I love were untouched in another country.

I didn't feel it right away, the desire to fuck until I fall apart. That's the cliché, it's what I was waiting for: frantic fucking in a stranger's son's bed like it was up to us to repopulate the world. And it's true on the first night we kissed like we needed to take the other in whole, but we stopped there. I held his hard on as we fell asleep and mostly I felt nothing at any time, not even boredom. I may have finally been taught patience. Twenty four hours of house arrest, six hours at the consulate, eleven at the airport, sixteen on planes. I could sit anywhere. I could be empty anywhere. I spent days without a book or a pen or paper—things I have not been without since I became literate.

I did find many strangers sexy throughout it all. Everyone looked eligible, including other women in their days-old clothes. But this indiscriminate hunger came later, the sense that I could clear-cut any swath of men, that I could summon and fell anyone near me on the train or the street. I was already a perpetual yes before. I could look at someone and know sex with you would not be good. It would be awkward and unfulfilling and you would get emotional, but I'd do it anyway and I would get wet and I would be right.

That was the place I was in before. What place am I in now?

Sweet
December 11, 2008

I loved the FBI men. I didn't want them to leave. It's ok if it was brainwashing; it was magnificent. I want us to all go out to lunch once a week. I want to be an honorary agent. That happens in movies, doesn't it? They take you on because you lived your life on the bad side, which makes you better at being good.

> I've been getting an influx of emails from clients:
> *Hello! Can I see you soon? I miss you!*
> *Let me know what day is good for you and I will take care of the rest.*
> *Miss you . . . again . . . miss you and want to know about your trip.*
> *Despite the economic environment, I have been thinking about you lately*
. . . and so on.

One man sends me pictures of his (grown) children and updates me on their accomplishments. His daughter is an increasingly popular photographer whose work consists of naked people with their heads hidden. I believe some are self-portraits.

He himself is a cheerful, baby-faced fifty year old who likes feet and smokes pot. He runs what is essentially a den for Republicans and has a beautiful home with a beautiful view of the river.

Quite a few clients have shared their families with me in one way or another. When I worked on webcam, a long time regular once called his sister into his room during a session. He had me train the camera on my face, away from my mostly nude body. He handed her the phone. I asked her how school was and how her assignments were coming along. I told her I had heard a lot about her because I had. She said, "I've heard a lot about you."

I know it's easy to mock or pathologize that. It's easier to insult it or marginalize the impulse than to consider what circumstances made that choice palatable. He had his kid sister talk to a naked stranger whom he pays by the minute for masturbation. Why would he do that? I think you know.

I used to pride myself on "never getting lonely." It took me a decade to realize that this was true only because the loneliness was there all the time like a film on my skin. It wasn't something that needed to be brought on or achieved. I thought I was immune because I spent so much time alone by choice. But it's excruciating to be around vulnerable people and unbearable to be around anyone else. Being alone is just hiding, and sometimes it's horrible.

Thanks for asking about my family. David is back from Iraq, we are so happy to have him home safe and sound.

Last week I met with a man I hadn't seen in a year. He cradled to me his chest and called me precious. He said, "I don't know why I like you so much."
Don't you? I do. It's because I am here with you.

Generational Porn
December 25, 2008

My grandfather is like a Muslim Hugh Hefner. He's always dated and married younger women. His second wife was his barely legal second cousin. His third wife was the girl whose life he'd ruined decades earlier when she was only eighteen, shaming her through her illegitimate pregnancy and the subsequent leave taken from study abroad in America. He was married to my birth grandmother at the time; she died of a brain tumor after bearing him four children in as many years.

He wears only pajamas when he is entertaining at his home which is a right the elderly have earned. Although he's never physically hurt me, he has beaten his wives, his pets, and committed other wrongs against those close to him that I don't want to write about here. About a week ago, I had a dream that he was forcing himself on me while I cried. He was trying to get me pregnant.

During a recent family lunch, I was sent to replace the tango CD with gypsy music, and I took the time in his office to browse his porn collection. The best pieces are kept on display in a perpetually open closet next to a sofa and an end table supporting only a lamp and a pump bottle of Jergens lotion. At this point, seeing the sleaziest DVD among his things would not surprise me, but I had not expected *Shortbus*, *Lie With Me*, and Susie Bright's series.

As we were driving away, I told my brother, "I claim the porn collection."

He said, "You've told me that before."

My grandfather's sexuality has manifested itself in many ugly ways, so it's strange to want any artifacts of his libido. But some part of me also wants to rescue and redeem them. I don't blame porn, and the implications of dirty pictures change when in the home of a young woman as opposed to the closet of a man in his seventies. What seemed threatening becomes sexy. Acceptable.

I keep my smut in shelves and on coffee tables in common areas. No one would take my collection to be a testament to cruelty. I'm not only allowed to enjoy porn, I can use images that turn me on as a positive representation of my personality. I know few men can say the same.

2009

Sexual Jealousy
January 8, 2009

I'm curious about all things but about sex above all. I want to know how people behave during and after: how they move and the noises they make, when and why they come, what they say when the clothes are back on, what they text two days later. My ego is there, too. I want to know how they come with me, what they say to me, how they touch me. Even when it's bad, I'm not necessarily unhappy or even deterred from doing it again. Experiments don't really go wrong, they only yield disappointing results. You can always try again.

When I hear stories of sex other people have had, I become disconcertingly jealous. Even if it was bad for both of them. Even if it was good for them but is not something that would turn me on. I still want it. I want to be a part of every potential sexual act and circumstance.

Someone told me once that having sex with me sometimes felt like being with an anthropologist in the field. He was amused by this so it was not an insult. Besides, the novelty with which I regarded sex meant we had it multiple times a day, as many times as I wanted, or rather as many times as he could stand. The capacity for observation to the detriment of participation is not unique to sex for me, and sex is where I've probably improved upon it the most. I think it's common to many writers, or those who would be writers.

Because greed is about quantity and not quality, my excessive appetite for sex is not powered by lust exclusively although that often, obviously, plays a part. I almost wish my promiscuity were borne solely out of momentary, overwhelming desire. Sometimes it has been. But the fact that it is often purposeful, almost intellectual, seems to make it even more indefensible. Although I haven't figured out yet if non-monogamy needs defending. I only know that, sometimes, the idea of being on the end of someone else's profligacy makes me sad.

Control

"What are those?" I asked. I knew, but I wanted to hear it. I was wearing suspender pantyhose, the kind that leave your thighs and crotch bare. I felt the air under my skirt as we walked.

"Bulletproof. Shields, in case some crazy person comes out of the metro shooting. All of the windows are blast proof."

"Blast proof," I repeated, scanning the face, imagining slow motion footage of those imploded buildings with that leisurely, thudding impact, smoke billowing out.

When he closed the door behind us, I said, "I can't believe you're willing to lose your job for this. Would you lose your job?"

He shook his head, but he wasn't listening. He was taking off his suit jacket. When he met me at the entrance, I noticed the gray in his hair for the first time.

I asked if the war room looks like it does in Dr. Strangelove. I asked if there were maps and he said there were digital screens. I gripped the sink with both hands, bent over. I didn't look at our faces in the mirror. I looked at the black stockings and my skin. I tried not to make noise but I couldn't help it.

He made noise. He whispered to me the entire time.

On his lap, I leaned back and watched my patch of pubic hair move up and down. There was a faint pink stain on his white shirttail. I couldn't think of what it was from until I saw the bright ring of blood at the base of his cock.

"Oh baby," he groaned. I held the handicap bar behind his head. "You're going to make me come. You're so beautiful. Oh . . . "

Afterward, I wet a paper towel and tried to wipe it away. It was stuck on the underside and I didn't want to rub too roughly.

"It won't come off." I was still trembling. Sex with him involves so much adrenaline, and it starts before he's even inside. It's like he's caught me wild, escaping from a fire. Like I'm trying to run from him before he fucks me.

"It doesn't matter, sweetie. I'm going right home." I passed him dry paper towels and he wiped his hands.

"Does that always happen?" I'd asked him this before.

"Not always. Normally. We go really deep. And you're so skinny. I think you're skinnier than me."

"I'm not." I said.

He wrapped me in his arms and I ran my hands over his back, then up to his head. His hair was soft and short in my fingers. I kept trying to slow my breath. I wanted to lie down with him. He kissed my cheek and my neck, held me patiently. I didn't want to be that girl, using sex for affection. But I wanted so much affection from him. I was that girl. Did he know it? Is that what he was thinking? He has a daughter, a very young daughter. What would he think of his daughter someday bleeding on an older man's cock?

He asked me my real name. I'd promised I would tell him and I did.

"Oh Baby, that's a beautiful name," he said, as though I didn't think so.

On the escalator, he let his hand drift down my arm and pause over my fingers. He looked at me with that faint smile.

"There are a lot of hot women here," he said, and I thought he was joking, but then a petite brunette in a pink shirt walked by.

"She was hot." I murmured.

"She was. I liked her sweater. It looked so soft."

I stared out the windows as we passed. The trees in the courtyard were covered with snow. Nothing was coming from the sky.

"But not like you," he said, low. Men and women in wool coats moved around us. So much black and gray.

"Nobody here is like you. I fantasize about you all the time . . . "

"How many years in the army were spent at Telling Women What They Want To Hear boot camp?"

He laughed. "They don't teach that. That sounds like something you'd learn in law school."

I have to believe he's playing a game. I tell myself: *This is not a real connection. You are a foolish girl. You are easily taken in by men who know what they're doing.* But I don't know if he knows what he's doing. I only know that I don't.

Sunday

He pulled out and it laid wet and shrinking against his thigh. His pelvis was smeared with pink.

"I've never seen you soft before."

"Women tell me this is what most guys are like when they're hard."

"You're still bigger. A little thicker." I wrapped my fingers around it, holding him. It hardly looks real when he's hard. "I was hoping I wouldn't bleed this time."

There were crimson patches on his white duvet because we hadn't bothered to pull it back. Every time he came at me I spread wider, lifting my knee over his shoulder or dropping my collarbones to the bed to lift my ass in the air. Raw inside and still hungry for it. When I came the second time I said his name. I knew he'd like that. So then he tried it with mine. He'd never said my name in front of me.

"Me too, baby. But you're little. All the small women I've been with bleed. Or if they don't, I know they've had some really big dicks."

I thought I'd had big too, until I was with him. It wasn't his girth, it was his length and his head, which was huge, as though intended for battering women into submission. I was afraid forcing it through my throat would hurt him, so I didn't try.

I ran my hand over his chest down to his stomach. "Why did you shave all this?"

"I thought you'd want me to."

I laughed. "Why would I want that?" I touched his armpit. "I like your hair here." It was dark, not long but thick. Not curly. "Were you going to shave this too? And your legs?"

"I considered it."

"Don't. Stop shaving." When I was first with a woman, it was for an audience. She rolled over and presented her ass to me, exactly the type of tan bubble ass you'd expect on a 5' tall white-blonde with fake nails and a shaved pussy. And in the deep cleft of her round cheeks there was a thatch of silky black hair, like a secret even she didn't know.

He washed me in the shower, gently, as though the lather was abrasive. He handed me his towel and went for another one. And then he dripped dry on his mat, watching as I stood in and he stood out. I felt used inside but it didn't hurt.

In the car, he kept turning his head to look at me.

"I'm crazy about you," he said.

"I don't think so."

"Oh you don't? You don't believe me?"

I smiled. His hand was in mine, and I squeezed it.

Overnight

In the car, he stared. And again when I crouched in my shirt and panties digging for lotion; in the morning shower, washing off my makeup from the night before; as we crossed the street holding hands to get lunch; "I want to know you. I want to be your best friend. I've never liked looking at anyone as much as I like looking at you."

He showed me his badges from the 2005 inauguration, back when he was all flattop hair cut and broad shoulders. He looked younger and thicker. He'd been a father for two years and was about to leave the military. I was twenty-two, done with grad school, living in a different city alone in a two-bedroom apartment.

Now I'd learned to defend myself from his thrusts by squeezing against them, angling my hips or just putting my hands on his thighs to push back. But there will still moments where he plowed into my cervix and I cried out, expecting red. While the light bled between the blinds, he pulled me to the edge of the bed. I splayed my bent legs, the inside of my knees flat against the mattress, and here he managed to fit it all. For once I felt the pressure of his pubic bone against mine and I clenched my fists full of dirtied fabric and smiled into the cloth. It had gone from good to perfect.

"Did you hear me?" he asked when I woke. "Sometimes I talk in my sleep."

"Oh? What were you saying?"

"Something I didn't want you to hear. Something I don't think we're ready for yet."

I lied, "I didn't hear anything."

Us
February 12, 2009

"What do you want out of this?" He'd asked me so many times. I could never answer. "Besides sex?"

Tonight I finally replied, "It doesn't matter what I want. It's already here. We can't change it. We can't do just sex. It's either this or it's nothing."

The city night around us, black punctuated by neon. Wild wind and girls in dresses. I was late.

"Thank you for saying that," he said.

I took his face in my hands. "This is horrible," I said, and kissed him.

He'd fucked me hours earlier on the high counter in a family bathroom. Took my jeans down to my ankles and then lifted my feet to slide my thighs down over his body. I held the backs of my knees to get the best angle. It felt so good. Sometimes that's all I can think to say about sex with him. It felt so good. Someone pounded on the door. He flipped his tie over his shoulder. It was red.

Days before, in bed, he asked, "Are you like this with every guy you sleep with?"

I didn't answer because I knew he wouldn't like the truth. Which is yes. Sometimes. Often. I touch their faces. I push my mouth against their necks. I fall asleep on their chests. I stroke their hair, always.

The silence made him restless. He came on my face, then lifted my leg and fucked me for a few strokes, pulled out and came more. It was heavy on my eyelids, streaked through my hair. I wiped my face with the top sheet.

He was kneeling over me, his cock still hard. "It has to be just sex between us. Just business."

"Ok."

"That means no more touching my hair."

"Oh. Ok."

When he lifted his chin in a kiss request, I said, "If there's no hair touching, there's none of that either."

"Right. Just business."

"It can't be business if neither of us is making any money."

"We'll film it."

When I tried to sleep away from him, he pulled the length of my body against his. It never takes, no matter how hard we try. But we don't try very hard.

When we first laid down together, he cupped my pubic bone, splaying his long fingers down over my lips.

"You don't know what you do to me."

He said, sliding one finger inside. I arched against it. "I crave you." He slid in another. "I crave you."

"I don't want this to end," he'd said every time in the car, in his bed.

"I love you," he said in the bathroom before opening the door.

Away

This city used to be vibrant and amnesia inducing, but it's become dull. It wears its sadness on the surface now; I've never realized how sick the people here look. The tone is that of a perpetual come down, of gazing out into a gray dawn from the passenger seat of a car in a Pizza Hut parking lot. Rather than feeling plunged into something hot and shiny so I can come out brighter and better, I feel flattened.

My life looks funny from a distance. Decisions I thought were important seem now to matter less. Everything becomes diluted, easy to give up. So of course from this distance he and I keep trying to end it, but, without fail, when one pushes the other pulls. It's stressful and boring in the intellectual sense. Stomach-wringing in the emotional. But isn't that the way it always is? Heart and brain stranded from one another, not even glancing across the divide.

One night as we lay in bed talking, he said to me, "I think I've conquered sex, as a man." He meant that the quest for sex didn't haunt him like it used to because he didn't doubt his power to have it when he wanted, and so he didn't have it for his ego. He spoke of needing sex in an almost impatient, dismissive way, like he didn't find his id's demands particularly interesting.

During this same conversation, he told me he often felt used because of his cock, objectified (although he didn't use that word,) and he worried that was where my interest in him began and ended. He said a cheerleader called him in high school because she'd heard about his size, and asked him to come over.

"What if a guy was really cute," he asked me, "but had a really small penis?"

I thought on it, but he interrupted. "I mean really small."

I braced myself.

"Like . . . " He indicated about five inches, and I laughed for a long time.

Another man told me something similar when I made a joke about him being proud that he's been with so many people.

"Sex is easy," he said. "It doesn't mean anything to get someone to have sex with you."

I understood what he meant, in a way. I remember once in high school watching a group of kids roughhousing during lunch. They were the ones who spoke a little too loudly, were too skinny or too fat, took classes at a remedial level. They were, in other words, utterly unappealing to most privileged adolescents. One boy and girl, clearly a couple, were physical with each another in a way I'd never seen: oblivious, animal. For the first time in my life, I thought, no one has to be perfect to have sex. It was a revelatory moment on par with the one that caused me to abandon my father's religion. I had evidence that sex is not something anyone has to earn. And so it's not an affirmation of worth.

But I disagreed with him when he said that it doesn't mean anything: "It's nice to know that many people wanted to have sex with you. Even more wanted it, really, since someone can want it without making it happen. I think there's an achievement there. It at least means they're attracted to you. At least you have some people skills."

I was trying to convince myself, of course. Maybe I don't want to believe that everyone else is like me, desperate to give it away.

A client who's into spanking wants me to spend an upcoming weekend with him someplace sunny. I've never seen him naked and he has never come in front of me. Our time together consists of walking, talking, eating, or me laying over his lap while he spanks me for hours. After my first session with him, I was bruised for a week. He recently emailed and offered more money, but warned before taking the increase that I'd "be sitting down for the entire flight back."

It's good advice. Remember the consequences of getting what you want. Think of how you'll feel on the long ride home.

Endings
February 24, 2009

He often told me he loved me, that he daydreamed about us married. This when he didn't know my middle name or favorite album or where I grew up. Although what does any of that mean for love? "Your favorite food is tomato soup? Now I love you more." Like collecting a catalog of details proves an emotion.

When I told him some of the bigger truths about myself, when I hesitated before doing so, he said as encouragement, "You know I love you." Not necessarily committed to me but committed to loving me, to answering every aspect of me with love. If you believe that's love. If you believe love can be near immediate, that it can resemble infatuation. Maybe you believe there is no true love without something like infatuation.

One of my philosophy professors lectured wildly about love once, yelling: "When you're in love with someone, that person is the lighthouse of your universe." (I scrawled it inside *Science and Poetry* in pencil—lighthouse of your universe—as if I would ever forget that phrase.) He was a delightful caricature of his position. I could swear he literally tore his hair out while howling at us.

He went on, "Nothing means as much without that person."

One of the men in the class repeated, incredulous, half-laughing, "So you're saying you can't enjoy, like, a vacation, without someone if you're really in love with them?"

"Of course not," the professor replied. "Not completely. You recognize beauty, but beauty means less if they don't witness it with you. Beauty is less. You see something sublime and your first thought is that they should be there with you. It's not as good without them. They illuminate. They make everything more."

I've only ever been completely in love with one person in my life. I begged him to tell me he didn't feel the same, to say the words, to give me proof of what I knew but didn't want to believe. I'd keep telling myself what I wanted to believe if he wasn't merciful enough to admit it. And he wasn't, so I slept on the couch, crying all night.

In the morning, I walked him to work and then I walked myself to the train station. It was November. I didn't see him again for four years.

"I've been thinking about my father a lot since I met you," I told him once while we were at lunch, holding both of his hands across the table. "I don't mean that in a weird way."

Days before, when he was talking about what he had to pay for his daughter, I said, "My father never paid child support." The bitterness was there abruptly, like the smell of something burning. "And he had to pay so little."

"My father didn't either," he said matter-of-factly. "I still love him."

It was over before it began, he wrote me. I just didn't want to admit it. He was right. I would never have loved him the way he loved me. When he said he wanted to marry me, I said, "You'd be disappointed." But there was something there, and I wanted to enjoy it longer. To look at his eyes and eyelashes, to get wet from being near him, to feel him inside.

During my trip, my friend and I spoke at length about love.
"You're the better loved?" he asked.
"Yes," I said, "Always. But I'd rather be the one loving more."

His relationship with his wife, who is also my dear friend, is coming to a close. I had a dream before the visit that they sat me down at a kitchen table—not theirs, not mine, but somebody's—to tell me about their impending divorce.

I don't believe it's me. I believe it's a trick I've learned, some skill set I picked up from work. So when a guy does fall, it's not surprising, and it's somehow unreal. Like it doesn't involve me, like he's loving me while I'm wrapped in something opaque. If that's true, if it's all the work of a certain capricious cleverness, has that behavior become a part of me now? Is it something I can't turn off? What if I can but don't?

I once told my first older man, "It's not your fault if someone loves you and you don't love them back. You can't help that."

"Can't you?" he replied.

I came home from the gym and sat down, sweaty, with tea and clementines. I stared at the plate of jagged orange rinds and then I stood up. I did the only think I could think to do: I called my dad.

After High School
March 5, 2009

He said I shouldn't contact him. We finished in anger, although it was not nearly as nasty or ugly as it could have been, so I obliged. Even when he sent an email apologizing. Even when he sent messages saying he still needed me in his life. Now every few days I get a "hope you're well" or "how are you?" It's not me being strong for the both of us, thinking of his emotional well being; I'm afraid to respond for my own sake. I'm afraid it will start again.

My father spoke repeatedly of my happiness. This is the source of concern for both my parents. They won't ask directly if I am happy; we're far too entrenched in the slant method of awkward discussion.

In high school, when I stopped getting my period, living off of 400 calories a day and four hours of exercise, only once did my mother accuse me of being sick. She was scratching my striated back one night in the dark and she said my name, shrill, abruptly hysterical: "What are you doing to yourself?" Pushing her palms against my bones like a frantic blind person.

I said, "I don't know!" We may have both been crying.

Because I am bad liar and have lied awkwardly for years, there is no convincingly fabricated career, but both parents know that I never accept money and vehemently dissuade them from spending on me. Asking if I "need anything" is only met with "no," and since they're not sure what else to offer, they fall back on distressed (mother,) resigned (father) expressions of what they want for me, whatever they're left to hope I will find on my own.

"I just want to make sure you're happy and that you have your own . . . autonomy," my dad said, the latter a word I've never heard him use before and with which he was audibly uncomfortable.

When I was twenty-one, we stood together in the women's studies section of a bookstore and he asked, genuinely confused, "You honestly think women are treated differently than men?"

Moments later, we had the most blistering conversation of my life. I told him I was dating the older man—he asked how old, I told him, and I thought his anger would blow the building's roof off—and then my father declared (didn't suggest or propose) that my damaged relationship with him was to blame.

I called my mother from the road, driving like Cruella De Vil, and sobbed, "I never want to see him again, I never even want to speak to him again." I was wearing a long red wool coat. I remember because it made me feel sophisticated and mature, a big city girl deigning to visit her small town folks.

Sometimes going home feels a bit like being trapped in one of those time travel parables where no matter how many different approaches one takes, the outcome is always the same. In my hometown, there seems to be only one possible future for me, one mundane destiny I've temporarily cheated, still waiting, toad-like and smug, for me to admit its inevitability. And the skin of a moody adolescent whose chief talent is glowering, a suit I assume all too readily.

I didn't leave town that night right away. Instead I went to the sex shop nearby and looked past my reflection in the locked plastic panes to the shelf-aged Doc Johnson toys. It was, I realize, a transparent and pathetic assertion of independence but not entirely unsentimental. I'd bought my first sex toys there, a rocket shaped, Band-Aid colored vibrator, and a pink dildo that later made me bleed when I tried to fit it in. I was practicing for the webcam job I'd just started.

I took the second boy I ever slept with on the first shopping excursion because I needed the company. I knew he wouldn't ask questions and anyone he told probably wouldn't believe him. He was sweet and somewhat dopey, easily confused and distracted. I made him the scapegoat of all my bad behavior in high school rather than reveal the sheer number of friends who were all doing the same objectionable things. "Your dad hates me," he said often, apropos of nothing, and I'd have to agree.

We never dated, we were only friends, although he was the first boy to make me wet. He did this when we were lying in his bed with my best friend and his best friend, and he kissed my neck in a firm, exotic way. He and I had sex three times: once in his living room behind a Christmas tree while friends were over; once in the bathroom during a party; once in his bed while his mom was outside doing yard work. Because the town is small, my dad dated his mom in the past and they were still friends.

The time in the bathroom is the only one I can recall. People kept trying to get in and the bath mat was soaked, yet I gripped it, water leaching through the knees of my jeans. It was pitch black and I had all my clothes on. Sex then was always strange, intense pain, but that night more so than before. I gazed into the black space in front of my face, thinking, *nothing will ever hurt as much as this*. I was fucking this boy because the boy I was in love with hated him. Sometimes I think my entire vaginal history can be attributed to misguided revenge attempts.

We brought the toys back to his house, into the same bedroom where we'd had sex years before. We took out the vibrator and laid together giggling, crunching up when it tickled, holding it to one another's necks and faces and armpits.

Offering Yourself
March 12, 2009

I hate having my picture taken because I don't believe I have a beautiful face. It's not that there's a single feature I want changed. I'd be at a loss to specify any modifications that would improve upon it, beyond exchanging it entirely for someone else's. When I was young, I wrote:

"I was born already a failed thing/I do not contain all the beauty in the world." I think many women feel that way. Expected to be the loveliest of all because otherwise your prettiness is irrelevant, as if attractiveness were judged like hands in a poker game. You have to be the most captivating, or you are categorically, eternally inferior. Insufficient.

Yet I've found myself with a series of men who insist on staring at my face—partners and clients alike. When I spent a weekend with the spanker, we were lying together and his gaze fell on me while I looked at the ceiling. I recognized it as a restful gaze. It was a gaze that said, *I think I'll stay here a while.*

We'd never spent so much time together before and I was caught off guard by how romantic he was, waxing poetic about my "perfect" body. Sometimes men get carried away in this vein, enthusiasm spilling into more enthusiasm. Perhaps it's because American masculinity doesn't normally permit effusiveness, and time with me and women like me is permission to abandon those rules.

"Do you remember what I called you when we first met?" He asked me. "Shayna Punim. Do you know what that means?"

I understand beauty gives comfort. Some women's faces I love looking at because they are deeply beautiful, others because they are unusual and still beautiful. There's a certain brittleness in the most conventionally pretty faces, something unsatisfying, like cotton candy. A pleasant taste but nothing substantial. The older man told me, often, "I can't wait to see what you look like at forty." He stared at me as I fell asleep, as I slept. I'd wake up to him smiling faintly next to me, his head propped on his hand.

It was merciful of him to do it while I slept, or when I was too sleepy to protest. That's been the hardest demand of my work and of my relationships: letting someone look at me, for as long as they want.

Want Everything
March 16, 2009

At first, when I wrote him, I felt strong, superior to my old self in that ridiculously arrogant way. (*Last month me was so clueless.*) I felt capable of resisting, so contact was safe. But we resumed our old patterns almost instantly. There were a few warm lines about missing one another, his far more intensely worded than mine, and plans to meet again. Then his flash of bait, the predictable attempt at making me jealous, which I ignored, and then an equally predictable outpour of emotions: *she didn't matter, no one's like you, my friends think I'm crazy.*

It's been a relief to be without him because, yes, I am small enough to sometimes be exhausted by the constant venting of passion. It's like holding my face in front of a furnace. I need cool air. I need my oxygen back. And it was easy enough to push him out of my mind, to let the entire affair recede at warp speed. Hence the self-righteousness and miscalculation.

The sensible choice is to not see him again. But there's something there, a something that is not just sex. It's not the same for me as it is for him, but that doesn't mean I'm not aware of it or that it doesn't matter. It's like we're looking into opposite ends of a tunnel. The sight is composed of the same things, and there's another person at the end. One of us just has a clearer view.

**Indebted
March 21, 2009**

I tied the blindfold and let his head down on the pillow. With effort, he lay still. I smoothed lube down his taint and over his asshole, pressing gently with my pointer finger.

"I like your hair," he said quietly after a moment of silence.

"Thank you." I held his cock with one hand. I slid my finger inside. "How does that feel?"

"Good." He was holding the backs of his knees. I'd told him to show me the position he takes when he puts things in his ass. Then I asked him what he used.

"A dildo. A stick of celery."

"How was that?"

"Better than the dildo."

"Because the dildo was too big?"

He laughed a little. "Probably." He paused. "The handle of a spatula. A section of orange."

"What did you do with it afterward?"

A half-pause. "I ate it. And the celery."

"How did it taste?"

He shrugged, barely. "It was more the . . . eroticism of . . . doing something taboo." Another pause. "That's weird, isn't it?"

"No," I said.

"I didn't want to but—well, I guess, at that point I was begging. I promised."

"Did you eat it before you came or after?"

"After. Sometimes, she would put my come on it and make me eat it. Now that I'm thinking about it, that's really weird, isn't it? I'm sorry."

"No. It's not weird." I kept stroking with my left hand. I pulled my finger out and replaced it with the tip of the dildo.

"Where are your lips?" He asked.

I leaned forward, relaxing my stomach on his erection. I kissed him, he kissed back. He was a good kisser. (Before I tied the blindfold on, he'd said "Wait. I want to see your breasts." I took off my bra and he looked for a moment before saying, "Thank you," and lying down.)

I didn't want to stop but I had to sit up to get the right angle for the strap-on. I took his cock in my hands and rocked my hips slowly.

He came profusely on his chest and stomach. He didn't make any noise. I leaned in again, smearing it between us, and kissed him once more.

"Stay here," I said. I brought back a damp cloth. He hadn't moved, not even to take off the blindfold.

While I was cleaning him, I noticed the holes in his ears for the first time.

"You have your ears pierced."

"Fifteen times," he said.

"What, where?"

He gestured to the cartilage in his left ear. "Twelve here." He tugged his right ear. "Three here."

I could only see one on his right lobe. "I think they've healed up."

"I did them all myself."

"With a needle?"

"With an earring. I wanted to piss off my dad."

"Did it work?"
"He didn't notice."

When I first met him, we did an elaborate, hours-long role-play in which I was his little sister confronting him about stealing my panties. The scene was slow and detailed. I talked about feeling jealous when my friends said they had crushes on him. I said I didn't like it when he dated girls from school and that I was afraid of him going away to college. He said he was thinking about staying home, that he was afraid of leaving too. I asked him why, and he looked me in the eyes and said, "Because I'm in love with you."

It was intense. We each did community theater in high school—you know how those types are. He ran away from home when his parents wouldn't let him play Bernardo in "West Side Story."

We tried to set up another appointment but I was traveling then and not seeing many clients. When I finally started working regularly again, I emailed him and he replied that he couldn't see me because the last time had been too much. He said he had feelings for me and didn't trust himself to be satisfied with seeing me as a client. He told me he'd send me money if I ever needed it; all I had to do was ask.

But I could never do that, and never have. Asking for money feels degrading. I don't even like shopping when someone else is paying. The spanker bought me a shirt during our last engagement. The previous time we saw each other he'd bought me a laptop, but it was this purchase that made him say, "It makes you very uncomfortable when I buy you things, doesn't it?"

"Yes!" I said, relieved. The older man told me that I never asked for anything: food, a ride, for him to wait up. I realized he was right, and that it's because I don't want to owe anyone anything. And the truth is that I don't do this job for the money. I don't need money right now. I've never *needed* money.

When I greeted him at the door, I was wearing a red dress that he mistook for a nightie. We sat on the bed together, me barefoot and him in jeans and a polo shirt.

"It's not a nightgown. It's just a summer dress."

"You don't wear that out in public."
"Of course I do. I mean, I have."
"But you can see your underwear through it."
"Well, I wouldn't normally wear black with it. I probably wouldn't wear underwear at all."

He reached out and fingered the thin fabric.

"You whore," he said.

I Wanted To Make Strange Men Touch Me
March 29, 2009

Last week I met a new client. He had an odd face, with a gap between his front teeth. I felt something strange under his shirt while I was touching his chest. When he was naked, he said, "They're keloids. My body overheals itself. It's not contagious."

"Does it hurt when I touch them?" I asked.

"No . . ." He spoke like he'd never been asked this question before and was not sure of the answer.

When we lay down together he reached between my legs and I was melted. That's the consistency, not oily or greasy but soft and smooth like ice cream left out to thaw. I still blush when I'm that far gone and someone touches me. Embarrassed that they know how swollen and soaked I am. It took me very little time to come against his fingers.

I know it's hotter if I make all of these men out to be stars: tall, powerful, sexy, etc. The type you'd beg to fuck you for free. And some of them have been extremely good looking. One was a former wrestler who looked like the friendly jock crush in a movie for teenagers. It was hard for me to refrain from making his looks the subject of conversation every time we met. I insisted others must have told him all his life that he should have been an actor. I even talked about what scripts I imagined him taking. He was very indulgent of this and asked very little of me. I think he, too, expected something bigger of his life than a home in the suburbs, a nine to five job, and a paid girl in a room.

Another was a runner with a shaved head who also seemed like a Hollywood archetype, although he had none of the other man's boyish charm. Instead he was flinty and lean, on the verge of angry with his prominent jawline perpetually clenched. To make sense of him, I cast him as the cop whose entire family died some painful death at the hands of a criminal he had wronged. Now he hated the world and everyone in it because he'd never smell his wife's sweet hair again. But I didn't say that out loud.

I always felt ugly in his presence. Some of my mascara rubbed off on his face once and I made a move to wipe it off with remover on a cotton pad. He knocked my hand away, flinching.

"What is that?" He demanded.

"Just stay still," I told him. Thinking: *asshole*.

He wanted me to look up at him while he was in my mouth. He'd say it: "Look at me."

I would, and he would come. When he was on top of me, his body was hard and flat. It didn't last long, and I could feel tiny stubble in all the places he shaved. I can't remember anything about his cock.

During our last session, we were lying in bed together after he'd come and I said I was going away for the summer. He said, softly, not quite to me, "I bet all your customers will miss you." It was one of those moments when you realize that someone you believed doesn't really think about you, doesn't even necessarily notice you, actually thinks about you a great deal.

And the German with the British accent, my first big cock, with his four children and lawyer wife and big hair and big smile. Everything we did was fast and frantic. I haven't had that type of physical chemistry with anyone before or since. It felt like I wasn't even operating my own body anymore.

But the truth is some are plain yet sexy, some are attractive and horrible, and it doesn't matter what they look like anyway because they don't need to look good for me to be wet. This is either my talent or my curse. All I need is the hotel room, the silence before meeting, the adjusting and checking in the bathroom or a hall mirror, the unfamiliarity, the unpredictability, the newness. The fact that I'm pretending to be in control but really no one's in control, even outside the room. Especially outside of the room.

I found this line weeks ago. I can't remember when I wrote it or what brought it on. It was isolated on a sheet with other notes, none as dramatic. *I wanted to make strange men touch me.* When did I want this? Or rather, when will I stop wanting this?

Swimming
April 12, 2009

I met a new client last week, a very smart man who spends most of his time immersed.

"How many bodies of water have you been in?" I asked. "Do you even keep count anymore?"

He said no, but tried to name them anyway. Then he offered beautiful words in Hebrew and Arabic for highly specific terms involving man-made structures and oceans. He had shaggy dark hair with faint silver strands laced sparsely but regularly throughout, a close cut beard, and a tattoo of a lion that looked like it sprang out of an elegant children's storybook. I stared it for several minutes while lying against his body. His arms were strong and long, his torso flat. His was a carelessly cultivated fitness—my favorite kind. I don't know what I had expected, but it wasn't this, this effortlessness.

When I first put my hand on his cock, he asked, "Is there a particular kind you like? Some shape or size?"

I studied his. "You have good girth."

"Is that what matters most?"

"Every little bit helps," I said and we both laughed. "I doubt you've had any complaints, have you?"

"No, I haven't." He replied. "And I guess there's nothing worth than false modesty."

Towards the end of our time together, he asked me to squirt for him. Squirting is not the most flattering descriptor but neither is "female ejaculation" particularly appealing. I'd thought of some euphemism for it when I worked on webcam, where that ability became my most requested, but I can't remember it now. Gushing would be accurate in my situation, although that's still not quite sexy-sounding. I'm no Cytherea but I can hold my own. I've shot off the end of a bed before while sitting at the head of a queen mattress. On nights when I went on cam, I'd soak about four full size bath towels before calling it quits because I didn't want to do any more laundry.

It's a parlor trick, something I taught myself to make more money. It took one book, one afternoon, and one very frustrating hour of me burrowing with my fingers until I drenched my bed. I let so much go I couldn't believe I'd done it right, but it was definitely not urine. I pressed my face into the soaking sheets, sniffed it, licked it. There's nothing like the taste. The closest I can come to describing it is clean sea water, musky and salty but in a bright way. Fresh. The bed needed hours to air dry.

I held back with him because we'd still need some dry space on the bed but I'm a bad judge of volume and, even trying to restrain myself, ended up sitting in a splotchy puddle at least two feet in diameter.

"Do you want to taste it?" I offered. I had licked some off of my fingers during, then gone on my hands and knees to smell it. This is only partially to look wanton and whorish. Mostly, I'm still fascinated by the phenomenon. And I genuinely love the taste. He laid back to observe it, stroking himself while he watched. Then he asked me questions about how I did it.

"That's impressive," he said. "It's amazing that you're that in touch with you body."

"Thank you," I said. I wanted to go to the bathroom to let out the rest but instead lay down into his open arms.

He wanted to watch me come right away when we met, which I did expect. I'd saved it for him. I'd been closer earlier in the day but thought, *no, later, with X*, which is not exactly a premonition of some connection because I always choose the delay. I like waiting. The anticipation is better than realization, although the realization in this case was long and strong.

He asked what I was thinking the moment before, and I couldn't answer because then I was gone, and coming down could only laugh and shake my head a little.

"Nothing," he answered himself, above me. "Just drawing a beautiful blank." He pushed my hair back from my forehead and kissed me there while I was still trembling.

A Dream About Escape
April 16, 2009

Waking, I occasionally imagine apocalyptic situations to generate some response plan. For instance: Do you try to take your pets? Do you leave them alone and alive or do you kill them to spare them a slow death of starvation or burning? This may equally be the result of last November, and living in a city that invites attack by virtue of its unpopular role in the world. Or my inexplicable gravitation to dystopic literature: *The Road*, *Never Let Me Go*, etc. I was reading *Blindness* on the flight to India. Somehow this fits with my girlhood when I was most struck by *Lord of the Flies* and *1984*. When I was still in the single digits, I wrote several bizarre stories that consisted entirely of preparations to leave a home in a tornado's path or what to put in a hurricane kit before hiding under a card table in a closet. Listing is probably the most obsessive-compulsive activity of mine; I do it everyday, several times a day on paper, infinitely more in my head.

Of course I've had dreams since about menacing men with guns showing up in enclosed spaces where I then have to hide with loved ones. But I don't know what brought this one on.

The dream's was quiet, specific terrorism, not the grenade-hurling approach actually employed. We were in a hotel, and we saw men with guns talking to other men with guns. They wanted to round up all the foreign guests. We, meaning me and my dream friends and family, those characters that mutate and fade out and arrive without comment, tried to sneak out. A hotel staff member found us and ushered us outside to waiting cars. Thousands of people filled the sidewalks and the structure of bombed-out buildings lining the streets. They waved their arms, smiling, shouting, standing on the ledges of third story concrete floors. I didn't understand why they weren't afraid; then I realized we only had to be afraid because we weren't natives.

"Why are they all cheering?" I asked the driver.

"They want you to be safe," he said.

"You" didn't mean me. It meant all of us, everyone in the hotel.

After and during the actual attacks, there was much attention paid to the claim that the terrorists were targeting British and American citizens.

This may have been true for any number of reasons, including garnering more world attention or having "valuable" hostages with which to bait police. Yet in the end they killed very few foreigners and very many Indians.

Cheif Karkare was the first high-ranking official featured in the news coverage. He was a nice looking man with a trustworthy mustache. (When I was a child, I had an immediate affinity for men with facial hair. As I got older, I realized all of my father's church's pictures featured a bearded Jesus.) He was going to solve the problem. You could tell: here is the man to fix this. Minutes later, he was dead.

More and more officers were dying in every site and there as no gas in the halls, no shields, no helmets or body armor for the earliest men. We passed the Cama Hospital when running from the Taj. Our impromptu guide even said, "That's the hospital for women and children." We had to stand at the edge of its gates and wait while a truck full of soldiers drove inside. An hour later, the terrorists were there.

The day before the attacks, I heard horn music while in my room. I opened the door to the balcony and stepped outside to see a trio of men in white shirts and pants, standing on a rooftop next door in front of a microphone, holding trumpets. It was wedding season. They played "Moon River" and then they played "I Can't Help Falling In Love With You," twice.

Only Connect
April 20, 2009

I had a strange regular when I worked for someone else, a criminal defense lawyer who would say breathtakingly terrible things when he came to see me. For instance, "I feel like I'm at a carwash," or "It's like being at McDonald's." He was an unhappy man who spent a lot of time with escorts in Vegas. He would call my booker while on vacation to give her messages: "Tell Charlotte I'm surrounded by gorgeous women and I'm thinking about her." I never had sex with him.

Once he took me to a Starbucks nearby rather than staying inside for our appointment. He showed me pictures on his cell phone and accidentally called a dog a pig, which made me laugh very hard and made him deliver a flustered confession about watching *Babe* the night before and having pigs on his mind. It's possible to feel affection for any human being, I think, if you catch them at the right moment. Even those who've proudly defended child molesters.

He often suggested setting me up with his son, Seth, not for a session but for dating. The selling points were how rich Seth was going to be, and how good-looking he already was. (Judging from the pictures I saw, that would be "very.") I wish desperately I'd agreed to it for the delightful weirdness of the situation: "Your father pays me to look at me naked. And what about you, do you have any hobbies?"

Unfortunately, it never happened. I lost contact with him after I went solo although he found me a few weeks ago. In his email, he said something about seeing me "before the plumbing wears out." I replied asking if he meant mine or his.

After our Starbucks outing, we sat together in his car in the parking lot of the condo building where I worked and he told me that he and his wife slept in separate rooms. I asked him how his most recent experience with an escort was and he said, "Unpleasant."

When I pointed out that we had a few minutes left and I didn't yet have to go inside, he flew into a strange fit, asking, "Don't you understand? I would have paid and gone if you didn't want to leave with me . . . I've wanted to tell you about myself for so long!"

He had those moments occasionally. They usually ended in him yelling, "It's not about the money!"

I used to think I wasn't a very good girl for hire. I knew I was expert; I made a lot, and if I saw someone once they'd ask to see me again. But I was convinced I fell short of the platonic ideal of sex worker. I never got manicures and didn't really know how to use makeup. Then I realized that what sells best in some cities is probably glamour but what sells best here, for me, is tenderness. Lust can burn out but everyone's in the market for solace, always. It's why I can't properly quit this work. It fulfills me too.

Several days ago, the diver wrote that he was surprised and "unsettled" by how much he'd been thinking about me. "You may be a victim of your own success," he said, before explaining that he couldn't see me again unless he could get his mind right about how he felt. This has happened before with clients. And there are non-clients who've told me the same thing, albeit in different ways. What kind of success is this? To make people feel for you when you can't or won't reciprocate.

The paradox is how vehemently I'll claim that I am my real self with these men, then think *he doesn't even know me* once they start feeling more. And sometimes it makes me angry. Sometimes it ruins whatever beautiful residue I was basking in: our connection was real and perfect, and now you're destroying it because you can't accept what it is. Suddenly I'm in a position of diminishing what happened between us, degrading it in an effort to erase that intensity. Because it seems the only acceptable reactions are to admit, "I want more, it amazed me too" or to say, "I'm sorry you feel that way, best to you in the future." The first option wouldn't stay true for me as long as it would stay true for him, or as intensely. I'm already in a relationship with someone. I can't date, and I don't want to date. I don't want to feel pressured to be constantly accessible because his way of loving makes him needy. That goes for any "him." I'm not going to say "I love you" back, because I wouldn't mean it.

I worry—I know—that I tend towards carelessness and selfishness in these situations. I'll mine a relationship until I've satisfied my curiosity and as my interest starts to wane, his intensifies. Someone once told me that he'd give up everything to be with me, any women he was dating, his home, any pre-existing plans. All I had to do was to say I wanted him. Have I ever felt that for someone? Do I even want to? I've upended my life in the pursuit of passion once but it was unintentional. Not regretted, but heedless rather than purposeful. And the relationship I was pursuing would not last. I knew that at the time and it didn't matter. Its transiency only made me more urgent.

If I could, I would keep the diver in my life on whatever terms we both needed and it would be enough. Even if it means I don't get paid. The aspect of service helps us find each other but then we can do what we will. When the bond is that true, it's not about the money anymore.

N.B.

New Leaves Shuddering In The Breeze
April 26, 2009

I stared out the window over his chest, watching the top of a sparse tree. The wind dragged back the small leaves, which moved a little like fringe, like a boy's long, unwashed bangs being swept to the side. Each one the shape of a daisy petal.

"When you die, what do you think you'll wish you'd done more of?" I asked.

A moment passed. "Spent more time with you."

"Come on."

"That's my response. What about you?"

"Swimming," I said. I pictured myself bobbing in the water as the sun crouched down above the dark waves. I learned to swim in the Atlantic, and I love the dirty taste and dingy look. One wrong mouthful drains in my sinuses all day. Every time out is a negotiation with the ocean's own mind.

I need to be in waters that boast about their danger with fat waves and thick froth to have that joy. It's a unique type of freedom, to kick out and release yourself into the occasional chaos. Coming back is not entirely your decision. Although I suppose that describes every day—but some circumstances make the reality more clear.

The last time I swam for a full day was three years ago off the Mediterranean coast of Spain. It sounds glamorous but it wasn't. The beach was full of naked children and topless mothers; the sea was placid and bland. When I tried to swim far out a man in the water yelled at me to come back.

A year later, I was in the Persian Gulf and it felt like being pickled. Staying in was a test of will. My skin burned from the salt. I hate pools, but I'll take what I can get.

The day before this reverie I lifted my leg before a kneeling client whose hands I'd bound as he kissed my inner thigh. I held his head against my crotch and told him to smell me. Then I undid his wrists, covered his eyes with the same tie, and guided his fingers into my cleft. I was slippery. Gloss spread over his skin and over his wedding ring. I kept thinking about that for the rest of the day, but in an idle way, like turning over a small object in my hands. No revelations, no emotions. The next day I leaned against my boyfriend's ribs as he slept supine on the couch, and I felt a light tapping on my back. He was snoring but his cock was hard and dowsing. Only one of these two moments made me happy.

I've been thinking a lot about joy. I don't know that I'm very good at it. It's been a long time since I've felt angry, but recently I cry easily, although I'm not necessarily unhappy while I do it. I cried while I watched the leaves.
"What were you thinking?" He asked.
"That the tree is beautiful. And then I imagined being in the sea."

Wizard
May 4, 2009

He picked up my hand and held it in front of his face, inspecting my fingers.
"Are my nails too long?" I asked.
"No," he said. "I like to observe you."
After a moment, he set my hand back down and said, "Impeccable." It's amazing the things these men will compliment. Teeth. Hands. The same features used to judge a horse or a dog.
When he was down at my feet, he said, "You need new shoes."
"Because of my callus?"
"No, you have a . . . bubble."
"Oh, right, a blister."
"I will get you some new shoes. What brand do you want?"
"I don't know. You choose."
"Jimmy Choos? What else do you need?"
I couldn't think of anything.
"Come on," he said. "Don't be shy. Take advantage."
"A bike." I've told several clients this but a bike is not a sexy gift. No one wants to give a bike.
"What else?"
"I don't know."

"Tell me! It would be my honor."

Earlier he asked if I worked for the FBI: "You give me amnesia. You could get men to tell you anything. You're even worse than the water board."

"What year were you born?"

"1982. I'm a dog."

He looked up, thinking. "Yes, you're a dog."

Later, he bit my nose and said, "A nose is very important to a dog." Then he asked me to do full lotus while we lay back, naked.

"How long could you hold that?" He was incensed.

"A long time. This is comfortable to me."

"How long did it take you to do it?"

"I've always been able to do it."

He talked about how valuable it was that the men he deals with think they're superior. He called it a "privilege."

"They know they only got their jobs because they're lucky. It is not because they have a shiny degree from an Ivy League school, or because they are the most qualified. It's because they are on the right side of the party." I knew he meant in the right party, at the right time, but I rather like picturing politics like one big middle school dance complete with crepe paper and snacks. "That means it is good for me if they think I'm funny, or can't speak English. I don't care. They need to feel better. I want the contract.

"Do your friends tell you how your beautiful you are? Your classmates?"

"No. Why would they say that?" I don't think anyone told me I was beautiful until I started charging them money. When I was young, I'd sometimes sneak looks at myself in the mirror and think it, but adolescence cured me of self-confidence. From age thirteen on, I hung lace over my bedroom mirror and avoided all others, even reflective glass.

He swept his hands through my hair, over and over. "It's black."

"Yes . . . "

"Where are you from? Were you born here?"

"Of course."

He made a disapproving noise. "No Americans are born with black hair."

The woman who blew it out that morning asked if I was Slovakian after she saw my light roots. When my hair was red, everyone guessed Irish-German. The way you look is a Rorschach test for everyone you meet. You can learn so much about someone else just by looking like you do.

Sometimes I think my alter egos are knockouts. Of my webcam persona I frequently said, "She's a babe." Because black eyeliner and a blond wig go a long way.

Before this appointment, I caught myself singing Hall & Oates' "Man-Eater" while doing my makeup in front of the mirror. A few moments later I realized I had switched to Nina Simone's "Chain Gang." It's wonderful to be so cheerful that you lose all pretense of being cool. I think biting the nose of a stranger falls into this category.

"You're like a wizard!" He told me twenty minutes after we met, eyebrows raised. It was the best thing he said all night.

Men and Other Animals
May 7, 2009

This new eccentric and I spent the afternoon together and in between his orgasms he alternated talking about Paris runway shows and his work in Africa. He spoke about being fed already-eaten food at restaurants in Niger, and being escorted across borders by UN armored trucks.

"You could come sometime," he offered, meaning the Congo. Because with any aspect of his life we discuss, he invites my involvement. He described the job I'd do, which sounded perfect for me. "But you have to train. I mean, you need to be able to outrun a twelve year old with an AK-47. In the jungle. At 12,000 feet."

"Oh boy," I said. "I'd love it."

"You run into these kids who've been trained as soldiers since age eight and they're on drugs and armed and . . . there's no reasoning with someone like that."

He paused, thinking. "I feel safe there. But the poverty . . . I mean, we complain here because we're in a recession but those people have nothing and they're happy. They're kind, they're dear, they speak softly."

When we first met, he gave me a handmade box that held small carvings of gorillas in different poses, each wrapped in a piece of hand-dyed, patterned cloth. He'd commissioned them from some men in the jungle. And he didn't even know I did yoga.

He was easily impressed. "You're insane," he said. "You're so powerful." And I was worried he was bored. How could anyone wow a man like this? It's his openness. He's ready to be thrilled by every aspect of his life. Predisposed towards enjoyment.

I asked how much a baby gorilla costs on the black market.

"20,000," he said.

That's so cheap, I thought.

"It's cheap," he confirmed. "But not to people who are used to making a dollar a day."

What They Like
May 25, 2009

His apartment was pure liberal arts academic, full of Eastern artifacts and old books. The windows looked out on black treetops, bushy leaves barely visible in the slick dark.

He was intensely interested in domination, forced orgasms and chastity and that type of thing. Plenty of men are curious about this in an unstudied way, but it quickly became clear that he was someone who'd done his homework. He was particularly taken with the idea of CFNM parties and a group of women keeping male slaves—in a sorority house, for instance—where they would make the slaves rub against each other if they wanted to get off, or have masturbation contests after long periods of chastity where whoever came last was rewarded and everyone else locked up again.

He could endure an impressive amount of abuse on his balls. When I wasn't giving him enough, he'd push me for it. At one point, he said, "You're not really controlling me. You're just pretending." He was right but I pulled him by his balls off the couch for saying it.

He'd been hurt in a humbler several years ago by a professional domme, and by hurt I mean permanently damaged. We talked about it for a bit until he looked away and said, "I don't want to dwell on that." Not bitter or angry or even sad, simply ready to move on. He told his doctor that he'd done it to himself by tying up his balls when masturbating.

Diana Krall played for hours. He said his live-in girlfriend was so sick of her music that he could only listen to the CDs when she wasn't around.

He bought a pretty pair of black stripper sandals after this same girlfriend mentioned that the local tradition of men running a race in high heels aroused her. But apparently when he showed her, her reaction was not a positive one. He wore them for me, shuffling on his hardwood floor naked. His hairy calves and the top of his thigh muscles flexed.

"They make your legs look great," I told him.

"Yes, well, they make everyone's legs look great. That's why women wear them." He stepped out of them immediately.

He'd grown increasingly talkative as the night went on, once he'd had several orgasms and emptied his wine glass several times. He even told me about a girl he dated in high school who wore stockings and garters, not (of course) as something sexy and retro, but because those were her functional undergarments. He loved reaching far enough up her skirt to feel the skin just beyond the rim of her stockings, but he knew the moment he reached it she would slap his hand away.

"In the pictures of escorts today, it's all about the woman's achievement. She's looking as hot as she can and it's all about her working hard for three years or something to get this body. It's 'look at me. Look at what I've done.' It's all her ego. But pin-ups used to be about appealing to men, about seeming available to a male viewer. That's not in the equation anymore."

"I guess you're right," I said. "I select my pictures based on how much I like the way my body looks."

"My favorite pin up ever was of a topless girl in overalls bending over near a pick up truck, picking up basketful of a harvest. And she's smiling and the caption says: it's corn . . . but they like it."

He insisted on walking me out of the building. It was a charming and curious co-op, built many years ago and uniquely purposed for a more conservative life. Everyone's mail was held in shelves of small open boxes behind the hotel-like front desk. Open alcoves on the second floor looked out into the spacious lobby and he explained that these were the places where single women entertained a gentleman caller when it would have been scandalous to bring the man into her room. It was pouring outside and he waited with on the street corner with me under his huge umbrella until we flagged down a cab and said goodbye.

After his first ruined orgasm, I went to wash my hands in his bathroom. As I passed by the open doorway, I saw an unexpected yet entirely familiar scene on the daybed in the library. A stuffed moose sat at the head of a semicircle. He was flanked by an assortment of makeshift toys, anything that could be anthropomorphized. A snowman ornament, a Virgin Mary tchotchke. A child had been here enacting some funeral or football huddle or party. I didn't want to linger looking it for so long that he noticed my absence. But I noticed there was a mirror in the center. They were gathered around a lake.

Into The Void
June 1, 2009

The last time I saw him his grandfather was dying—although I suppose there's actually never been a time I've known him when the grandfather wasn't on his slow way out. He's not a good client because he can't grasp the boundaries; he keeps asking me out on dates, presses for personal information, wants to spend all the time talking and only attempts to come at the absolute last minute. The last time I kept staring at his face while I worked his cock, trying not to feel that easy whore anger and thinking to myself: "his grandfather's dying, his grandfather's dying."

Now his grandfather is dead and as I laid next to him on his bed tonight, he said, "I was thinking about your role, in my life I mean, and about what I want from this, why I do this—not criticizing myself—"

"Just introspective," I said.

"Yeah. I really like it about you that I feel like I've made this cool random friend and we have this secret life together that no one else knows about . . . But I mean you're a therapist really, right?"

"Sometimes." I hate that attitude, maybe because it's so common and so incomplete.

"And you're also a distraction. I mean some people read a book if they're upset, but if you're really upset then a book isn't even . . . because you can't . . . "

"Concentrate."

"Yeah and so some people do physical things, like run or . . . " He shut his eyes. I knew what was coming.

His face grew wet in an almost sweaty way. It's strange to watch how grown men cry, small tears disappearing in the fine lines of their faces. I put my hand in his and held it. Pressing myself against him felt artificial, so I stayed propped on my elbows and rubbed his chest with my free hand. I thought about a mom slathering vapor rub and did that but gently, gently.

He still pushed our time limit—he always goes over—and I pushed back. I gave him a kiss at the door. He asked for another one. He made kissy noises down me at the hall and I laughed obligingly. When I got home I took out his cash and saw that, for the first time, he'd tipped. And he'd given me the money as soon as I arrived, before the moment in his room. I sat down and started writing this, feeling like a little shit.

Something You Can't Lose
June 4, 2009

On the phone, I finally said, "Why don't you think about it and call me later? You seem a little taken aback."

"No, I—if I'm nervous it's just because . . . " he lowered his voice. "I know I'm in love with you."

We hadn't met before but I went ahead with the appointment. You're probably thinking that was stupid. Maybe. But I screen extensively and I wanted to hear what he had to say. Even tiger tamers get arrogant, or maybe they have to come to the occupation that way. One of the people closest to me criticizes this constantly: "You have this funny idea about the world and how nothing bad will ever happen to you . . . " It's less that I don't believe there are bombs and more that I'm sure I can diffuse any one I come across.

As soon as we were alone, he pulled me to him. "Am I like you expected?"

"I wasn't expecting anything. You're tall."

"Did it upset you, what I said on the phone?"

"What did you say on the phone?"

His voice dove down again. "That I'm in love with you." He dragged his hands up and down my back in an odd stroking motion.

"No."

"No?"

"No. That's sort-of your own business, isn't it?"

"I want you to marry me." He squatted down, knees splayed on either side of my legs, to whisper in my ear. "Does that concern you?"

"Not really," I couldn't stop laughing. "I don't think that's something you can do without my consent."

"What?"

I repeated myself but he still seemed not to hear.

He wrapped his arms around my waist and pulled, lifting me up en pointe, and slid me to the bed. He started undressing me. At one point, he said, "Just stay there, just relax," and disappeared for a while into the bathroom. Then he came back and straddled my torso.

I looked at him rearing above me and thought, *how does somebody that good-looking get to be so crazy?* Good-looking was perhaps a stretch, but he was forty-nine and looked closer to thirty-five. He had dimples and a defined but somehow delicate jaw. An abundance of hair. In another life, he would have been a pussy magnet. He complained that it was harder to flirt now because everyone was uptight about the economy.

"Do you have a boyfriend?"

"Yes." I never admit this.

"They all say that," he muttered. I repeated him in disbelief. "But you're not like the others. I loved what you wrote on your website. You're an excellent writer, very candid. You have a very distinct voice."

This happens often. Some clients specifically say before meeting, "I want to talk about what you said on your site." They recite lines of it back to me. I've forgotten what I wrote but it does a marvelous job of finding men who want to pay me to do very little. This man, for instance, explicitly said he didn't want to come. When I was younger, I briefly wanted to go into advertising.

"Man, you're pretty. Like beautiful pretty."

"Thank you."

"You're probably the prettiest person I've ever seen."

I gave him a look.

"Move in with me."

"But I already have a home."

"Where?"

"Here in the city."

He rolled abruptly onto his side. I'd plugged in my iPod and "Cowgirl in the Sand" was playing. "He wrote this song in one day with a fever of 102. Did you know that?"

"I'd forgotten it," I said.

Hello woman of my dreams, Neil sang. My client and I regarded each other.

"You're really not uncomfortable at all, are you? You're so relaxed. How do you do that?"

"Are you trying to make me uncomfortable? Why wouldn't I be relaxed?"

Later he said it again: "Move in with me."

"No thank you."

"But . . . if you move in with me, everything will be ok."

"I don't think my boyfriend would like that."

"Ugh, your boyfriend. You've got to get rid of him."

"Why would I do that?"

"Because we're engaged."

"Oh. I guess that is a good reason."

He smiled. "I like your answers. I like that you're willing to go along with the facade." Then later: "But I am in love with you."

"Ok."

"It's kind-of nice. I mean what do we have in this life? We have our iPods, some of us have jobs . . . but if you like somebody, it's just . . . out there. You don't have to worry about it."

When we parted ways, he said, "Write for me." He didn't mean write a specific piece for him. He meant simply commit the act.

Earlier in the day I walked towards a father lifting his young son to touch the leaves of a tree. The child let the leaves drag over his palm and his fingers squeezed only reflexively in delight, not in an attempt to clutch or pull. The father set the boy down as I approached and he stood on his stocky legs with that faint drunken sailor sway of the newly bipedal.

"Hello!" I said to him, looking down at his face while I passed.

He stared back at me for a moment before he began to beam.

N.B.

Fishes
June 9, 2009

One of my oldest clients has been seeing me for so long that we've built up a peculiar, childlike style of intimacy together. Two or three years ago during one of our afternoons, he launched into a storybook way of speaking: "I love you more than all the stars . . . and all the fish in the sea . . . and all the sand . . . combined!"

I laughed and he kept going. "More than all the people . . . more than all the cars . . . "

I said, "You sound like you're writing a children's book."

And he said, "Yeah." Then in that coy voice used to address kids: "There are many different fish in the sea, but the sea is lonely without this one fish. You're the only fish for me!"

I liked that he used the pathetic fallacy. That's something children do a lot. One of the toddlers I babysat for in college told me, "The rain will stop soon because it gets tired of coming."

I had no idea the client too remembered that particular afternoon until several weeks ago when he whispered, "You're still the only fish." His new nickname for me is "The Best," as in "simply," as in Tina Turner, who he loves. He'll send me text messages before he goes to sleep reading: "Goodnight, The Best!" and whispers it when he's clutching me in bed. We talk about how we'll be the new John and Yoko with our bed-ins. We spend most of our time together in a nude, full-body embrace. After I fake an orgasm while he fingers me, he'll squeeze me so hard it hurts, and gasp, "Oh, I love you," in my ear.

The last time I saw him Tina Turner was playing and when the CD came to "Private Dancer," he said, "This one's my favorite. She's so . . . primal? It's like they're not even human."

I assumed "they" meant the private dancers, but then he said, "I hope you think of me as human."

"Well, I did notice." I said.

He looked at me, nervous.

"I noticed that you are one. From the very first moment I met you. I thought, there's another one."

"Another human being," he said, laughing now. "I can spot 'em from a mile away."

The Truth
June 17, 2009

One of my clients has had tremendous physical pain in his life. When he was in his twenties, a freak accident wrecked havoc on his pelvic region. Sex is painful, touch can be painful. He has to wait two days between orgasms. If he forgets, if he comes too early, it might be a year before the pain subsides enough for him to do it again. He's lived this way for over thirty years.

"I saw an escort in San Diego," he told me early in the session, "and while she was stroking my cock and getting me very close to coming, I said, 'My favorite thing about you is your face.' And she just looked at me and said 'classic.' I thought that was pretty funny. I guess you get that line a lot?"

We lay together clothed, listening to the music and stroking each other. His touch is tremendously gentle. He's missing the first joint on his right hand's fourth finger. The scar sealing the nub where the rest of his finger should extend is delicate and thin.

He asked me if I thought of myself as a courtesan and I said, "No, should I?"

He said yes.

He also said, "I want to make you feel as good as I felt the first time I saw you." So I did my best realistic fake orgasm and he hugged me tightly and I could swear he whispered, "I love you" while I was in the false throes.

When we said goodbye, he dropped extra cash into my bag. "I wanted to give you something more for being so kind."

"You don't have to do that," I said, and I was almost hurt by it. Like he thought my being kind to him cost me something.

He was one of two new clients I've recently spent time with. The other was equally easy to be with but far less soothing. He told me he became open to the idea of paying a woman like me when he had his first (non-sexual) massage at a hotel one year ago while on vacation. At the end of it, he thought to himself, "Well, I wouldn't really mind if she wanted to finish me off."

When he was in college he was in a fraternity known as "Skull House," although it attracted such well-behaved members that people started calling it "School House." He described how tame their pledge week was; it consisted of some fake story about one of the pledges embarrassing the house and there being an annual blackballing ceremony as a result. Then everyone chosen got a marble that was both white and black on the big selection day–which was a joke, I guess?

I'd mentioned something about being a wild child when I was younger, drinking too much liquor and not being able to stomach it anymore. He asked for an explanation so I gave him a bit about my role as the abstinent one, my parents mistrust when I wasn't doing anything wrong, and my subsequent decision to do what they already presumed I was doing. He asked if my relationship with them had recovered since, to which I said, " . . . " and then he asked if they knew what I did for work. They don't.

"Well, you have your dark side and you have your . . . regular life and you keep the two separate, that's fine," he said.

"I'm a white and black marble," I said.

"I'm a white marble," he replied. "With just a speck of black."

"A speck of black in the middle, where no one can see."

"Yeah," he said. "That's the truth."

Glory Days
June 21, 2009

I've never been as devoted to anyone as I was my high school friends. I was quiet, self-conscious, anorexic, in physical therapy after a serious injury, with braces and a perpetual ponytail. Yet somehow, I ended up in this crew with some of the most amazing personalities I'd ever meet. It had something to do with the fact that I thought the foul-mouthed tough-guy act of one of the bullies was funny rather than intimidating. And I had a car.

We created our own list serv for planning parties and taking polls on who was the smartest, most lovable, prettiest. (I only won one. Guess? The funniest.) It was still the 1990s and our average age was sixteen. I wasn't truly a wild child, particularly not compared to they who'd been drinking and making bongs from beer cans for years already, but I got drunk and stoned a lot in the summer. Once I was older I branched out to mushrooms, K, and so on.

While I don't begrudge anyone the use of drugs to obtain momentary transcendence or illumination, that's never happened to me. I've only had nights of brilliant fun. My nineteeenth birthday was all lights and euphoria, thanks to one fat line of what I later learned was crystal meth. One New Year's Eve, I swallowed ecstasy with tap water in a casino bathroom, and fifteen minutes later was filled with a slow, thick joy. I petted the passenger seat as I sat in the back of car, saying, "Is anyone else, like, having a really great time?" I could have been left in the car the whole night and I would have been delighted.

The only incident close to an epiphany came after an all night coke binge and it was nasty, the lowest moment of my life. I was sitting in a car this time too, the front seat of my own, which I'd left in a fast food restaurant parking lot. I prepared to drop off a friend before I took myself home to fumble with whatever lame lie came to me at the last moment. The sun was rising, so I couldn't leave yet—I had to wait until it would be plausible that I'd slept somewhere else and woken up at a more characteristic time.

As the sun burned a slow track up the barely blue sky, I thought, *This is it. This is the rest of your life. Every day as pointless and empty and painful as the next and it will never, ever change. It will never get better. Because it is all meaningless.* It was unfathomable that anyone could bear to be. But I didn't see what the other options were.

So I drove home and went into my room, fell asleep and woke up a few hours later with a bloody nose and no appetite.

That night kicked off like so: I'd been left in a house alone while others went to get beer, and when the dealer came I befriended him. Then his eight balls were ours for free as long as I could convince him to party hop with us. Several nights afterward—I think I had his phone number?—a girlfriend and I ended up at his house in a bedroom with him and a friend. We did a few lines and then one of them asked if we'd ever put coke on our clits. I said I had to go home but I couldn't get my friend to leave with me. I never asked her what happened after I left.

None of my guy friends from this high school gang wanted me to try cocaine. One of them, the bully's older brother, very angrily told me that he'd never allow any of his friends to sell to me because I was better then a "coke whore," which he was sure I'd become since he'd seen it happen to many other girls. I was both infuriated and flattered by his concern, which was echoed by the rest of the group.

It meant so much to me to feel valued by these young men, more than they knew or probably will ever know. I told them I loved them, I hugged them and slept next to them, lied to be near them, forsake my family for them, and then love stopped being a big enough container for how I felt. I can't think of what I wouldn't have sacrificed if they'd needed it. Except, I suppose, my own willfulness.

My nineteenth birthday I spent with the boy I called my "big, big love" when writing in shorthand years after our time together. It was the first and only night I met the girl he was already falling for, although I didn't know it then. I thought she was merely an acquaintance of the man who sold me my meth line. She didn't say much to me and that was because she had more information than I.

I can't remember her well: dry natural blonde hair, straw-colored, and something about her skin—maybe she had a lot of freckles? Very small brown ones and otherwise not tan, not pale. Maybe a pug nose.

I could never recall anything concrete about her beyond what she was wearing. We went to her apartment first, before the dealer's, and she was in makeshift pajamas, a regular daytime shirt with comfortable lounging pants. And a long, loosely knitted sweater, heavy and cream colored without any fasteners in the front. She didn't change when we left her place to walk a few blocks over, and it was messy winter outside. She was so nonchalant as she dragged the hem of the sweater through puddles and piles of old snow, hugging her elbows. Like she didn't care how she looked or what she ruined.

I recognized the sweater and it took me a few weeks to place the maker but when I finally did, I bought one for myself. I never wore it, outside or in. I only ever packed it in the bottom drawers of my dressers and in boxes every time I moved, for years. Until one day it was gone. I don't know where it is. I may have given it away. I may have put it in the attic of my mother's home. Its disappearance distresses me a little; I don't know why I would be so careless. It's still the best birthday I ever had, because I spent most of it with him.

Eventually he wrote me a letter telling me how in love with her he was. They're not together anymore, but I wish I still had the sweater.

Getting Off
June 29, 2009

I don't masturbate anymore. When I was younger, I was a fiend. In the shower, in tanning beds, in the home where I babysat after I'd put the children to bed and locked myself in the bathroom with the father's Penthouse. I think I was eleven when I started playing with myself—the same age at which I got my period. And it's astounding to reflect on how much time I spent getting off.

Part of this recent abstention is due to the fact that I like coming with someone else better than coming alone, and orgasms aren't particularly interesting or necessary to me unless another person is around. I'm sure this is temporary and correlated to work. I actually can't even remember how I used to come when I was alone; I've done it as a performance far too many times to have any natural instinct for using my fingers anymore. I'm deeply uncomfortable and self-conscious if I try to do it in front of anyone who really knows me, unsettled in the way of any animal when a physical routine is challenged.

Without a gaze, masturbating is foreign and awkward. All the aesthetic adjustments—spreading my thighs back and close to my chest, pointing my toes and curling my arches, reaching under my ass and nestling my wrist in the cleft of coccyx so I can still use my left hand to spread or finger but my arm isn't in the way—are moves I still make now and they have nothing to do with my pleasure.

Or they may. Sometimes those vestiges of being watched can make me feel sexy, as my habit of sympathetic noise occasionally does. Another reverberation of work is the sounds I make during any sex, not only PIV. They aren't verbal or loud or even insincere. They're a cross between a pant and a moan, and they're designed for encouragement, not outright deception. (I started catching myself on moan autopilot with personal lovers years ago and was never quite sure what to do about it. The unthinking sounds may be here to stay, at least for another year or two.)

My orgasms have become much more powerful this year, by which I mean longer, stronger, and deeper. More muscular and less superficial. I'm told that when I come my pussy clenches in a distinct front to back sequence of squeezes, a transparently logical series of pumps. (I can feel the squeezing but can't pay enough attention to notice that much.) And now I'm more relaxed afterward. There's increased sensitivity but it's not as uncomfortably intense as it used to be. I feel like something in me has changed, something has happened, rather than just brushed by. I don't know what I should attribute this shift to. Stronger PC muscles? Greater flexibility? A different type of sex?

But even as my orgasms are better, I care about them less and less. Clients often regale me with stories of particularly intense orgasms, in which the climax itself is what was so memorable. But I don't know that I could remember any single orgasm by sensation alone. I remember some as hallmarks: first time I came with a toy—while I was working on webcam, with a man who became one of my best and most loyal clients; first time I came with a man—also the first time anyone went down on me. I was twenty-one; first time I came with a woman—about four minutes into a show, with a vibrator.

Those moments might be valuable or meaningful to me but they aren't what come to mind when I think about the best sex I've had. Because the best sex I've had hasn't been about one instant at the end. It's been about everything that comes before.

Full Moon
July 8, 2009

We have amazing physical chemistry. It's good with many clients but not always this good. He holds me down with one hand, yanks me into a tight triangle with my chest on the bed and my ass in the air, stomach on my thighs, and smears my wetness up and down my pussy lips while whispering, "Good girl." He pushes my hair over my eyes and then pulls it away, hard enough to make me yelp a little while I'm underneath him, and then he growls, "This is where you belong." It doesn't take me long to be ready to beg for it.

"Do you know how much self control it takes?" he asks when he's pumping a finger in me. "I want to fuck every hole in your body." His fingers are long and thick enough so that the first time he put his thumb in me from behind I thought for a moment that it was his cock. Although his cock is much bigger. Fat.

Tonight he had me pinned on my stomach as he worked me into a froth with his hand, laying his weight on top of me. He'd already come once but I hadn't. I thought he might slide in without a condom and part of me didn't care. I was aching for it. But I kept my hips angled so he stayed between my thighs. Then he reached down with one hand and positioned himself against me. He rocked a few times but his head didn't split my lips. I started trying to move away.

Maybe he thought I was playing, or struggling because it makes me feel sexy. I knew what was happening between my legs and held it in my head in the same time, not as an image but like an outline or a memory or the impression of a sensation no longer there. Maybe that was the fuck up; I watched when I should have been in control. I don't know why else I didn't speak. You can hold that against me. I do.

He repositioned his cock with his hand and started pushing against my asshole. I was trying to crawl forward on the bed. I was making distressed noises. Then a slow tearing pain. I cried "no" from deep in my throat and it sounded like a sob when it hit the air.

Then the pressure was gone but the pain remained. He rolled over and took me with him. We both lay still, breathing. My mouth pulled back at the corners. The hurt was so sharp and ugly—still the impression of being stretched, of my skin there thin and tight as a sunburn. He wrapped his arms around me and clutched me as we lay our sides, spooned together like two stuck mating animals. He might have been kissing me.

I pressed my forehead into the mattress. I'd been here before. The first time a client stuck his cock in me without a condom. The first time a client I liked did it and even though I fought and said no, he didn't stop until I cried, then stood outside the bathroom door calling for me to come to him, using his Greek pet name for me while I stood in the shower sobbing. I don't like this man the way I liked and trusted that one. I don't feel bonded to him. I don't think he's a kind person.

This man stroked my back with his fingertips and it felt good. I

N.B.

thought of things I might say to him. *We were both being reckless* or . . . I don't remember the other ones. I didn't hate him. I didn't even feel angry. I just wished I wasn't there, in that place, in that place in that way. I wanted to be far away from what had happened and I didn't care how I got there.

Finally I lifted my head and turned slowly to face him. None of his features formed an expression. At least nothing I could name or recognize.

"I have to go," I said.

"You drive me crazy," he said. "I lose control."

I gathered my clothes from the floor, put on my bra and dress but dropped my white thong on my bag as I walked to the bathroom. *Please don't let there be blood*, I thought as I reached back to wipe. I pulled my hand away and looked down at the red. I dabbed again and brought back more streaked tissue. I lifted my dress and spread my ass cheeks. I looked over my shoulder at myself in the mirror.

When I left the bathroom, he was standing naked by my purse. I bent down and tucked in the panties.

"What would your mother say if she knew you were walking around without underwear?" He asked.

"I hope she never knows," I replied. I held open my purse and he put the money inside.

I'd told myself the only thing that would make this better would be him paying me more, but he didn't, and I already knew he wouldn't. Maybe that's why I made it the one salvation. I know the type of guy he is. He wants to toy with me. He does want me to beg for it, any way he'll give it to me. He wants me to be invested in how he sees me. He wants me to make myself fully his whore, to be ready to do whatever he wants for only his approval in return.

"You know, if I get too pushy, you can whack me," he said.

"Ok."

"I really appreciate you meeting me tonight. Tonight was . . . " he shook his head and sighed as in, *incredible*.

"Thanks for . . . having me." I said.

"You English majors and your word play." He opened the door. Neither of us said goodbye.

I felt like I was tilting through the lobby, listing a little like a drunk. I started walking home but was disoriented and kept going in the wrong direction. I should have hailed a cab but I didn't want to sit. I didn't want to be alone with a stranger. I was still throbbing wet between my legs and I thought about masturbating once I was home, an idea that was hideous and soothing.

A homeless man said hello to me gently and I lifted my fingers at him but kept my arm by my side. It was all I could manage. I passed a girl on her cell phone who was saying, "I want you to talk to me while I walk home so I'm not bored and . . . lonely."

Men in cars whistled at me. Writing this in my head kept me calm.

A few blocks from home I looked up and saw the quiet full moon above the roofs of town homes. It was beautiful. And when I was approaching my building I thought I saw the moon reflected high in the glass but it was only a round yellow light on an apartment across the street.

Ports
July 10, 2009

I saw the diver again. He looked the same, maybe thinner. When I held his stomach and kissed his thighs, I felt long abdominals rise like rails against my palms. He apologized for not shaving. When I asked him how long he's sported his beard, he said since the 1990s.

I love his hair, the thick cap on his head and the fine curls all over his tan torso and paler legs. I grazed the skin on the inside curve of his hipbone with my fingertips and he sucked in his breath. He laid still while I drew my fingers and mouth over all of him. I didn't realize how wet that made me until he parted my lips with his hand and I was suddenly slick up and down the length of my crotch.

I asked him if how I was touching him made him uncomfortable and he said, "No. I don't think you have a wrong move in your body."

"You know what I was thinking about you since I saw you last? You look entirely different in profile than you do head on. I mean–"

I opened my mouth and he caught me. "Everyone does. But from the side you're very defined and angular. And facing you, you're curvilinear. Soft."

He drew his finger along my cheek. "I've never known anyone who looked so different that way."

"You're right," I said. "My profile is very . . . severe."

"Not severe, just clean, sharp. It's not a bad thing."

I didn't know what to say so I said, "Well . . . now I have that information."

We laid in silence for a moment. Then I told him about meeting the musician who, within minutes of our introduction, told me I had a sexy jawline because it was so defined, then touched the back of my face, fingering the bone's edge to which he was referring. I thought everyone had that, and I told him as much, after which he lifted my fingers and had me touch him there to prove that I was wrong.

I didn't want to bother him—I assumed people were in awe of his celebrity on a regular basis and clung to him when they had the chance—so I tried to resume conversations with the other people backstage. At one point, he interrupted me with a roadie by asking me, "Why the fuck are you talking to this asshole?" We all laughed but it was awkward.

"So then I told him about what I do and he asked if he owed me money for the time we'd spent talking together and I told him he did."

"What did you tell him? Did you use the word 'courtesan'?"

"Come on. No. I think I only intimated it, I didn't come out and label it."

"You're a therapist," the diver suggested. I didn't say anything.

He touched my scar and said, "poor femur."

"It's ok. It's better now. It's bionic."

Then I wondered aloud what happened if you were cremated with metal parts, if it messed up the machine—the kiln? The oven? Whatever it's called.

"No, you can still do it. They collect it afterward."

"So you mean my body falls away and then the titanium is there and … what do they do with it?"

"They put it in with the urn."

"But!" I placed the edges of my hands at the top and bottom of my thigh for measurement.

"You'll have a really tall urn."

He told me about one of his brothers, a banker who blew through Ivy

League schools and whose partner is a former gymnast, a Texan, who once did a standing backflip in a suit to prove he still could.

"I wish they would take me in. They sound fun."

"They are."

"And sexy."

He nodded a bit. "My brother's an attractive guy. They're good together."

Then, abruptly, "Tell me there's someone for everyone."

"Repeat that back to you verbatim?"

"Not necessarily. You can do variations on a theme."

I was quiet. Finally I said, "I think there are many people for each person, don't you?"

"Yes, I do. I just . . . Chicks, man."

"Are you like Uncle Vanya in 'The Seagull'?"

"Uncle Vanya!" He laughed. "Good Chekhov reference!"

"I wanted to get married but I never did." I recited. "I wanted to live in the city but I live in the country . . . "

He told me a story about his brother playing charades at a family gathering, trying to mime being hit by a train because his clue was Anna Karenina, then yelling, "Don't you people read?" when nobody got it.

It's too easy to daydream with these pieces he gives me, weave together a pretty life in which I charm his erudite siblings, join him on last-minute flights to London to see his sister and nephews who name a Lego woman after me, sail with him someplace sunny and sweet, practice in the hull until he comes down from the deck and then suck his cock while he stands next to me and I kneel sweaty on my mat.

As soon as we were alone together, he asked, "Does this happen all time? Guys falling for you hard and fast? Am I unique?"

I didn't respond right away. I wasn't sure what he wanted to hear. We started talking over each other.

"Sometimes."

"So I'm a sap?"

"No! You're not—"

"I feel like such a cliché."

"Well, clichés come into being because they're based on some truth, right?"

We'd ended up on the bed, on our sides and facing each other, still clothed. He was looking into my eyes. Then he said, "I suppose you're right."

When we parted ways, I was sad for hours. I felt unambitious and stupid, filled with that melancholy regret that takes over when in the presence of highly educated people, truly smart people. I see a lot of successful men, but rarely do I feel intimidated by their intellect, even if they're trying to make me feel inferior (especially when they're trying to make me feel inferior.) He tipped me and somehow this was very upsetting.

Our time together was different than it had been during the first meeting. Somehow rushed or more confused. He was in a philosophical mood, and got particularly hung up on the idea of people changing, musing that after a certain age you can only ever be one person, that your experiences determined it irrevocably.

"Do you want that to be true?" I asked.

"I don't know. Can you think of anyone you know who has changed? I mean really changed?"

He kept returning to this idea of stagnancy, asking me if it was a fatalistic thing to believe.

"Well, it could be comforting because it would absolve you of responsibility for who you are. You can't think of anyone you know who's changed?"

"No."

"Maybe you should be the first then. Be the example."

"But I like myself. I wouldn't even know where to start . . . What do you want to be when you grow up?"

I took a breath, then said, "What do you recommend?"

"Well, if this makes you happy then, I guess . . . keep doing this."

On Timing
July 16, 2009

I wanted to lose my virginity to my first love. I pined for him painfully for about a year and a half with a devotion recognized by my female friends as a definitive aspect of my high school experience. When he was going out with a friend of mine for a few days, whatever that meant or means, she casually told me at a party that if he had any interest in me she would wouldn't hesitate to step aside. This was after he and I absconded to the hanging chair on the front porch of our friend's house and talked for hours about something I can't remember. All I can recall is that I drew my legs up to the seat, and he slowly rubbed the sole of my foot through my red woolen socks with his thumb.

High school was fully of luminous moments like that, romantic incidents at night with no adults nearby and no action of which to speak, just the heady sense of endless possibility and immutable connection. There's no certainty like that of adolescent emotions.

I became mildly infatuated with him before ever meeting him because of an email survey making the rounds among his friends, one of whom I was acquainted with. My address was in the clump included in his reply, and I was entirely taken with his responses: his sense of humor, the music he listened to. These quizzes/surveys/whatever they should be called were ubiquitous at the time. There was a new one every week, each composed of dozens of questions regarding what song you wanted played at your funeral or what food you could eat for all three meals. When I finally saw his face, it was across the floor of a dark room after our one mutual friend pointed him out. I thought: *he's beautiful.* I've never quite had that hammer-to-the-head moment again.

But I was not beautiful. So I was left to do what all unrequited lovers angle to do in their desperation, which was to become his friend. And his friendship was not a consolation prize. His company was too valuable for me to complain about it, no matter what form it took. Eventually I got over him, we fooled around one night after I smoked crack (I know,) and we're still friends.

When I was going through a very bad breakup several years ago, he took me into his home, a beautiful place on Long Island that was everything I needed at the time. This is some of what I wrote about it then:

We actually didn't talk much this weekend but I feel grateful when I'm around people who can let me be silent. Making conversation is probably inextricably tied to work for me, which also means that I do it instinctually around men I don't feel entirely comfortable with. Luckily Nick is not one of those.

I had a weird sort of melancholy time at his place but it was perfect.

I slept very hard and with his cat. In the mornings, it was chilly, with green outside of every window: trees all around his wraparound deck with the ocean wrinkling on the horizon. We drank tea. He made a fire in his wood stove.

Recently, he wrote me and said he first became curious about me before we met, when he read some of my responses to one of those email surveys, a decade ago. I don't remember him ever telling me before now.

Knocked
July 22, 2009

"Well, your test result was positive," she said, immediately after sitting down in the chair across from me. White paper was spread across my naked legs, my dress hiked up around my hips. The office that day was running about two hours behind. When I'd put my cup of pee in the steel window, there was another woman's still there.

"Wow," I said. "Really."

"We'll draw some blood to make sure but, yes, your urine was positive. How have you been feeling?"

"The same. Entirely the same."

"No nausea, or . . . ?"

"No, not at all . . . Wow. I think I'm glad you told me rather than a stick."

"Yeah the sticks can be not so . . . Is this a good or a bad thing?" She asked. I'd seen her only twice before, over the span of two years. She introduced herself when she came into the room; we essentially were strangers.

I paused until finally saying, "It's not a good thing. I mean, I know who the father is, it's my boyfriend—"

"How long have you been together?"

"Years. Three years."

"So maybe it will be a good thing. But we'll talk options a little later. You came here for yeast infections?"

"I did but it sort of pales . . . I've never been pregnant before."

"You went off the pill?"

"Yeah, because of the yeast infections. I thought the pills were contributing so I'd just try it without, and I read online that the sponge was more successful than I'd thought—"

"For a woman in your age group that's simply not enough. You need something that's about 100 percent."

"Apparently." He'd only come in me once. That was part of the shock; he'd been pulling out. I know that's the warning: it only takes one time. But I'd considered for years that I might be infertile. Probably the rural girl in me found it impossible to believe that a tiny pink dot would be warding off pregnancy—it was too much like magic. I'd never had a scare, but I was meticulous, before now.

We were looking at each other but neither of us could concentrate. It was like trying to watch a juggler while seated in a burning theater.

"So, do you offer abortion services here?"

"Oh no, we—"

"Do you give referrals?"

"No. Dr. McArthur is pro-life, so . . . Are you sure that's what you want to do?" Her face was not expressionless. Her face stayed poised with the same expression throughout, I was having a hard time figuring out what it was conveying, or trying not to convey. It was disapproving, of course. But restrained, even before she knew what I wanted to do. She probably had grandchildren. Her skin was lined and soft and very white.

"Yes."

"Well you can google it and places will come up."

"There's nothing specific I should look for or a place you would recommend?"

"I don't know. You never know what you're getting. It depends on the doctor. Some are good and some are . . . " *Going to give you a complete hysterectomy. Use unsterilized instruments. Smoke during. Send you into septic shock. Which you deserve.*

I looked at the corner of the drawers besides her and slowly said, "There's not any name you're willing to give me?"

She picked up on my word choice. "It's not that I won't, I—I don't even know anyone."

"And how far along do you have to be to get one?"

"I don't know. Eight weeks?"

It was naive of me to think that a private practice would offer all the options, or at least resources for all options. I read feminist sites, donate to

NARAL, volunteered for a while as a clinic escort. But I hadn't expected this response from someone who is ostensibly "my" doctor, someone I trust with my health.

It wasn't professional or competent or right to not even have information on the basics. There's no other medical condition for which this would happen. No doctor tells a patient she has cancer and then tells her to shop around for an oncologist on Yelp. I could have said I wanted hymenoplasty and gotten a more encouraging response. The sheet of paper between my updated medical history and my insurance information asked about my interest in a list of at least twenty procedures like Botox and laser rejuvenation. In a gynecologist's office.

"But we'll go ahead and draw blood," she said.

"Do you have to?"

"No."

This seemed to surprise her a little or make her angry. Angrier.

"Your urine was positive and you haven't had your period in six weeks, you're pregnant."

"Ok," I said.

"Ok," she said. And she left,

I stayed in the room for a minute. She hadn't left a piece of paper, hadn't said anything about copay or check out. When I let myself out, she was there in the hall.

"I don't need to take up a sheet of paper, or . . . ?"

"Oh, no, I already dropped that off at the front."

"Ok." I was not crying but I was not well.

"Ok, Charlotte. Take care." Then she lifted her pale hand like she was going to touch me. But I was already walking away, and her movement was too slow.

Rare Work
July 31, 2009

I don't know how men imagine the sensations of women when it comes to the cavities inside us, the space of the hall and the potential nest—if they imagine it at all. Are you wary of that allotted void? Do you think there is an insistent hollow, canal and pouch loudly empty when we're walking and moving in the world? Because it's not like that. I feel whole and sealed outside of sex. Insertion is an invasion, which doesn't mean it's a bad thing, but it's taking in something foreign. There's no mistaking that the accommodation is temporary. Keyholes are primarily quiet, singular. They are there for the rare work but complete all the time.

I felt nothing because there was nothing to feel. No effect from the hormones, no coalescing tissue making itself known. No impression of suddenly sharing my body. The sonogram yielded blank, black space. I wanted to keep the small picture, the cut section of a ring, that familiar circular sweep, grainy and dark, but it stayed paper clipped to my file.

"You're barely pregnant," the first woman who drew my blood told me.

The doctor asked how far along I thought I was and I said, "three weeks."

"That's about—you're right," he affirmed. Then he told me my options: shot, pill, or surgery. He strongly discouraged the pill. He listed the options for surgery, twilight sleep or total anesthesia, and then he said, "Or you could do nothing, which in your case I wouldn't recommend."

I didn't realize he was talking about drugging options until I'd left the office. I thought he meant ways of responding to the pregnancy. Which made it very funny when he went on to say, "That's for women who have had four kids and just don't care."

He was a nice man. When he came in, he said, "You're twenty-six and this is your first pregnancy? You must be terrified."

"I'm ok," I said. And I was.

I had a coach, my best friend, my abortion midwife. She recommended the clinic, recommended the shot, explained the basics, drove me, came in with me, sat next to me through the blood tests and even the sonogram. I didn't even know the shot existed. It's a drug used to treat cancer. Make of that what you will.

I don't mean she pressured me one way or another. She was resolutely supportive of each possibility. This is someone I met when we both worked for a woman who ran an agency. Our friendship was instant. There is nobody like her, for me. When I called her once to complain about an accusation that I was incapable of making friends who weren't also sex workers, she said, "Sex worker friendships are so intense that it's hard to see the point with anyone else." Which is exactly true. There was no one else I wanted with me. My emotional life always gravitates to her.

At one point she said, "It's sort of exciting, isn't it?" referring to the pregnancy. It was, even though my knowledge of it was academic rather than felt. The bare knowledge managed to engender many qualities, often times in equal parts. It wasn't hard and I won't pretend it was. Or it was hard, but for reasons beyond the assumed. That is part of the story of my abortion.

The Gift of Embodiment
August 2, 2009

At first I thought—I hoped—it might be hemorrhoids. I asked my friend if she thought this was due to the pregnancy, since that effect is a common one, and she said "I don't think you can blame this on the baby." A week after the bad appointment I felt healed, but a few days later, I wasn't.

It's been going on for two weeks now and getting worse. It flared again after I was hurrying to obtain an abortion, while I was traveling and loathe to see another doctor. When I sit on the toilet, I try to imagine the pain of women with fistula, of all animals with wounds that will never receive proper attention, never heal, that they will either die with or be killed by. Try to fathom the suffering most beings endure, try to develop compassion, try to minimize sensation. I sit tall, breathing firmly and telling myself, *there will not be pain, there will not be pain,* but there is, precise and exquisite, and afterward the water is clouded with blood. I used to bring a thick cloth to bite down on, to keep me from screaming, but I think the less stressed approach is better.

In the wake of the rushed abortion and with the backdrop of this searing between my ass cheeks, which sometimes wakes me at night if I spread my legs too far apart, I've had no interest in sex. But I think of the many writers, including all the obvious suspects (Bataille: "In the excess of raptures that shatter me, I seize on the similarity between a horror and a voluptuousness that goes beyond me, between an ultimate pain and an unbearable joy!") who insist that sex be coupled with pain. My dreams have been richly horny, unfolding in that space where I'm as fully wet and swollen as I can possibly be, and I stay that way until the end.

A friend told me he thinks I'll need stitches. I was, I admit, terrified. I said I couldn't imagine a worse place to feel a needle except possibly the genitals. He said, "Definitely genitals," but I could bear this injury better if it were at my vulva or vagina. It's often the site of blood and trauma. PIV sex was intensely painful for me for some time; I would cry and cry out although my hymen was long gone and there was never any blood. I had to train myself to relax. I had to teach myself not to hurt. Still, it sometimes does. And for every cunt, suffering is part of its job description. I suppose that's the truth for all of the body.

When I was leaving the clinic, a protestor shouted at me, "Don't take the abortion pill! The abortion pill kills women!" This is true—it has killed several women—but of course childbirth has killed millions more.

Tricky Women
August 6, 2009

An earlier appointment ran long, so I called to let him know.

"I'm so sorry," I said. I hate being late. "Is it ok if I still head over?"

"Charlotte," he said, laughing. "You are a classic art-history major. You are so right-brained. You are so non-math, non-numbers . . . When do you think you're going to be here?"

"8:30?"

"Oh, 8:30? You mean the time we actually planned?"

I started laughing too. "Well, according to you, but I haven't decided if I trust your memory yet!" I was glad I made the mistake, speaking with him cheered me up so much.

Once I was there, he sank into the philosophizing that alcohol so often brings on in older men: on how different he and I are, how uncomfortable he is naked and how nonchalant I am, how my comfort enhances his. Then he asked, "Do you have friends you see infrequently? Once a year, once every two years, every three?"

I nodded.

"And have you noticed that with those friends you can be more candid than you would be with friends you see more often? You can share things with them more intimately?"

"Yes. Definitely."

"I think that's natural," he said. He didn't offer a context for his musing. He didn't need to.

"It's because you get to tell your story," I suggested. "All of the information is filtered through your understanding. Because that person isn't in the same circumstances with you, with the same people—and so you know they can't think 'that's not how it happened' or 'but she wouldn't do something like that.' They're not going to challenge your . . . reality."

"Yes, I think that's it." He said. There was a pause and then he told me, "One more outburst like that, young lady, and you're going to get another reddening."

In the interludes between spankings, he doled out his reflections since we'd last been together, about how comfortable I am with myself and also about how "careful:" "You don't say what you're thinking. You don't reveal much." I wasn't sure how to respond to this.

He asked me if I actually liked being spanked, if I enjoyed it or hated it or tolerated it, and prefaced that by saying he shouldn't even be answering the question because he wasn't sure he wanted to know the truth.

"Should I not answer then? Should I save you from yourself?"

"That's good," he said, impressed. His drinking, apparently, makes me seem like a genius. "You're ahead of me. You're tricky."

"Tricky? I like that."

"It's a combination of street smarts and intelligence and . . . craftiness and . . . self-preservation."

When we'd met in the lounge, he was holding a copy of *Island*. I asked him if it was good and he said it had several great lines. There's one that I'd love to find an opportunity to use in conversation, but it seems to be the domain of earnest yet neurotic men, British journalists and hardworking Jewish boys-turned-elderly-gentlemen: "I won't take yes for an answer."

Girl Dream
August 7, 2009

I was at a pregnancy retreat. Women there could bring two guests, two people to keep them company and help with the birth. Most of them had their mothers and fathers. I had my mother and a man who was either my brother or my boyfriend. I was the only girl not showing. *Why am I here?* I kept thinking. *They'll kick me out if they find out about the abortion.*

One young woman had red hair and a wide, pale face. She was charismatic in an irritating way: obnoxious because of her arrogance and insecurity, compelling but not beguiling. I wanted to be her friend. She stole my long, ugly coat. Then someone evil came and put each of us alone in a tall rectangular hole. I wondered why we would give birth in holes. Then I realized we were left there to die, before or after or during it.

The sun was bright and the grass around our graves almost neon green. There was a breeze. It was a ridiculous place to feel fear. I was mostly confused, especially because the holes weren't so deep that we couldn't climb out with a little help. We escaped with our families. We weren't pursued.

I ended up in a small dive with one of the other girls. We sat together at a table, drinking or maybe not drinking. The redhead came in, wearing my coat. I was surprised to see her, and angry. I accused her of stealing, which she denied. Finally she admitted, "I said I would give it back! I told you, you just had to wait and I would give it back."

I said, "I only wanted to be your friend! Because you remind me of my daughter."

The word came out like a punch to my own face. I'd never for a moment thought I had any ties to this girl, but is that who she was? Was she my potential daughter at my age, of my generation?

Someone was at the jukebox. I heard the strains of "Just Ain't Gonna Work Out" and thought, *Hey, I know this song.*

Hit Me Harder
August 9, 2009

With him, there's no playing along. I'm rarely so insolent and uncooperative. He brings it out in me.

"Look at her, standing there like 'when will this be over?'" I don't know why he talks about me in the third person. I don't know why I even agree to see him. Except that August is slow. Everyone's gone or lazy with heat, busy with the family and broke from vacations.

He was holding my legs between his thighs as I stood in profile to him. I kept my face still and waited for the impact.

"There she is, bored. Acting like there's nothing strange going on."
"What's so strange?"
"You're in a hotel room with a man you barely know, naked."
I rolled my eyes. "Stranger things have happened."
"Oh really? Really, what type of stranger things?"
"We're not the only ones," I said, disparagingly. Ridiculous to pretend we'd invented nudity, or hotel trysts. I was being a killjoy. That's supposed to be part of the fun: the naughtiness, the unseemliness, the uncommonness. Except this is all so very common.

One client is wildly into being watched. He desperately wants women to catch him in his underwear, so our time together is molded around him standing nearly nude in front of a window for hours, pretending to be on the phone, while I lie on the bed behind him in lingerie, with binoculars, watching for those who might watch in return. Much effort is put into selecting a hotel room that faces an office building where unsuspecting ladies do their daily work. We routinely remark on what hard workers the women are; they rarely look out into the sky or the street, daydreaming.

The last time I saw him, he occasionally urged me to move further back from the window, so far that I was kneeling on the other side of the bed in my bra and panties, peeking over the edge as though I were ducking from bullets. Early on, he said, "Don't look, but there are some guys watching us from that office. They have binoculars too."

I should have suspected this—another client told me he kept binoculars in his desk when he used to work opposite a hotel—but I hadn't, and I was delighted. I did look. I saw them, two of them, heavyset and in Oxford shirts, and when they knew they were seen they'd move to a different window or crouch down at the corner of the glass, heads still visible.

"Oh, people are so great," I kept saying, laughing. "People are so great." And so arrogant, to think no one else is like we are.

At one point in the middle of beating me, this other man told me to turn around so he could see my "pretty eyes." I say "beat" when it's with his belt or a strap or particularly roughly with one of his paddles. And I say beat because he complains about my non-response ("you're so stoic") and tries to hit me hard enough to get a reaction.

"I realized I know how many dimples you have in your butt, but I didn't know the color of your eyes."

"Really? Well I hope someone knows to call you if my body ever needs to be identified by my ass alone."

"I don't *really* know," he admitted.

Sometimes I get irate enough to ask what I should be doing rather than taking it without complaint: "Weeping? Screaming?"

"No, no, I know you're not a screamer."

"Ok then . . . " I suppose that's a yes to the crying.

"You hated this one last time," he said, drawing out a tawse. I didn't recognize it and I told him so.

He struck me twice.

"Oh right, I remember," I said. And he kept going.

Girl Talk
August 11, 2009

I held it in front of my face and touched it. It felt like the inside of a cheek, firm but silky. It was the size and shape of a slug, clinging to my tampon. Shiny and slimy with blood. It probably did not yet have a heart. It was alive only to the extent that my own life was working to assemble it, which is to say not at all. An empty, barely-built house.

When I was sixteen, I went to Planned Parenthood with my best friend so she could get birth control. It was located just off of our town's main strip and there were never protestors because that branch didn't actually provide abortions. When we entered the small waiting room, we recognized a relatively popular girl who sometimes hung out with our guy friends. She wasn't friendly towards us, though, so we didn't speak beyond (possibly) a hello. She picked up something from the counter and left.

Knowing that she was having sex was exciting and scandalous, and for the rest of high school her last name was synonymous with "fuck." ("Did you booth?" "Are they boothing?")

Several years later, I came to that same PP for a morning-after pill. This was before it was over the counter and still highly taboo, so taking one felt illicit and dramatic. When I told the boy I'd had sex with that I got my period, he replied "Oh, that sucks" and I had to remind him why it didn't.

Another high school friend, Kelly, once told us, our all-female core group, that her mother had an abortion after bearing Kelly's little brother. I remember all of us being inexplicably disapproving, probably because we had a hard time reconciling motherhood and abortion in the same individual. Abortions seemed like the domain of the young and wild. Kelly, though, was proud of her mom and declared that she would have done the same thing.

I've gotten quite a few emails recently from women whose emotional experience seems to mirror my own. They were pregnant, they didn't want to be, they had an abortion, there is no drama or regret. The common theme is of certainty, of the lack of waffling and the absolute clarity with which they made their choices. I resent the cultural script that all women afterward are crying and broken, haunted forever. A lot of women only feel relief, and crying might never occur, or only be brought on by dealing with shitty health care professionals—one employee of Planned Parenthood told my friend she thought all surgical abortions should be done without anesthesia, as an extra incentive for the girls not to get pregnant again—or crazed family members. (The father's mother screamed at another friend of mine, "You killed my grandchild!")

For any man who knows a woman about to have an abortion, here is my advice: just don't make it hard for her. This includes talking about what a profound impact it will have on her—even if the intention is sympathetic—because this assumed devastation might very well be nonexistent and then you're piling on to the cultural guilt trip.

I wasn't sure that I would tell my mom, but I did. She asked if I didn't even think for a moment about keeping it, and I said no. She said having an abortion shortens your lifespan, and I laughed and said that was propaganda. She said she wished I had spent more time thinking about the psychological ramifications. I told her I didn't need any time at all to know that the psychological effects of having a child would be far more profound than those of having an abortion. And then she told me she'd had an abortion before I was born.

I cried because she cried. She had the surgery and she named her baby, which she either knew or suspected was a girl. She thought about it when she was trying to conceive and when she miscarried before getting pregnant with me, thinking God had given her her chance and she'd lost it. It was my father's. With him, she experienced every outcome a conception can have: live birth, abortion, miscarriage, stillbirth. Women. They amaze me.

"Don't tell your brother," she said "but carrying you was the happiest time of my life." We cried some more. I am crying a little right now. She told me about other family members who had an abortion, including my great grandmother, who had two in Turkey and lived into her 90s.

One friend emailed me and said he was sorry for my loss. I told him not to be because there wasn't one, but that's not entirely true. I forfeited one future for another, which is something all of us do everyday in small and large ways. That's the bargain of being alive. You don't get to have it all.

Abundance
August 15, 2009

Ever since I've been doing some form of sex work, I've been paid more than I ever expected. I began doing it in grad school, and the truth was that I didn't need much money since I already had a stipend, a scholarship, and was paid for teaching. Rent wasn't much. I didn't have any expensive habits. My recreation was hanging out with other poets, talking about art and walking around the city, or watching Futurama and eating instant oatmeal with my beloved housemate who was also a writer and a musician.

When I moved to a different city and lived alone, I did the walking by myself. I read a lot, wrote some, watched films, and bought clothing and used books. I made well above what I needed, and sometimes I would look at the number at my bank account and try to think of new things to buy. That's what a good American I was; I'd wrack my brain for something I didn't own that I inevitably needed or had use for. A digital camcorder, for example. I shopped for one with the older man and the salesperson kept referring to the man's son as my boyfriend, even after I'd told him the father was who I was with.

What did digital camcorders cost then, five years ago? A small, tidy one with good quality? At least 1k, I think, but I don't remember. I never used it. A friend of mine from that time called me once asking me to give her suggestions of things to spend money on, because she'd already bought everything she could think of. Clients compounded this because they'd always want to give presents. We had to find something tangible to point them towards and after we were exhausted by clothes and shoes, we'd turn to curtains and kitchen appliances and luggage. But that same friend would also call and say she was broke. One week she'd be getting extensions and laser hair removal and the next she was worried about making rent. I always saved, and figured out fairly quickly that I liked hoarding better than spending.

I relocated again, started work for a woman, and culled clients down to only those who tipped the best or were the least demanding. I'd count my cash every night, religiously, put it back in my hiding place with a yellow legal pad where I kept track of what I'd made per appointment, added up to what I made for the day, added up to what I made for the week, then the month. The moment that really screwed me was seeing the cumulative, realizing what my yearly income would be if I kept up at the same rate. Once you have that number in your head, I think, it becomes nearly impossible to settle for less. Even if it's double what you want. Even if it's three or four or five times what you need. And even if you're beyond knowing what either of those other numbers might be.

It makes me uncomfortable and it always has: how senselessly satisfying it is to count piles of bills, bind them with rubber bands, label them with the amount, tuck them away together. (For some reason, there's no satisfaction in depositing them in the bank, although I do that on occasion.) I joked that the nightly counting was my Silas Marner ritual, but that's really no joke, only an accurate analogy. I have enough sense to know money only means something to the extent that it's useful to you and cash sitting in a dark place for months or years isn't improving my quality of life.

But it was an epiphany recently when I thought about my target salary for this year and realized it was entirely arbitrary. It was a number without any effect on my lifestyle, although I suppose I sometimes rely on it as proof of my value or how good I am. Really, though, it's nothing. The months when I fall short are no different than months when I go over. I couldn't even tell you, without looking at my notes, how much I made two weeks ago or last month.

I was recently with another woman who told me about her goal amount, the point at which she'll leave the industry and put her money towards another enterprise. And she mentioned managing to pay off all her debt several months ago. Somewhere in the back of my head, I was finally getting the most basic of concepts: *so that's how people figure out how much money they should make—they figure out how much they need.*

Another friend recently retired to pursue another business. This impressed me greatly, because she was incredibly successful and it was hard for me to fathom that anyone would turn away from that much money.

Both of these women are older than me, which I should probably take as encouragement. Even Silas Marner was eventually redeemed.

Marriage
August 17, 2009

They were simply wonderful, fun and funny. And the husband truly seemed to only have eyes for his wife, which makes any man instantly endearing. When he touched me—it always shocked me a bit since he seemed so fixated on her—he made sure his other hand was still on her skin. At the end, he asked if she had been jealous. She replied, "Yeah, kinda." But I couldn't think of why that would be true.

As we were getting dressed, I told her she had beautiful breasts and it took her aback. She asked if I saw the scars. I hadn't. She told me she had a reduction when she was only sixteen.

She came down to the kitchen dressed to go out to dinner in a black minidress, and her husband said, "You look hot. I love how that necklace dips down into your cleavage . . . Are you showing off because of what Charlotte said?"

"Oh yeah," she replied. "That made my week."

"I meant it," I said. "I'm jealous."

"You? Oh please. You've got a whole—" she gestured in the air with a bounce of her hip, "a whole situation going on there."

They were so frank as we sat talking in their living room. The husband recapped what had happened since we last saw each other. "Well, there was a time there where our sex drives were dead, I mean . . . we had sex maybe once for the whole month?"

"Noooo," she said. "How do you know that?"

"And then we were on a safari and before that we got really fat."

"You're not fat," I said.

"Well, we lost some of it."

"But we're still a little roly," she said, leaning back on the couch in a way that suggested she really didn't care.

I love going down on a woman. She'd never had a woman even touch her before but she seemed relaxed and receptive. This may have been because I switched with her husband and she later confessed she wasn't sure who was doing what. Too many hands and tongues and sensations at play.

Afterward, she wanted to ask about my work. Every female client I've seen is like this and most male clients too, but the women are more blunt. One, a professor at a university in New England whose husband arranged our encounter, asked if I'd ever been sexually abused. I indulged the wife's questions for a while. She wasn't rude. ("So, this isn't part of your sexual life? I mean, you keep that for your private life?")

I talked with the couple about recently cutting off someone who'd become too invasive with regards to my privacy, who figured out my real name and scoured the internet for information to then suggest ways he could advise or assist in other aspects of my life.

"He must have been a little in love with you," the husband said.

"I guess," I replied. But I don't like the idea that love and infatuation are interchangeable.

"Have you ever seen a client in public? What happens if we see you in public?" he asked. She and I were flanking him. Everyone was naked and lying the wrong way on the bed.

"I'd say hi!" I laughed. "I don't have to say hi. We can ignore each other. I'd probably at least smile at you. That doesn't happen very often though. I've only had it happen once, when I was at a play with a girl friend."

"What happened?"

"I tried to ignore him but unfortunately we had seats near each other and I don't think he was being particularly discreet. But we didn't say anything to each other. I hadn't see him in a long time anyway and he was with his wife, so . . . "

This seemed to stun them a bit, sweetly enough, as though this complication hadn't occurred to them.

"Are most of your clients married?" the wife asked.

"Probably." I felt ashamed to admit it to them. And for a moment I thought they might even ask me if I felt guilty or had some ethical problem with it. One of them may have asked that, but the other cut them off. And shortly after that began the business of gathering clothes and blowing out candles and complimenting bodies and saying goodbye.

Being Over
August 23, 2009

Again, we decided it was over. He said he couldn't bear the unhappiness and while he once saw a way to make things right, he couldn't see it anymore.

"I'm not angry," he told me.

"I'm not angry either," I said, shaking my head, tears leaking into my mouth. "But I don't know how to fix this."

He'd been having dreams at least once a week about the baby living on, us with a doctor, looking at a kicking ultrasound image. And he told me about something he did alone on the morning of my clinic visit, something he asked me not to tell anyone so I won't even write it here.

When he said he didn't know why he was so affected by it, I said, "Maybe you think that was our only chance. That we won't be together for it to happen again."

And he nodded, "maybe."

We lay together and combed the past. I thought of how different I was a year or two ago, what I dreamed then and wanted and believed about the future. I didn't say it aloud but I felt the thoughts punching my chest: *I should have been braver. I should have done it alone. I made so many mistakes.* How terrible it is to sit with the knowledge of the ways you've made yourself less because you were afraid.

He said that from the first day we met—when he was still married and didn't know my real name—he knew he wanted me in his life forever. He said my work now tortured him not because I was with other men physically but because he knew the amount of energy and attention they gave me, an expenditure he felt he couldn't match because he was so drained by his obligations. There were many revelations like that, of the truths that I should have seen more clearly but didn't. Evidence of all the ways I'd misunderstood him and vice versa.

This fight began when we were talking in the rain. He asked, rhetorically, "And how many friends do you have?"

Not many. Very few. I catch myself staring at groups when I'm in restaurants, wondering how those laughing people know each other and what it would be like to be surrounded by a fan of people who like and love me beyond sex or some lonely need. I wanted to say that it was the nature of the work—one of my webcam friends has called me for years to mourn the fact that her only friends are her rotating drug dealers and lovers—and the nature of being in a relationship, where other connections are stifled. But I couldn't say anything because I was too gripped by the fear that maybe it's just me. Maybe I'm not likable or nice or interesting.

When I told my first real love that I was in love with him and I knew he couldn't repeat the words to me, I curled on my side in his bed and sobbed, thinking, *who will ever love me? If he can't love me, who will ever love me?* I couldn't fathom anyone knowing me in the way he did. But I think I believed my baring myself to him meant he saw me, when really all it meant was that I was naked and he was looking the other way.

And I chose this work, so what then does that say? I choose writing, which is even more solitary. I design my life around being private, either alone or with one man.

Later, when we were lying together, he apologized. He said he took my few friendships as evidence of how selective I am and the type of intensity I need, and that that made him feel special and lucky to be included in that circle. He listed each of my friends he knows and said that each loved me: "There's no one you keep in your life who wouldn't go the distance for you."

He proposed a series of living situations, ways he could still give to me even if we weren't together but I said no, he didn't owe me that and I didn't want that from him. He said there was nothing he wouldn't give up to be with me, because there was nothing else that mattered as much.
"When you were against the wall," I said, meaning the moment when we agreed we couldn't go on, "I thought about how I'd never be naked with you again. And that made me so sad."
I was surprised by that impulse, because our sex is sometimes awkward and depressing. But intense physical familiarity with someone seems to merit eternal accessibility, like the taste of an apple or the feel of water on your skin.
I cried into his hair. He kissed my chest violently, crushing my body into his.
"Oh baby," he said. "You're the love of my life. I'm not ready for it to end."
So it didn't. It hasn't. But now we have to make a change.

Two Types Of Release
August 27, 2009

We met in Rittenhouse Square, three years after the last time.
Finding him with my eyes birthed a deep bloom of happiness. My smile surfaced like it'd been pushed up mightily from the pit of myself, lifted with joy and a tinge of relief, although joy may already encompass relief, unburdening, a sloughing off of everything heavy and wrong.
We hugged.
"You look different," he said in his suspicious way.
"You look exactly the same," I replied.
Both of us were surprised by how hard he still made me laugh. We

watched a child riding the statue of a goat–it was our release. Children, like animals, are good diversions when conversations are awkward.

Last night, my boyfriend and I returned to the ending—we are eternally walking a cul-de-sac of ending—and at one point he gestured for me to sit in his lap. I said no, that was the release valve, the cheat. When he looked confused, I said that in asana there is an instinctive way your body will move to try to escape whatever stretch or exertion it's feeling, and part of your job is recognizing that and not allowing it. That's the work: holding onto the discomfort. Sitting with the moments that are hard. He gestured again and I said no. Then he came to me instead.

As I've matured, I've begun to contemplate that thought which I refused to entertain for years: maybe there will never be another who I care for as uncontrollably as I did my Big Big Love. Maybe that's the epitome of naiveté, the belief that life is an endless stream of people to pour your love into cleanly, individuals whose mere existence turns that other, inner valve until you are nothing but release, all your good intentions set free.

Years ago in the park, the wind gnawed our bodies as it so often had during the cold seasons of our heyday. It all felt familiar yet unique. I'd thought of the moment for so long and now I was in it like a firefly in an overturned jar. I crawled the walls calmly, feeling out every contour. Surprisingly, I didn't cry.

I haven't seen him since and I don't think I'll ever see him again, so I'm even more grateful for that last time together. There was no thought in my head; I was full of being with him. But it was not as it had been before. This time the delight I took in him was burnished, aged, existing in a place without a future. Promise-less. Absolute.

Bless him. He let me see him once more, plainly, so I could see how right I was. So I could affirm the absence of regret. So I could continue to believe in the infallibility of my heart.

VOLUME I

Believe Everything I Tell You
September 3, 2009

I didn't want; I wondered. Would the sight of him still spark that nervy charge between my legs? I've never had that so powerfully with anyone else, a physical memory that didn't erode. The thought of him literally makes my pussy clench, probably in defense as much as yearning.

Many of the times we were together I didn't come, but quantifying the quality of our sex with an orgasm count would be insane. The sensation of him fucking me didn't fit into any ideas I have about what is hot or sexy or even good. The compulsion to get his cock inside was as uncompromising and mindless as the urge to eat or drink. It wasn't about pleasure. It was about need.

And I'd take more even after I was sore and bloody, tired, hollowed by the blade of my bad choices. There was something special about that. I never felt I was performing with him or that I could even if I wanted to. I barely felt like I participated in our sex. It was effortless—not easy but spontaneous, undertaken without intention.

I don't believe I could see him again and not have sex with him. I don't think it would be possible for either of us to resist whatever wretched glue binds our bodies. It's why we so often ended up in bathrooms and cars. It had to happen. The how and where were irrelevant.

He'd been emailing me and I wouldn't reply, but I finally did after I dreamed of him. I explained I hadn't written sooner because I didn't want to interfere with his new relationship. A torrent of confessions and lies followed—he said his girlfriend knew about the past and then claimed she didn't; that he'd decided to be loyal to her but only if I didn't want to have sex again; that we should never contact each other but we should still email. These emails make me hate him a little, not because he'd betray this other woman but because his volatility makes him unattractive, and, worse, not worth the risk, which means I have to surrender the hope of immolating myself again in that particular fire.

A wise friend reminded me that when things burn too bright they burn out quickly, and staying past a natural expiration is "like seeing the inside of a bar at the end of the night after they've turned on the lights." I love that comparison, because there's nothing quite so sad as being present in the moment when a space that was once sexy and slightly mysterious—and by extension, made you feel alluring and powerful—is revealed to be sad and common. But don't you sometimes get to a point where you can't force yourself to relinquish that feeling? When you should go out into a truly beautiful night and carry your fading good impressions home, but you sit on the stool anyway, because letting them go on their own feels harder than having them wrested away?

Labor
September 9, 2009

Sometimes my work makes me angry.

I've never been a naturally affectionate or physical person. There's only a short period of time during which I can stand being twined with someone else and once my limit is reached, I need space immediately. If space is not afforded, I start to feel venomous. I think mean things about the man I'm with, even if he's someone I like, someone kind and honest. These thoughts are mild, often sarcastic, not violent or cruel, but they feel rotted and wrong anyway.

I stop working to keep up the glamour. I don't pretend to enjoy the way he's touching me. I keep my lips closed when he tries to kiss me. I use my own hands more roughly. I want it to be over and I want to be alone. I think about how right my friend was when she described sex with a client as "just some condom-covered thing moving in and out." I think, *this is stupid and gross*. With the exhaustion and hopelessness of an overburdened mother: *this is just so stupid*. I get bored right in the middle of all the rutting and rocking.

This doesn't happen all of the time or even most of the time. But it happens some of the time.

Sometimes I don't want to go to an appointment. Usually I'm only indulging in whiny, childish resistance to giving up my time—the same irritation most people feel when going to work—but occasionally it sprouts claws. I'll feel a little afraid, anxious, almost panicked. I press the edges of the nervousness to see if there's some valid hesitation there or if I'm being plain lazy. I try to be honest with myself about where the emotions are coming from, to see if I'm being melodramatic and playing the part of every damaged whore in a movie or TV show or activist's mythology. Trying to figure out the truth. Then I get ready to meet the man.

Sometimes in midst of these jaded or bored moments, I come. It might not be during the sex. He might be rubbing me while I lie next to him without his dick inside me and I come with my legs split wide, one knee bent and one leg straight, muttering a generic internal monologue like *you're such a slut, you were just full of a stranger's cock, you fuck for money*, etc. etc.

None of that actually turns me on. My fantasies are highly specific and don't involve being degraded, at least not in that way. I go to something easy and obvious when I can feel how close I am because I want my brain to have some role, to grant me the illusion that the experience is equally mental and physical. Really it's my hormones and the pressure on my clit or the friction of my g-spot a moment ago when I was riding him—in other words, the machine of my body functioning to design, going about its business—and when I come it's very much like a sneeze. I'll feel unaltered afterward but the tiniest bit disoriented.

Those orgasms are either that mechanical, or they are so deeply psychologically induced that I'm not sure I even want to know the root.

I hate their mouths on me more than anything else, anything else that could happen in a rented bedroom or out of it, even when I'm not angry. I know some prostitutes are repulsed by penises because of the association with dirtiness, disease. But cocks never bother me. It's the saliva I can't stand, the sensation of a tongue pushed against my vulva. Even if he licks me in way that feels good, which is very rare, I'm full of revulsion.

Kissing is disgusting. Good kissers are even more rare than those who give good head, although it's not really about quality. Even if I'm surprised by how pleasant kissing him is, I don't want to keep doing it. The longer it lasts, the more I feel like someone's earnestly reading me their bad piece of writing, waiting for affirmation while I mentally grimace and wince.

When I told one of my escort friends that I'd moved into the realm of full blown prostituting, I remarked on how much easier it was than all the policing and boundary keeping and diversion tactics that came with hand job and fetish sessions.

"Yes," she emailed me. "It is quite easy!"

Exclamation point.

She Of Sorrow
September 13, 2009

Only once did we speak on the most obvious aspect.

He began, "For my family, your grandfather dying so soon before you got pregnant would have meant—"

"I know what it would have meant," I said. His soul come back to the earth, newly bodied.

Though it was to be a girl. I was convinced by my most recent dream, unprovable and superstitious though my conviction is. A day or two later, when I was still preoccupied with that vision, her name came to me instantly: *Mariah*. I imagined holding some type of ceremony for her, making a garland of flowers and burning it in the wind. I saw myself doing it on a cliff with friends, warm and gentle people, all of us saying goodbye. I told myself that was ridiculous. *You are a parody of a hippie.* I couldn't think of anyone who would do it with me or where I would go.

I didn't know where the name came from; it had no significance in my life. I thought it might be one of the names my mother wanted for me. Her favorite was Leisel, but my father convinced her of his selection instead, which he told me he first heard as a teenager. He saw a beautiful blonde girl diving at the neighborhood pool and asked someone who she was.

But I called my mom, and Mariah hadn't been on the list, so I looked up the etymology. Leisel means something like "God's promise." But Mariah means, according to various sources, "bitter sea," "sea of sorrow," or "rebellion." It truly is her name.

Several nights after the dream, I began crying in savasana, that soundless, tears-only yoga cry. Responses welled up against the void, the unanswered questions no one had posed.

Of course I would have loved her. How could I not? I didn't ask for her, but I would have loved her: flesh of my flesh, blood of my blood, heart of my heart.

In a Body
September 24, 2009

There's one man whose mouth I tolerate much more than any other's. Sometimes I think he may be my favorite client. He is married and unashamed; he doesn't shunt aside his family life the way some clients do.

One day, years ago, when I was working for my lady pimp, he presented a CD he wanted us to listen to. It was the Bee Gees' *Greatest Hits* and he was so excited to play it.

"Do you want to dance?" He asked. "My kids and I dance to this all the time."

So we did, to "Night Fever" and "Love You Inside Out" and I felt like his children were there with us, moving in bouncy, uninhibited ways. It was so wholesome and I was so happy for no reason except the surprise of it, the right dark light in the room, the winter outside.

Our time together is always highly predictable, ritualistic. He licks me everywhere, lingering on my ears and armpits and soles of my feet.

"I don't have a foot fetish, you know," he said once, tongue out against my instep with my other foot on his cock. "I'm not one of those foot lover guys." One day he dragged the tip of his cock over my back and limbs. That was a good sensation and something no one else had ever done.

When I saw him recently everything started as usual, but this time he planted his face between my legs and stayed long after he would usually move on. His licking was enthusiastic and noisy and it was repulsing me. I'd been reading *Living Buddha, Living Christ* earlier that day. And now I was blindfolded on a hotel bed letting this father of four eat me out, thinking about mindfulness, about *breathing in, I am aware of my heart; breathing out, I smile to my heart*—sometimes, when I'm not paying attention, I slip into ujjayi breathing during sessions—and trying to figure out if I have to be mindful even through moments I don't necessarily want to be in.

The motions of his tongue were starting to feel good and that bothered me even more. *Why does this bother me?* I asked myself. *Why do I care?* I'd looked at myself in the bathroom mirror moments before and felt a little thrilled over the impending action. Not that our chemistry is even that good, but I was in horny whore space, looking forward to getting fucked and getting paid for it. Now I wanted to be away from him. I knew I could come. Should I not come. Should I come. Which will make me feel worse? My brain was like a pinwheel in wind.

In class that week, one of the teachers had been joking about the retreat center I went to after the abortion. "We call it the Krip," she said. "I mean you go there and have the silent breakfast and only drink tea and it's good . . . it's good." She was delivering this information with the implication that it wasn't necessarily good, just silly. But I was thinking about the silent breakfasts and how novel an idea to me that was, and how grateful I was to not have to speak to anyone in the mornings. How easy it was to go without sugar and how better I felt for it. The heavenly absence of TVs.

I thought about the silent breakfasts now during the licking, about mindful eating, which I don't do enough of. Mindfulness. Mindful coming or not coming. I pushed myself towards it and then fall away—it felt like that between my legs, a softening and swelling when I was ready for it and then a tensing away when I changed my mind.

I let it happen and I let all the feelings about it happening go out in the air. I didn't make any noise but I spasmed and clenched. He still didn't want to stop so I had to push him away.

He gave me a box full of food at the end. He joked about it being a care package and explained he'd accumulated items that made him think of me. "My daughter's becoming a veggie, you know. She's had some problems though, with anorexia and such, so the doctor said 'absolutely not!'"

"Yeah," I said. "I know a lot of people get concerned when girls with . . . unhealthy pasts chose restricted diets because they assume that it's a cover for more poor eating. But it could help her get engaged with food again."

He set the envelope on top of all the chocolate and crackers. "For you, my dear, my friend. My dear friend. Thank you for seeing me."

I walked home mindlessly; I'd had enough presence for one day.

Emerging
September 27, 2009

I haven't gotten wet with him since the accident, the man who tore me. That's not intentional. Either he handles me differently or my body is boycotting. I saw him the day before the abortion, early in the morning before he left for a trip, and I was like a corpse. That was his punishment, or a lesson he either ignored or didn't get: *I choose how to be with you. I choose who I am with you. Your appeal is not what you imagine.*

In the times since, I'm less cold but it's still not the same. We begin with conversation that feels scripted. Apropos of nearly nothing, he inevitably makes a sarcastic aside about how elitist or snobby or classist he is. I've never met anyone so self-conscious of his arrogance. He complained about the marble in the hotel bathroom and I said that marble was an excellent investment nowadays.

"Planning to buy low, sell high?" He asked.

"Sure. Plus when the revolution comes, gold, silver, jewelry—those are all portable, they'll be easy to steal. But the masses aren't going to bother chipping apart and carrying giant blocks of marble out of your home."

"I don't think the revolution's coming anytime soon," he replied.

"That's what they want you to think," I said. "To be successful, revolts need the element of surprise."

He came only once and then laid near me, stroking my back. We chatted just a bit and then lapsed into silence, and he slid his body down the bed to better reach my inner thighs. Sometimes a person touches me and I question everything I thought I knew about him. His hands were so tender. Through his fingertips I could feel the effort, the thought flowing down from his head through his skin. Could feel but not decipher. His gaze was on my vulva and like most men, he wanted to stare for a long time. How can two people experience one another in such radically different ways? And does my personality create or hinder his reverence?

A different client once told me I was his Galatea. He meant that I was his ideal, that if he had crafted a woman to suit his aesthetic, I would look like her. I think he was right in ways he didn't immediately realize, though. Part of my work is being a blank, offering a surface for projection. When Pygmalion falls in love with Galatea, she is nothing but a surface, and she is not human. She is a pleasing object that closely replicates a human appearance. And she is created out of his revulsion for the behavior of living women.

This client though, the would-be Pygmalion, is nothing like that. He and I have engaging conversations about art, travel, history. He is gentle whenever and wherever he touches me. I felt flint struck from our first few moments together, not sexually but intellectually—although I did come from his sweet fingers.

"From the first few moments I spent with you," he told me months later, "I thought, 'this is someone I'm going to be glad to know.'"

I venture more honesty with him than with others. I told him about my allegiance to my brother, about the strange ways I feel crushed and helpless when life is not as good for him as I want it to be.

And one afternoon when we were facing one another while lying on the bed, I saw this man's age fall away. I'd never witnessed a rejuvenation so stark. It was raw light taking over. He went from late sixties to early twenties, late teens.

"You look so young right now," I told him, in awe. I hope he believed it. He was boyish, beaming.

When we last said goodbye, he took my hands in his as I stood before him. "Charlotte," he said with that warm emphasis, the extra weight you give the name of someone you love. "Is that your real name?"

"No," I said, leaning in, shaking my head a little, smiling.

"Ok," he said in the same tone, smiling back. He asked no more of me.

At The Door
September 28, 2009

The party was hosted by a friend's older siblings, two grown women who left high school long ago. It was not particularly fun or wild. The most interesting moments took place out of view. One of the boys in our crew, we later learned, lost his virginity to the oldest sister. He was fifteen and she was twenty or more. Their sex would not be a singular occurrence. He cried over her, sometimes in these semi-public places, many times before it ended.

Well after midnight, I found myself in a vacant bedroom with a man of similar age difference. I too was a virgin, in braces and athletic sandals. He had a horrible goatee and a gaunt frame. He convinced me to drink beer with him, and I was repulsed by the taste but pretended to keep sipping. Our conversation turned to my recent surgery and I showed him the scar curved long on my flank. Everyone else had gone home or passed out in the house's various corners. When he left to get another beer, I realized this was not an ideal situation and I crept down the hall testing doors for a space to lock myself inside.

One bed was occupied with a boy I'd sleep with years later. Clothed, he spooned one of the queen bees, a girl who would months later offer me her boyfriend like he was a shirt I wanted to borrow. This sleeping pair had been friends since they were children and they were one of the few potential figurations that never materialized during those adolescent years of playing musical chairs with sexual/romantic partners. I whispered to them but they were both deeply asleep, so I laid on the floor below the bed in the dark, listening as the older boy slurred my name outside and tried to turn the knob.

I wasn't accustomed to coed communal sleeping yet but soon would be. When I hosted an illicit and disastrous party in my father's house, I slept on the floor between that same boy and his best friend, a frantically energetic computer geek who bragged that foreskin gave him an advantage over circumcised guys. He spent copious amounts of time trying to show me (and other women) his collection of sex manuals and once asked me to hold his cock while he peed: "Aren't you curious about what it feels like?"

Of course I was, or else I should have been, but I didn't do it. I knew girls were supposed to say no and act scandalized by anything explicitly stated. We were to be cajoled and handled, not clearly asked. (I'm turned off by outright questions still. "Can I kiss you?" could never receive any answer other than "no.")

He was ahead of his time—what a sexy thing to ask; what a brave thing to suggest—and sadly, I was oblivious to his affinity for me until friends confronted me. ("Why else do you think he always gives you a ride after you sneak out?" they asked, rather angrily.) After that, I was cruel.

It may have been a predictable teenage power game, a nasty instinct to exploit a devotion that, in retrospect, was considerable. Yet I was cruel or at least callous to any boy who tended to me because I disbelieved his interest was true. I was too insecure to trust that anyone could want me physically and I scorned the idea of being liked for my personality. What type of sex, I wondered, was based on responding to someone's personality? I longed painfully to feel desired (those hours of exercise, the abstention from food) but was terrified when I was.

I remember once complaining that my hair looked tangled and stupid blowing in the wind from the open windows in his car and he replied that it looked beautiful. I think he was one of the first people to tell me that, to call me beautiful. When I cut off all my hair before graduation, he was one of the first to see me.

"Oh Char, your curls," he said as he stood on my front doorstep, face slack with a sense of loss. He cared for me even then, knowing that I'd mocked him. The thought that I'd killed some of his kindness and enthusiasm, or made him trust women less, haunted me for a while. In college, part of me hoped to visit him at the campus where he was socially excelling, let him feed me drugs, fuck his revenge, be careless and cold with me afterward. I was ok with that if it would restore some of what I'd destroyed—although now I see it would have only torn open any scarred places I might have had a hand in wounding.

But before all that, back at this earlier, boring party, I slept the night on the floor and woke to the faces of two of my friends.

"Hey, Char," the boy said, sleepy and accepting above me, as though I were not an uncommon fixture of his mornings.

"I'm sorry, I—I needed a place to stay. That weird guy was talking with me, and . . . "

"It's ok," the girl said next to him, regarding me with that mixture of amusement and confusion the popular harbor for the self-conscious, telling me with her eyes how silly it was that I thought I was intruding. How silly to think I didn't belong there with them, allowing our young, yearning selves innocent rest through the night in a stranger's home.

Present
October 1, 2009

My father bought me a bracelet for my seventh birthday. It was gold with only two charms: a horse and another object that now escapes me. Probably a book. He explained that he thought we could add one charm a year or one for every special occasion. It would be a type of project for us.

Writing this now reminds me of the tree he planted for me in the backyard of the home he had to leave and how, many years later, it was dug up and discarded because its roots would interfere with a new structure. There was a consensus not to tell him about it, although it was inevitable that he would discover it on his own at some point—playing basketball with my brother, say—and be forced to ask, "oh, you got rid of the dogwood?" in that trained half good-natured, half nonchalant tone he adopted so often around us in the space we all once lived but he was now a restricted visitor.

In the more-is-more child aesthetic, the bracelet was near unwearable; it needed more dangly things to really please the eye. But I was excited and I did wear it, studying the tiny pieces and letting their movement surprise the skin on my wrist. When my maternal grandmother took me to the mall for the usual birthday shopping spree, and she saw the same emptiness I did, I didn't try very hard to dissuade her from filling the spaces.

What was intended to be a few supplemental charms turned into a collection of as many trinkets as the links would bear—a dog, a dolphin, a star, things that had nothing to do with who I was or what I valued. It was not that my grandmother didn't understand me, just that she wanted to please me with gifts, with the gratification of receiving. She was a quintessential doter, soft and warm and perpetually smiling, and not related to me by blood although it took me years to fully understand that.

When my father saw the augmented bracelet, he made his frustration known. Whether it was his reaction or the sheer chunkiness of it, I never wore it again.

Made Me
October 7, 2009

For most of my life my body has been something unruly, like a strong wire structure I can never bend into the right shape or a collection of pieces I can't properly assemble. Regrettably, I was stuck with it. I do not think there's ever been a more gullible target for the advertising industry. I used to think the three tiny, faintly purple spider veins on my upper outer thigh were a guarantee that I'd never be loved. I guarded my breasts, which dominated my chest from age twelve, as though baring them would be the equivalent of opening the ark of the covenant. I convinced my parents to get me braces, unwarranted in terms of dental function but necessary to close the gap between my front teeth. (It was a cunning move; for years, people complimented me on my teeth. Some clients actually touched them, as though it were implausible they could be real.)

That insecurity was relieved, in a large part, through my work. Not through working on webcam—that involved being subjected to a constant stream of YouTube-like commenters, people who tell even the thinnest girls that they're fat, the most radiant girls that they're ugly, and toss in other charming bon mots like ,"I bet your family is ashamed of you," and "you're going to die from AIDS." But seeing men in person, where they were generally thrilled by my mere presence—that was a revelation. I don't recall a client ever insulting my body, not while we were standing face to face. That may be due to the vulnerability of their own. Being naked in front of a stranger will make you acutely aware of your own glass house.

But only yoga has given me the gift of bodily joy. When I'm moving through poses, I feel beautiful in a unique and clean way. It's a beauty that doesn't depend on the appreciation of others; it doesn't even involve others. It exists beyond the register of sight. It's about the breath billowing up in my chest, stretching open my heart, and the reliable power of my legs, the fluidity with which they bend and flex. I wish I'd known all my life that such an experience was possible.

It's not like dressing up for an evening and feeling glossy and groomed and glamorous. There's real pleasure in that experience, too, but it's dependent on anticipation of the pleasure others will take in how I look, in their approval. That's where the power in that sensation comes from as well: I have confidence that I look so good other people will make themselves pliant for me.

But yoga's not about manipulating anyone else, and there need not be any other person present for me to love it. When I'm full of its beauty, I'm the only one who is pliant. And I supplicate to my own body, to the life and energy there, that I am graced by but not the source of.

Years
October 9, 2009

"I love you," he murmured from on top of me, while inside me. We hadn't seen each other for a few weeks and the last time, as with this time, he didn't come. He has no trouble getting hard but struggles to finish no matter what the means. Although I've only faked orgasms under his hands or mouth, he works intently at making me come with his penis, moving his hips like he's stirring a pot with his cock.

"How long have we been dating?" He asked. "Two years? Three years?"

"You don't know the first day?" I said. "You don't have that written down somewhere?" I have records but I didn't say so.

"I spy on your smile," he told me. "You don't know that. But I do." That's how he found me after I left the agency—he recognized my mouth in a picture where my face was otherwise obscured.

"And I know your body. Your hips." He held me there with one hand. "I could pick your hips out of a line up."

"Well, let's hope it doesn't come to that."

I'd decided not to see him again—I don't know why. He hadn't done anything wrong. Flights of fancy are his specialty. I've written about them here before. Every time we wrap ourselves together, he sighs and says, "I could do this for the rest of my life." And he hadn't even done anything different except tell me he loved me while our bodies were stacked instead of placed side by side. But I knew as soon as I saw him that it was time for it be over. It's the time of year for change.

I saw a new client who told me, "I've looked at your picture, your site, for years. First you were there, then you were gone for a while, and then you came back . . . It took me so long to work up the courage to email you."

"Years?" Only two, I think, although I avoid quantifying my life whenever possible, my mind sift out any identifying dates. People ask how long I've lived in this city and I never know the answer. Of course I have records of my website, my leases. I keep all sorts of records but I don't consult them. They exist to be ignored.

"Does that—I'm sorry, does that make you uncomfortable?" He asked.

"No. I'm just surprised because you don't seem like the indecisive type."

"It wasn't indecision, it was life's . . . other restrictions."

I'd felt a little anxious about meeting him. We'd had to reschedule so many times that I'd lost the impression formed by early correspondence. But being with him was easy and when he slid his hand into my panties, I wanted it. I wanted him to know how wet I was. He was so gentle he barely parted my lips with his fingers. *Feel it.* I arched up and squirmed. *Feel what you did.* He stayed high, sweeping over my clit in little half moon shapes, and then all it took was the sensory shock of one finger slipping down and curving inside for me to come.

"You're a good hugger," he said once we lay down.

"Well, you're good to hug," I replied, a little emptily. Not because it was untrue, but because complimentary conversation always feels superficial and he was stuck on saying nice things: "You're like an Ivory soap commercial." "You're better than I imagined." Etc. Etc.

"Thank you." He said. "I don't hear that often enough." Those words and the way he said them—focused but not emphatic, no self-pity—told me so much. They told me everything. I kept hugging him, my arms around his back, my toes curled on his, my thighs squeezing around his hips. He moved my hair with his hands like it was a curtain. We ground against one another slowly. When I came, I latched my lips to his, not for his sake but mine.

Before he left, he said, "You're a kind person." But that makes me sound too intentional. My best sessions are instinctual, not only the sexual chemistry but also whatever subtler connection is forged. He—the other, the client—has to let go a little, subdue his ego so I can release mine and not be preoccupied with performative banter. We both have to cede control so that we don't merely play out refined version of our public, social selves but instead drop all pretenses and explore what's beyond all that.

I don't like calling this work "therapy" but I know it can be emotional medicine. Sometimes when I cup my palm around a scrotum or pull the pad of my fingers over a man's taint, he reacts in a way that makes me think no one has touched him there in a long time. I like finding those neglected spots and returning there so the first time doesn't seem like an accident. There is a way to touch another person that tells them: "all of you is good, none of you is wrong, no part of you doesn't deserve acceptance." I know what that touch feels like, and it breaks open an inner yolk. You can actually feel the giving way inside, the slow flood filling your heart. When I find someone who hasn't had that touch in a long time, giving it to them doesn't feel kind, it just feels decent.

The Good News
October 14, 2009

As we rode, my cab driver chatted with his young front seat passenger, an androgynous pre-adolescent who may or may not have been his child.

"Man, that movie, *Fighting*?" the kid said. "That was a good movie. At the end, the black guy? The black guy was going to beat the white guy but then the white guy decided, no, and he beat him, and he won the fight."

"That was a stupid movie," the driver replied, unhurried but emphatic. I think he was Haitian. I tried to stifle my laughter.

"No, I think it was ok," the kid countered. "There was that scene where they were training. That was cool."

N.B.

"Excuse me, sweet young lady," the driver said after I'd stopped paying attention for a moment. "Do you see that over there? What is that?"

I looked up to see a black poster with "2012" printed at the bottom.

"It's an advertisement for something." I answered. "Probably a movie. But they don't want it to seem like an advertisement, so they just give you a name and hope that you're going to spend your own time looking it up on the internet later."

"Miss," the kid asked, "have you heard of the movie *2012*?"

"No. Is it a real movie?"

"Yeah. It's . . . it's because some people think that's when the world's going to end!"

"Oh, you're right! A lot of people think that. "

"Is it a Muslim thing?" the driver asked.

"No, it's Mayan." I replied.

"Muslim?"

"Myyyyy-aaaahhhnn," the kid said.

"Man, those people? Why would they bother making a movie if the world is gonna end? Why would NASA be bombarding the moon? Pfft. They gonna make a lot of money telling you you gonna die. You know some churches tell everyone Jesus was going to return in 2009. Do you see Jesus? Is he here? They were . . . embarrassed. They had to do a whole lot of fixing when that didn't come true."

The kid said something about Jesus that I didn't hear, and the man started in again. "Jesus was just a prophet. There are other prophets."

"Right but Jesus was like way, way . . . He was like, the most."

"What about Abraham? What about Moses?"

"Yeah, but Jesus is above them all."

"Look, use your common sense. You're just a child. I'm not going to discuss this with you."

They were taking me to see the Dalai Lama. It was my first time.

When I was very young, I prayed every night while lying in bed. My form of prayer was thanking God for keeping all the people I loved safe, thanking him for whatever nice things happened that day, and then reminding him of all the people I'd like him to look after tomorrow.

I included my pets, distant cousins, everyone I could think of until I fell asleep. It was a better version of counting sheep. Sometimes I even mentioned my stuffed animals, just in case. I don't think anyone taught me to do this.

I also had an idea that death meant Jesus took me on a personal tour of the universe, showing me the planets and stars and explaining what he thought when he made each one. Death, or at least afterlife, sounded pretty awesome.

That all eroded at some point after I intellectually rejected my father's religion. In third grade, I made a Jewish friend. She was perhaps one of three Jewish students in our entire private school. When I visited her home, we sang "Hava Nagila," a melody I loved and craved hearing again for years without knowing how to ask for it by name.

Our friendship led me to ask my father if she was going to hell because she didn't believe in Jesus. My father said that after she died, she'd have a chance to say she did believe. I asked if inquiring this at the gates of heaven wouldn't make the answer obvious and therefore meaningless.

The conversation devolved to the point where my father called our pastor so he could speak to me directly and he tried to assure me in a less convoluted way that my nine year old friend wouldn't burn in Hell for all eternity. Whatever his explanation, I remember thinking that it was ridiculous, indicative of a incoherent philosophy, but I had to pretend it was plausible just so I could get off the phone.

The Dalai Lama had an excellent sense of humor, which I'd suspected from his books, but seeing his comic timing in action was delightful. He acknowledged that Buddha sometimes seemed to give disparate teachings and began chuckling as he said, "Perhaps Buddha, with respect"—and here he shook his pressed hands behind his shoulder at the giant tapestry of a blue Buddha—"sometimes forget what he said one morning, so say something different the next. Or perhaps, with respect, Buddha was drunk!" Everyone laughed. He became serious again.

"No," he said. "It is because one philosophy is not enough. We need all variety. If your tradition is Christianity, good. If your tradition is Islam, good."

Towards the end of his time, while talking about anger, he leaned forward a bit. "We know, real troublemaker," his voice was low, conspiratorial, as he pointed to his own chest, "is here."

On my birthday, I rode in a hot air balloon. I watched the city emerge incrementally on the landscape around me: the dried blood color of the Eiffel Tower, the towers of Notre Dame, Sacre-Coeur white on the muddled green hill. There was a small group of people doing qigong in the park below and I looked down at the slow repetitions, their arms drifting with rapturous patience. I'd take in the horizon and then check in on them moving like weighted ballerinas. I always thought I was a little afraid of open-air heights but I didn't feel fear at all. Nor did I feel exhilarated. I felt calm, as though this was where my body belonged, suspended in the cold air.

The man who sold me my lecture ticket couldn't attend because of a family conflict. He asked for precisely as much as he paid and insisted on meeting me near my home but far from his, at the fountain in our city's most famous circle. We spoke for some time and hugged good-bye at the end.

When he asked how I came to Buddhism, I said it was the only organized religion that seemed trustworthy to me. I talked about attending some lectures and wrestling with the idea of non-attachment when so much of what I love in others is their wild passion and enthusiasm. "I really don't know what I'm doing," I said finally, and he seemed to approve of this.

I said I couldn't believe I'd managed to find him when so many others were posting ticket requests online, and he replied, "You know, they say when you aspire to meet the Guru, you have to start cultivating merit. Then when you're ready, it will happen. This means you must be ready."

I'd never thought before about the curious semantics of the Dalai Lama's title, which is not "the Holy" but "His Holiness," a synecdoche that makes the focus of appreciation and reverence not the person but a quality of that person. And what if everyone was named for their best quality? His Inquisitiveness. Her Hopefulness. His Forgiveness. Or not necessarily their best quality but their most prominent? His Mistrustfulness. Her Seriousness. His Anxiousness

Her Restlessness. Her Lost Thankfulness. Her Readiness.

Strange Life
October 19, 2009

Occasionally I'm struck by how odd it is to move through life looking out of this body, a form I will never completely, truly see in action. If this thought occurs on the street, I start to summon the subjectivity of whoever I tilt my gaze to—today, the a woman in her forties getting out of a car as she says, "Thanks, Mom." I try to imagine living her life, looking out of her face, believing that her experience at this moment is like mine in that we are each the center, each inside a vehicle, forever ignorant of the way we look to the rest of us who are outside, observing. Her subjectivity is, I assume, like mine, but radically different too, in a way I will never be able to access or even plausibly imagine.

Of course our bodies are ours intimately, ours in a way they can never belong to another, yet in this respect they are a little alien. We can never experience ourselves as we experience the rest of the world: that is, as a recipient. We take in the endless barrage of noises, images, smells and sensations that constitute reality, but we will never be confronted with ourselves as an external other. This sometimes has the effect, for me, of making me feel in the world but not of the world.

I can touch my own skin, but that won't reveal to me what it's like for another when I touch her. Notoriously, our voices, as they issue from us, sound different to our own ears than they do to a listener's. The discrepancy is shocking; we can never believe it when we hear our voices recorded. Nor can film recreate the experience of being physically with oneself. When I see a person familiar to me on camera, it is only an approximate version of them, their energy flattened and lines somehow fuzzy. They are, necessarily, less luminous and a little cold.

I think this is why it's so easy to think of oneself as invincible or otherwise perpetual. My body will never belong to the world of others, of objects, and never has. I am observing the world, which involves others observing me, but my experience is ultimate. It's very hard to imagine billions of subjectivities, each as rich and confused and unique as mine, coexisting.

There are certain work moments that seem lifted from a film. Like I'm wearing a beautiful dress, not just something business-y (they request that look so often) but simply sexy, and he's got the room's sound system tuned to "chill" or "lounge" or whatever channel plays only songs you'd hear during tasteful sex scenes. And I sit on a red leather ottoman in black high heels and stockings and start sucking his cock as he stands, my legs spread on either side of his, some Hôtel Costes selection throbbing around us. Or I'm walking through an infamous hotel's lobby and male eyes are tracking me, thinking whatever they think about single women who look like me when they're striding towards a man waiting by the elevators.

This can be funny, like my client and I are both in on a joke, both playing dress up. It feels silly in an almost innocent way, as artificial as childhood games in which the carpet was lava or all your friends were superheroes. Other times I do not feel like a real person. I feel entirely like a character in a script. It's liberating because it absolves me of responsibility. All the moves I should chose become obvious and therefore barely choices at all.

With the more prominent clients, there is a different type of oddity. One showed me a large article in *Business Week* about his rivalry with a man he used to work for. He rifled through his elegantly bound dossiers for tomorrow's speeches. He celebrated getting the opening and closing quotes of a *Times* article. When he mentioned his first introduction to a senator from a certain state, I supplied her name.

"Do you know her?" he asked.

"Well, I don't *know* her," I replied. "But I know who she is." I'd recently written her a short letter thanking her for doing such good work even though I'm not a constituent. Those intersections are nice. They make me seem more well read than I am.

These scenes are strange only because of their mundanity. I thought proximity to power would be more fulfilling. Or more accurately, I thought it would be personally validating and I would feel like I'm an exciting person. I can't really tell if it's working. Sometimes I think I get so wrapped up in the idea of living a good story that any thrill comes more from bragging rights than from glamour inherent in the moment.

But I appreciate the exchange; I like the businessman. He's pleasant and down-to-earth. I respect how ordinary he remains in spite of his extraordinary circumstances.

I had two outbursts recently, the kind of pressure-cooked emotional declarations that are blasted out of one of your dark corners, so you're unaware of their truth until you speak them aloud. The first involved me defending my work and I said it quietly, with as much control and sincerity as I could.

"This is the only thing in my life that makes me feel independent," I said. "I can't afford to give it up." I've known for a long time that sex work was a way of preserving my wildness. I can never have too many adventures. That's what I want more of, that's what I've specifically asked of friends, sometimes. More adventures, please.

The second occurred on my birthday and it was markedly less composed. "I feel so alone all the time," I said, slowly, so I could manage speaking at all, "and I don't know . . . how to fix it, or . . . if that feeling is just something I'll have to live with for the rest of my life." "Alone" is one way to put it. "Unknown" would have been another.

It made him angry. He took it personally. He asked, "How would you feel if I told you I felt alone all the time?" What he meant was: *how can you say you are alone when I am right here with you?*

I said I would be concerned for him.

He said, "You wouldn't be shocked?"

I stared at our hotel window. Its drapes were drawn. "Honestly, no." And I laughed a little cracked laugh. "I've felt this way for so long I think part of me just assumes everyone else does too. I can't imagine anyone being any different."

The man from this winter, the one from my affair, was one of the few to email me on my birthday. I couldn't believe he even knew the date. I don't think I told him; I think he did research. Or maybe I did tell him, once. We're the same sign.

Recently, he's mostly left me alone and I rarely think of our time together. It was so intense, consuming, torturous—fraught would be the best word—and now it's barely part of my personal history. When I think of him, I think of a story he told me one night while we were in the car together, after he mentioned he'd considered becoming a Baptist minister. This surprised me but then I didn't know him very well. I still don't.

It was a story his mother told him about her father, who was a preacher, and who was one day driving his two children down a narrow, winding mountain road. He took his hands off the wheel and held them there in the air, palms out, while closing his eyes.

"The Lord will steer this car," he said.

His daughter was terrified. She was certain they would die. But the truck curved gently along the road. They arrived at the bottom undamaged.

Daddy Issues
October 21, 2009

I have a pretty strict policy when it comes to my writing here and that is only to tell the truth. I realize truth is a silly idea when it comes to personal recollections, but I at least endeavor not to fabricate things intentionally. And I've always kept to that policy, with one exception that weirdly bothers me. I did not really call my dad on that night I said I did back in February. I thought about it. I wanted to. But as the evening slipped by it became too late to do it, and so I called him the next day, or the day after that—I can't remember. Calling him a few days later, though, isn't a good conclusion to that post.

When this blog was still very new—I had maybe ten posts total—a representative of a media company wrote me to propose buying it. Or buying half of it. Splitting the rights when it became a book and a movie and slapping up ads in the meantime as I continued to write. You can trace the point at which I started writing about my father to shortly after this initial contact because with it came my awareness of a message board debate about the veracity of my identity, and one of the claims put forth (you will see this one coming) is that I was too literate and self-aware to be an actual whore.

This made me angry and I was worried about showing that anger because I thought anger would probably be the response of someone who *was* a fraud. Why wasn't my first reaction just, *how ridiculous, how laughable?*

Regardless of how I should have felt, the way I did feel was: *fuck you.* You want me to be some damaged, emotionally crippled dove to prove that I'm real? Alright, let's have out with it. My parents are divorced.

Sometimes my father disappointed me. He is not a very active figure in my life. There are my credentials, now I fit in your box, now you can take me seriously.

I know that type of resentment was in the back of my mind during the earliest posts about my father. I wasn't making anything up, but that frustration was there like a little mole's nose, rooting out moments I hadn't thought of in a long, long time.

During my first long term romance, with the much older man, I mistakenly thought that affair would be the albatross around my neck in terms of throwing up the daddy flag for every passing armchair psychologist. Now of course, it's been superseded by this, my work, but my reaction to both is still largely the same: *so what?* Am I supposed to pretend it's outrageous that my past has coded my present? Or that I'm the only human being on earth like this? Like we don't all act in ways that kowtow to our upbringing, the good and the bad and the *what the fuck were you thinking?*

When I was maybe seven or eight, my father had been living in his own house for a year or two. He was always extremely particular about the house and the items inside. If we spilled something on the carpet, it was a Very Big Deal. One morning while my brother and I were watching cartoons, he came down and asked us if we had any idea why the upstairs terrycloth toilet seat cover was wet. We each said no. I went about my day.

Later, when I was playing in my room, I felt the tingling horror of a slow, dawning memory. In the middle of the night, I'd gotten out of bed. I wandered down the hall to the bathroom. And I'd sat right on the toilet seat cover and peed. I could even remember the nappy feel against my bottom as it grew wetter against my cheeks.

I started to cry. In my mother's house, where I spent most of my time, there were no toilet seat covers and the toilet seats were always up. I'd been too sleepy to realize the difference.

I did not want to tell my father. I knew there would be yelling and punishment, and I could not fathom a worse offense than peeing on some part of his beloved new home. But I was afraid my brother would be punished if I didn't confess and so, crying, I went to him.

He put me on his lap. I told him what had happened. And he laughed and laughed, wiping away my tears. "Well . . . that's ok!" He said, matter-of-factly. Like everyone sometimes peed on carpeted surfaces.

He was also very good at getting out splinters. And he bought me a special after-shampoo spray for years and years, because my hair was thick and curly, and I'd cry when the tangles were combed out. He'd spray as much of it as was needed to let the comb just slide through.

I think the anger all those months ago came from the fatigue of bearing the stereotypes that haunt sex workers because, look, sex workers are my people. I'm far from setting the bar for the smartest one. And when someone throws around those clichés about hookers beings stupid and uneducated and incest victims, they're spitting in the face of my dearest friends.

I'm bothered that I let people I don't even know shape some of what I've done here. Yet in a way, I'm grudgingly grateful. Because I think it's changed my relationship to my father—I'm not yet sure it's "with" him—for the better.

My love for my mom is like a great gaping maw at my core. I used to pray I'd die before she did because I didn't think I could handle her being gone. My love for my brother is a mace, solid and uncompromising and dangerous. There's nothing or no one I wouldn't tear apart if I thought they were making his life harder. My love for my father, to put it inelegantly, is a big question mark. I don't know anything about its shape or size. I'm sure it's there, but it's confusing.

But I've written about my father with more regular tenderness than almost anyone else. Or so it seems to me.

Austerity
October 27, 2009

There's been a slackening in me lately, a relaxation. There's an absence of craving for many things: food, the gratification that comes with others' desire. And sex. I don't want to apologize for it or try to correct it or pretend that it bothers me because it doesn't. I don't get horny and it's rare for me to respond to any type of stimuli with sexual arousal.

I still have fun with my clients. Last week I saw one of my oldest, a baby-faced man who comes only once, quickly, and spends the rest of the time talking. I mentioned on my long-ago blog that if I were to relate having sex with him it would only be a turn-on to the people who got hot thinking about Jabba the Hut with Princess Leia, which is pretty unavoidably cruel. He is big but that doesn't matter. This time, he wanted me to pretend I was a sex starved former law school classmate who came on to him strongly, with a lot of dirty talk, and while I was playing that up, I got wet.

When he was over me, a drop of his sweat fell onto my face.

"Excuse me," he said, right in the middle, and reached to wipe it off.

It was so sweet. Virtually every guy sweats, most far more profusely than he, and I've never had anyone apologize for it before while in the act.

It's temporary because everything is temporary. But it feels pretty amazing to not have this strange burden of feeling like my sexual conquests are not good enough, that they should be more exotic or more organic, and the fact that I've never been in this situation or that situation is proof I can't attract people, or am not good in bed, or whatever. Whatever crazy stories I used to tell myself around sex, constantly, to maintain a sense of self-doubt and worthlessness.

I went someplace special this past weekend to do something special with people I thoroughly enjoyed. At night, while there was drumming and young children, one little girl, probably four years old, went wild with dancing, exploding her limbs out around her in all directions. Someone later described it as her wondering, *Oh my God, what is this body?* She was astounding. I would have paid money to watch her. She was wearing pajamas at first but the room was warm and she soon stripped them off, leaving herself free to stomp and spin in pouchy cotton panties, of which she'd occasionally finger the elastic. You could see her thinking, "can't these go too?"

The abortion made me realize something I'd never known before, by the way, which was that I do want to have children and it is something I'm willing to sacrifice my body for. I mean, I would part with my vanity, if that happens to me again, if I get pregnant accidentally or intentionally. I don't regret what I did, but I don't think I could do it again, because in its wake I saw all the spaces in my life that could expand for a child and how whatever sacrifices I imagine making would pale in the face of being with this other human being.

On the way home on the weekend, I sat in the front seat of a bus with a girl who had a sweet dachshund in the bag on her lap. She was friendly and soft-spoken, and we chatted a little bit about her animal. The sunset laid out long before us through the windshield and windows.

"Look at how beautiful the sky is," she said. "And we have the best seat in the house."

Later, in the train, I sat next to a girl with a tattoo of cursive writing along the inside of her ankle. The top was cut off by the hem of her jeans and I tried to make out what it said. *Pleading?* I thought. That's strange.

I looked a little closer and saw that the "d" was actually a "t" and the entire word was written in lower case letters.

It said *fleeting*.

Sowing
November 2, 2009

The problem with this line of work, for me, is how directly it seems to quantify what I am worth as a human being. Even keeping in mind the myself/not myself paradox that I've written about here before, I do believe I'm primarily paid for my qualities, qualities I really possess. The physical interaction is important but I'm paid for time, and that's not how the time is mostly spent. It's spent talking.

So my permanent instinct is to refine more, charge more, present clients with more hoops to jump through. And it's not because I've learned some new technique with my tongue or been kegeling for a half hour every day. There's nothing I can point to that suddenly makes the product I'm offering new and improved. But I want the proof that I am an asset that keeps appreciating. (I feel that I am. I feel better with age in so many ways.) I've never tired of wanting to test the limits of what someone will offer for my company. Clearly, this is a type of sickness.

One of my easiest clients is into bondage; being tied requires very little exertion of any kind and I wish more men liked doing the binding rather than vice versa. While I've never had the patience to learn much of it myself, I'm fascinated by the cleverness of rope work and I like the sensation of being tied up. It doesn't arouse me but I appreciate the process, which is predictable given my predilection for methodological, visual progress. I like cleaning surfaces with sprays and a cloth. I like watching hair be cut and the clippings swept up in the dustbin afterward. I like packing and unpacking as though my belongings were Tetris blocks.

During our last appointment, he wrapped me in swaths of Saran wrap and later nicked me with the scissors he was using to shear away the strips of plastic. The cut stung as I went about restraining him afterward, his cock hard and dripping precome profusely throughout. That is the stage at which I get turned on, although I don't know why that particular form of sexual arousal is so contagious for me. It has something to do with frustration. As I alternated locking my panty-covered crotch down over his mouth to smother him and sliding forward to squeeze my tits together around his hard-on, I realized I was close to coming. I considered this response. Did I want to come from bumping my clit on this man's nose?

At one point when he was mummifying me with the cling wrap, I started to giggle.

"What's funny?" He asked. He lets me be cheerful–I love that. I love that I'm not expected to pretend to be distressed or uncomfortable or scared.

"I was just thinking of how mean it would be to do this to someone and then just push them straight backwards," I said, arms strapped my sides. "It would be like one of those trust exercises gone horribly wrong."

"This is already a trust exercise," he said.

All I'm encountering lately are pregnant women. Pregnancy is practically an epidemic at one of my studios, where yet another teacher showed up for class today with a low, stretch-mark-less belly swelling over the rim of her waistband.

I don't know how to talk about what the abortion did to me, about this residue of desire it left behind that has nothing to do with and is not even brushed by regret. To be terribly unoriginal, I feel as though I discarded one pair of glasses and received another that are much clearer, and that the giving up of the one was necessary for the other.

Gradually I've become inclined to not just see the way things *could* be—in terms of accumulating more or making the same circumstances "better"—but simultaneously the way things *don't have* to be. This means realizing I can release myself from ideas about who I am and what I want, how much money I need and how I'm going to get it.

I'm not in linear improvement mode anymore, assessing the best ways to intensify colors on the canvas; instead I recognize spaces where there doesn't need to be color at all. There is a core of certainty that this new want—to someday have a child—has a purity more profound and less reckless than that of any want I've ever felt before. I know it may not ever happen. But the conviction itself is what matters right now.

When I recall the period in my life in which I was having a lot of unpaid sex with a variety of men, much of it not very good, it's characterized in retrospect entirely by desperation. Not the wild and needy kind but something calculated and focused, like a craftsman searching a junk box for the tiny, precise piece he needs. My surface was one of calm motivation but underneath there were plates shifting, chasms breaking open. And those subsequent sexual encounters were the equivalent of throwing single handfuls of soil into the divide.

I read an article recently on praying, about the value of petitioning and bargaining and cursing a higher power. It included a Sufi story about a man who lost a very valuable ring and begged God to help him recover it.

He closed his eyes and offered to give half of the ring's value away in exchange for having it back in his possession. When he opened his eyes, the ring was before him.

"Never mind, God!" He said, "I found it by myself."

Gift Horse
November 9, 2009

During certain appointments, I start arranging my thoughts like I'm deliberating over wall art, lifting up one and taking down another, placing two together to see if they compliment one another. While one married man's tongue was skimming my clit, I thought about how I'd licked his wife there when we were all together for the first time. When he exclaimed over how much he loved my stomach and hovered over it, holding my waist and kissing my navel, I thought of her slack belly with the fold of skin as though she'd perhaps lost a great deal of weight. Also, of juxtaposition, how two disparate things might make the one you're least familiar with seem more desirable, special. I wondered if she would be hurt if she saw him doing this and if it was actual proof he wasn't loving enough or entirely devoted to her.

He'd been annoying me a bit at first with his nervous talking/British neuroses but once he started touching me all my irritations fell away. The drag of his fingertips combing my inner thighs was a mental eraser. And I squirmed and lifted without coming, enjoying it nonetheless.

I don't trust men when it comes to female beauty. If a man tells me a woman is beautiful (or "stunning" or "gorgeous" or even "attractive"), I picture something bland and Photoshopped, plastic and purebred. Haughty. Empty. I start to think less of him immediately for even addressing her looks or at least acknowledging them in that way. I associate our cultural beauty standards too strongly with effort or luck, and neither seems to me anything to admire.

It's the same effect whenever you're exposed to someone's bad taste in a field you seriously value, like music or literature or even food. You think, *oh, they're not like me.* You decide there's a certain worldview you two do not and cannot share, and afterward there's a permanent distance; the river has bled a little wider.

One of my clients once described seeing a girl at a pool who he was deeply drawn to as having, "A body that only a nineteen year old could have. The kind of body that's so unfair to other women."

You idiot, I thought, a little sadness running parallel to my contempt.

His tastes in women would fit inside the tiniest ring box—not even limited to nineteen year olds but to a particular subset of nineteen year olds, the type who look as though they haven't actually used their bodies for living, like they're fresh out of their packaging. As though that's something other women should or do spend all their time lamenting the loss of. I like my body so much more now than I did at nineteen. I would never exchange this for that.

It's a privilege to see a couple and feel entirely ancillary to the session—and that effect is dependent on the guy's cues and reactions. When the man keeps all of his attention on the woman he's with, it's amazing. I love it. I love being treated like I am not that big a deal, like I am ignorable, like I am not the most appealing female he's ever laid eyes on because here is another woman who he actually loves and everything about her renders me invisible, or at least shadowed.

The most recent couple I was with had this dynamic; all of my energy and all of his energy were directed towards her. She seemed mousy at first, hair up and glasses on, the hint of an overbite and a faint smudge of hair at the corners of her upper lip.

But when she later laid back against his chest as I fingered her, I finally properly saw her beauty. Her skin was soft, clear, and her waist tiny. Her breasts were natural and large, with pale brown nipples, spreading out over her ribs not formlessly but just a little loosely, the heft of them receding as she reclined. Her back was flat and defined without being starved-looking or overly muscular. And her ass was round and strong, the hamstrings and outer thighs below curvy and slightly dimpled. When I looked at her legs, it was impossible to imagine anyone—including her—wishing away her cellulite.

I met with a friend again for a double and while we conspired together before the appointment, she mentioned she had a new scar. I saw it later and it looked as though it was from a cesarean. It ran along the curve of her low belly, red and raw, punctuated by two short slashes higher up, which she later told me were from some liposuction. When she was underneath me, glowing and tan and soft, I took in all the incisions on her torso: the new work, the breast implants, the scars over the implants that looked like she'd had a lift done either before or after.

She had one of the best bodies I'd ever seen in spite of all the breast work—*flawless* was my primary thought when it came to everything else—

but she'd gone to Miami for a tummy tuck. Drinking with her boyfriend had caused her to gain some weight. They'd since broken up.

"He was a good escort boyfriend," she said. "But not a good boyfriend boyfriend. He was very high maintenance . . . He used to want all this crazy sex with wild positions and I mean, that's ok. But not when you've been doing it at work all day."

"You're so beautiful," I told her later in her car. And she still was, although I hated to see her hacking at it, especially when she herself admitted that the tummy tuck had barely had an effect on her already tight stomach. "You could charge a lot more."

"People tell me that," she said. "I have one client who gives me $1,000 an hour because he thinks that's what I should be charging. But I'd rather have people think, 'Whoa, she's worth way more,' than go away unhappy. I like feeling like I'm giving these guys their money's worth. What I charge is still a lot. I don't want to be greedy."

I was with a client last week who told me to lie down and relax while he gave me a massage, a common request but one difficult to obey. I'm used to keeping my hands or mouth moving, or both. But he pressed my hand down on the bed to still it and so I then kept my body quiet.

"You're going to make me a religious man," he said, as he's said before. "Because only God could create a body like this."

He ran his fingers over my back and arms, then put two fingers to my exposed temple and gently rubbed. His lips followed with a dry kiss. Then he leaned down to rest his cheek flat against mine, just for a moment, before drawing away.

Victories
November 16, 2009

Earlier this year I read a news story about a college student tortured by a homeless man for, if memory serves, almost forty-eight hours. He was mentally ill, she was disfigured and raped. It was one of the few times in my life when I thought "I wish I didn't know that." If I could have erased that knowledge, the particularly graphic knowledge of what she underwent, from my mind, I would, because it haunted me.

It's strange which stories fleece your brain and which don't. It's not as thought there's any lack of exposure to disturbing information day after every day. But sometimes something lodges inside me and I can't shake the sense that humans are irredeemably, insensibly prone to evil and there is nothing that can change it.

When I was reading this week's *New Yorker* I came across a story about the brutal murder of a family in their own home. I teared up while reading. I was alone but and the reaction made me feel insincere, insufficient and selfish, like I was somehow using a tragedy to prove I'm an empathetic person or—I don't know. It's hard to parse my reactions to my reactions.

I suppose it feels somehow shitty to cry for someone I don't know, like I'm making their pain my pain even though I'm at a remove, in a comfortable place. If you believe in unity and energetic cohesion and all those things then the point is that another person's pain *is* your pain, is everyone's pain, but it just makes me feel. Voyeuristic, like I'm an emotional ambulance chaser.

I don't know what to do in the face of human brutality. Tonglen seems laughably insufficient, which may mean I'm doing it wrongly or not sincerely, or am not practiced enough. Or maybe tonglen is insufficient because most of what we do as humans is insufficient, even when we are doing our best, but we're supposed to keep at it anyway. What else can I offer? Abstention seems to me all that I have: I promise not to rape someone. I promise not to set someone on fire. I promise not to kill a whole family. The problem with abstention is that it is not very active or very satisfying, and it is unlikely that my abstention contributes to others'.

I don't think much about what happened in India. Sometimes I look at the picture taken of us right after, while we were at the party and everyone was too drunk to even understand what had occurred, let alone foresee the tenacity of the attack. We are both smiling, laughing even. That's due to the adrenaline and the clash of two worlds: the eerily silent outside, with people on the street blinking at us from the dark like owls as we trotted across empty roads, and then the cheerful chaos of the dinner club's top floor where everyone repeatedly offered us alcohol.

But occasionally I think about two of the Americans who died, a father and daughter on a meditation retreat who ate dinner at the Oberoi. Some of the Oberoi escapees were with us at the American consulate; they talked about listening to the gunfire and hiding behind tables, running when the staff told them to.

In my mind, the father and daughter are crouching under a table and all the father wants is to save her. This trip was a gift to her, an opportunity. What went wrong? Is this even real? Even though he's not that type of spiritual, he tries to make a deal with God. He is willing to die to keep her alive. But then she dies in spite of him dying, dies with him, maybe even while he watches.

After living with this story for so long, I finally investigated the details of their deaths. He was shot first and the daughter second, immediately upon the terrorists' entrance into the hotel café. He and she may not have even had time to feel fear. I hope they did not have time to feel fear. The daughter was shot in the back of the head; I hope the daughter did not see what happened to her father. I hope he was dead before he saw what happened to her.

This weekend I spent much of my time around a woman I am becoming friends with, someone warm and generous, strikingly pretty with an accent that brings waves to her words. I knew her first husband died while she was pregnant, but I hadn't pressed for information. At breakfast, another woman we were eating with asked her how he passed away.

This woman with us, Theresa, made a remark earlier about her past as a trader and the many friends she'd lost when the towers fell. And she nearly gasped now when—I'll call her Brea—answered, "9/11."

"He worked in one of the towers?" Theresa asked.

"No," Brea said. And she proceeded to tell us her story.

Brea wanted to have children. She consulted a doctor who told her that because of her history with cervical cancer, she would never be able to. She relayed this news to her husband; they took a weekend together to mourn the lost possibilities and tried to celebrate the lifting of the burden of birth control. That weekend, she got pregnant.

N.B.

Three weeks later, she was due to present at an office in the World Trade Center but her morning sickness caused her to miss it. Her husband, meanwhile, was at his office in Manhattan where his boss was looking for someone to cover a meeting. The boss asked three people and all said no because of other obligations. Then her husband volunteered.

She took the subway from Brooklyn into the city to meet him for lunch. Almost as soon as she stepped out onto the sidewalk, she heard the first plane collide, looked up and saw the fire. She thought her husband was at his usual office, and it was his secretary who told her he'd gone to the second tower. No one could get through to him, but he managed to leave several voicemails on Brea's cellphone. She was listening to the last one while watching the second tower collapse, his voice telling her he was safe on one of the upper floors and they were preparing to evacuate.

After his death, she became convinced her child was a boy even though she'd previously thought she'd have a girl. She began having dreams in which people asked her what the boy's name would be and before she could answer, she would wake. The name she heard was not the name she'd chosen for him, but rather a name that had no meaning for her. It happened three times and by the third time, she looked it up. The name she'd been told meant "victory of the people." It was the name she gave her son.

"There are no coincidences," she repeated occasionally throughout, no tears, her voice a sweet step above a whisper.

"How old was he?" Theresa asked.

"Twenty-seven," Brea replied, adding, "I went through my whole pregnancy alone. My parents were back in my country and I couldn't bear to be around my friends. They were all pregnant, too, but they had their husbands."

Gently, she handed a brown napkin across the table to Theresa, who was crying. I couldn't cry in front of Brea because of the aforementioned reasons. But I did later, on my pranayama blanket, picturing this exceptional, radiant woman curled alone with her swelling belly and the treasured piece of her dead husband held inside.

I was in a workshop once with a married couple I'd met several times before. The husband's mother had died only hours earlier but he'd flown across the country overnight to be here with us and was as calm as ever, even summoning up the usual faint smile to his lips during meditation. If we hadn't been told about his mother's passing, we would never have suspected something so emotionally affecting had occurred. The only mention of it came when he was trying to impress upon us the ordinariness of spirit, how we don't come up against it but are up against it all the time, every day, like a sheet billowing around us.

He said, "When my wife arrived and we were in the room, my mom's body was still warm and it was like . . . "—he was smiling again, that distinctive smile of happiness and incredulity—" . . . That's not my mom. That casing isn't her."

Later, his wife called from the back of the room, "Are you looking for me? I'm right here."

And he said, with a slightly self-conscious laugh and the hint of a little-boy voice, "Yes, I was looking for you. You're supposed to stay near me when I'm lost." And he walked to her and sat down beside her in the place where he always is.

This Is Who You Are Now
November 18, 2009

"I had a bad dream," I said under the shower's spray.
"What happened?"
"I can't tell you."
"Come on."
"You weren't in it," I said sharply. "It wasn't like other bad dreams. Whatever you're imagining, it's worse."
"You can tell me."
"I don't want to talk about it."
Later, remembering, I thought: *my name has been fulfilled.*

Because some names seem like prophecies. This somewhat name, Nightmare Brunette, is stupid and was selected stupidly. Years ago, I got drunk with a friend at a hotel bar. A man implied I was easy because of the negligible length of my skirt.

"Me?!" I pretended to be outraged and pointed at my friend, "But she's the blonde!"

Her mouth formed a laughing little "O," and then she replied, "Oh yeah? Well, last night I had a nightmare. I dreamed I was a brunette."

I liked the way those words stuck together in my mind: nightmarebrunette. I didn't realize it was a t-shirt slogan. I thought, in that sly, liquored way: *yeah, be afraid. Be afraid of having to attract men with other things besides an imitation of idiocy and a sunny scalp. Be afraid of being taken seriously.* Those thoughts did not/do not have a lot of integrity but, as I mentioned, we were hard at work on intoxication. And I have always liked the archetype of Difficult Woman, which was what the phrase conveyed to me.

I once came across a sketch of a woman with a bull's head in her belly and I liked it so much that for months afterward, whenever I was angry, I imagined my uterus glowing an apocalyptic red. If what is inside me gets out, it will burn this world down.

Several weeks ago, I spent time with my mother. Long periods of time. And sometimes a strange vision would slide over the edge of my mind, that of me kissing her on the mouth. This is not something my family does or something I ever remember doing with her. Nor was the tone familial and chaste.

A lot of yogic and Buddhist instruction basically boils down to nothing more than "notice that," so I tried not to panic, disturbing though it was. I tried to think simply, *ok,* and look no closer. I'd seen an unusually high number of women and couples recently, most of whom were fairly older than me, so I told myself it was some strange crossed wire as a result of that work.

I'm not attracted to my mom. I am not even often attracted to other women. But the bloom kept at me like a lazy gnat, passing near me maybe three, four, five times over several days. That's how it occurred: not a flash but an image becoming briefly, slowly more distinct on a screen and then fading away. A calm gray blooming and retraction, unemotional as a pulse. Ok. Notice that.

Much later I thought of how trained I am to hone in and treat sexu__ lack, to respond to it in a professional (skilled, often dispassionate in spite of the show, but still quietly kind) way, like a doctor on a battlefield. You notice, you treat, you move on to the next. And lack is the right word, not necessarily lust or desire but rather simple absence. I am so often the redress for that particularly need going under-acknowledged. Perhaps my unconscious energy is reaching out to touch sexual dormancy in others all the time now, my little electric tendrils moving like the strands in one of those plasma globes, waiting for connection.

Pema Chodron writes, "What happens when you begin to feel uneasy, unsettled, queasy? Notice the panic."

That's the mantra. Notice that.

The Pieces in Place
November 24, 2009

On top of me, the man half of the married couple growled, "Last time I saw you, I smelled like you for hours." When he kissed me and I kissed back, he looked surprised.

"Is that ok?"

"Sure," I said. "Is it ok for you?"

"Oh, I have no constraints."

"Ok, I didn't know if you and she . . . " That was my boyfriend's rule during my first personal life threesome: I couldn't kiss the other guy.

I generally try not to mention the man's wife when we're together but he brings her up. If I see him two times in a row, he calls it "skipping the queue."

Earlier he fingered the line of my scalp and said, "Great hair. I'm not normally into hair but I can see how this would be fun to shampoo massage." Then he used his pointer fingers to trace the sides of my face, his touch passing over the edge of my brow bone, cheekbones, and then running down my jaw like drops of water. He did this several times, staring at me.

Surely the tenderness would bother her, but maybe not. I know nothing about her other than how she looks naked and how she speaks when she's nervous. Maybe she's transcended insecurity and jealousy and only wants him to be happy when she's away.

Last week I met a (different) married couple in a hotel bar. The woman was drunk. Upstairs, she used the rest room and I asked the husband if there was anything he wanted me to know. He said they'd been married for seventeen years and he'd never had another woman touch him.

"Wow," I said. "You must have been children when you got married." They both looked young to me. "Are you nervous?"

"I'm a little nervous."

The wife emerged and went to the CD player.

"We picked out these songs last night," she said, and she presented me with a jewel case with a cover comprised of different images from my website neatly fitted together.

"This is beautiful!" I looked at the body in the pictures, the colors of the lingerie and the textures of the fabrics and furniture behind. I laughed, surprised both by how glamorous I looked and the effort they'd put into it. "This is really beautiful."

"We went through a bunch of combinations to make sure nothing clashed," she said.

When we were all on the bed, she'd laugh at almost every song that came on, one of which was "Milkshake." She gave me a sharp, funny look at the "I can teach you/but I'd have to charge" part.

I've written about her before; I first met her with her lover. It made sense to me now that I was here with her and her husband, the man who had never been with another woman. She was assuaging her adulterer's guilt, which was probably more considerable than most as she'd had a lifelong monopoly on his sexual expression.

He told me she woke him up one night and said, "I found us a girl." (His response: "I didn't know we were looking.")

Sex workers are all supposed to have an exquisitely tuned sense of what men want and how they want it. They're supposed to be absolute masters of intuition and manipulation. And a lot of prostitutes and strippers brag about that in their memoirs: "I could know everything I needed to know about a man within sixty seconds."

But that's not how I move through the world, thinking that about myself. I know I have some ability and I wouldn't be working regularly if I wasn't doing something right, but I still sometimes have doubts. I wonder if I should be more bold or more clichéd, more slinky and cooing.

I was gentle with him where maybe I should have been ravenous. I imagined how my friend would have handled the appointment: she would have begged to see his cock and then told him it was hot, talked about what a sexy body he had as she ran her hands over his chest. That's not my style. Of course I want his first time with another woman to be special. But my version of special looks nothing like a porn movie. I'd feel I was cheating someone if I my behavior were that contrived.

One morning, while I was still in grad school and driving back into the city after a weekend in the country, I sat at a stoplight and watched two young men in dress shirts cross the street. I'll never forget it, the contempt and revulsion that flooded me as I thought, *I bet if I knew what gets you off, I'd want to vomit.*

I was despairing because that's what's deep under the overwhelming anger that comes with despising half the human race: despair. My work on cam was making everything toxic. Anal was de rigueur, the request for it perpetual, rude, clueless. Men sent me links to women being fucked with baseball bats and Coke cans and none of my customers could spell. I was trying to stay raw and capable of writing poetry by listening to *In the Aeroplane Over the Sea* constantly, "Communist Daughter" and "Two Headed Boy Pt. 2" especially, over and over again. *Semen stains the mountaintops, semen stains the mountaintops.*

Maybe that's the first stage of becoming familiar with the male mind; go to the dark places and stay there until you're brave enough to strike a light.

One regular cam client would ask for anal rape simulations, nothing but.

"More tears," he typed. "More struggling."

Finally I stopped—ass to camera, lying on my stomach, dildo in hand—and turned around to ask, "Ernie, what's the deal with the anal rape?"

You might think that breaking script means the customer leaves. That was true for the guys who didn't have much time, who could barely afford the minimum thirty dollars for five minutes. But with the guys who bought forty-five minutes or more, I learned I could actually talk to them. I learned that if you earnestly ask someone about themselves, they will usually try to answer. Or if you sass someone in the right way, he will not leave.

A different client instructed me in grueling self-bondage with ropes and dildos. Sometimes when I was feeling stressed and exhausted and didn't care about the money, I told him "no" for some step of the process.

"I don't want to do that," I'd say.

"Just try," he'd type.

"You try," I said. "It hurts."

"It won't hurt."

"You can do it to yourself if you like it so much."

"Haha," he'd type. "Ok."

Ernie told me his girlfriend left him because he was a sex addict. It would be more accurate to say a commercial sex addict. He spent much of his time and money not only on the cam site but also in strip clubs. He was obsessed with anal and he started to fantasize about forcing the issue. He admitted anal did not feel so different from vaginal sex; it was the probability of denial and not the sensation that drove him wild.

We spent most of our sessions afterward talking. He'd tell me about his most recent strip club escapade and I'd ask how it made him feel, not because I was into playing therapist but because I was genuinely curious. I'd never been in a strip club before.

I had another client who went by the name "sickboy." He and I, too, mostly talked and I don't remember him asking for any act other than straightforward masturbation. He was recovering from a suicide attempt.

Recently I met a client with a very specific fantasy, one that is not entirely unusual. I was to pretend to be his wife. I had poisoned him. I used him as a footrest as he lay slowly dying on the floor. I made phone calls to friends and to a pretend lover, stepped on his belongings and important documents, channel surfed, ate an apple. He booked far more time than we ended up using. I'd only been with him for about thirty minutes before he abruptly sat up and said, "Ok, we're done."

I was worried. I thought I'd really fucked it up. "Are you—is everything ok?"

"Yeah, I had my relief." He shook his head a little as though he were shaking water off his hair. "Thank you." He was a very serious, good-looking man with scars on his torso and a thick wedding band. He held an important job, not important as in pays well, although it does, but important as in his work keeps thousands of people alive every day.

"Ok. As long as you're happy."

"Oh yeah, you were great. That was great. Sometime I have to get it off my back." That was his exact choice of words: get it off my back. *In your heart there's a spark that just screams.* "It's been like that ever since I was little . . . "

"I feel really bad that you paid for so much time." I said.

"That doesn't matter to me." He busied himself in the bathroom. "The money? Doesn't matter. I've got to get back to work."

I kneeled on the floor and gathered up the things I'd stepped on, tapping the papers into a pile and setting them all on the coffee table. I pressed them smooth with my hands.

"You're a nice person," he said before I left, standing in profile to me as I put on my coat. His voice was weary, his words delivered from the place that opens up when you've been doing something hard and you're so consumed that you forget yourself in the struggle—but then you come out of it and see another person with you. I was down the hall and he was in front of the big window. "I hope I didn't upset you."

But other people's desires don't upset me anymore. I'm not afraid of them. And if on this good man I could lay my hands like a tent revival healer's and draw the shame out of his body, I would because I feel immune to shame. I feel like I could take on the shame of so many others and it would dissolve inside me like sugar in hot tea. Disappointment, loneliness, indecision—those are my poisons. But shame? I don't think I believe in shame in any more.

N.B.

The Women's Room
December 4, 2009

It was a rough week. Too much work, too little yoga, too, too little sleep. And then the full moon. While I was waiting to cross the street, a man next to me said, "Can I get a smile?"

I looked at him. "You already have a smile," I said. "It's on your face."

At the clinic I waited almost two hours past my appointment time to be seen. A diminutive older woman with a heavy accent assembled the needle, vial, alcohol wipe.

"Do you faint?" she asked.

"No, but I don't like it. I look the other way. I know that's silly."

I opened the inside of my elbow to her gloved hand and turned my head.

"Deep breath," she said, and then after a moment, "deep breath."

It was so gentle. I've never felt anything so gentle. My whole body was flooded with relief. Something that should have hurt not causing any pain—it was the best thing that had happened to me in days.

"Thank you," I said. "I didn't even feel it." I'd worried the steely pinch of the needle would make me cry. I've cried in so many Planned Parenthoods, overwhelmed by the sad energy there, the sense that all of us are shameful and strange, even the rare wonderful boyfriend and the toddlers pushing trucks on the carpet.

When I dressed that afternoon after yoga, I put on knee high socks and thought of my abortion midwife who once said of our wintery days at the incall, "You were always wearing tall socks and leg warmers under your jeans. I thought that was really sexy."

Suddenly I missed that time painfully. I missed her coming to meet after work, stuffing a washer full of sheets and towels while I recounted whatever irritating thing had happened earlier. I missed our competent, clever lady pimp and the quiet in the apartment when I was waiting for her call. This sense of a lost sororal conspiracy overtook me the way I was once sometimes overtaken by teenage nostalgia. *Back then, we had so much fun, we were so young and untroubled . . .* It's the time of year, maybe.

As I was leaving, an elderly woman on the sidewalk held a rosary. In her other hand there was a homemade sign reading: "Ask to see your sonogram."

I thought about telling her that when I'd had my abortion, I did see the sonogram, and nothing appeared. I'd told myself that if there were protesters when I went, I'd talk with them, really try to talk with them. But as I passed her, she said something like, "blessed are the women," and I didn't have any argument with that.

Packaging
December 11, 2009

He took my coat and scarf before serving me water with crushed ice—my only drink request while working.

"I know this song," I said and gestured to his docked iPod. "So Long, Marianne."

We talked about his running soundtrack, which doesn't include Leonard Cohen. ("That would probably lead to only walking," he said. "Or lying down.") He told me he was going to start doing yoga because he wanted to look like me.

"You know, you look very thin but you're actually just perfectly proportioned. I mean in your clothes you appear very slight but when I see you like this, you're not too thin at all."

"What a great compliment for a girl," I said. "'You look thin, but you're not.'"

"You package well," he clarified.

"I think I'll put that on my resume," I said.

"Do you remember last time I said I wasn't getting physically aroused even though this is an erotic fantasy? You with your quintessential quickness just looked at me and said '. . . thanks.'"

We laughed.

"But this time around," he went on, "I'm incredibly aroused."

"Very weird," I said. "Must be a solar flare."

He drew his fingertips over my reddened ass. "I wonder if it'll ever wear off. Do you ever think I'll get over it?"

"It doesn't look likely," I said. I refrained from pointing out his age.

I lay nude over his lap while he sat in a velvety red armchair. He told me to promise him that I would never put my toe in his glass.

"Why would I do that?" I asked

"I don't know. You just said it last time I saw you, something about putting your toe in someone's glass."

"That sounds like something I would say," I agreed.

Later, he brought up another exchange: "You know you said something very strange to me once. Well, not very strange but . . . the first time we met I asked what you did when you were with someone who seemed to be enjoying trying to hit you as hard as he could. And you said, 'I just endure it.'"

"Mmm," I replied. This sounded less like something I would say but more like something I would think.

He'd prefaced that with, "Now that I like you so much, it's hard to spank you."

As he held the collar of my coat so I could slip my arms into the sleeves, he said, "I think you're probably a great teacher. I bet you make people feel really good about themselves even when they can't do something."

"Thank you," I said. "That's a lovely compliment."

"I mean it," he said. "Goodbye, Charlotte."

And then I was back out in the world, bundled and sealed from the bitter cold, my package not in any pain.

Alone Anyway
December 14, 2009

I saw a familiar client who told me I was a good kisser, an incredibly rare compliment for reasons I've detailed before. "And I like the way you fuck," he whispered, one hand hoisting the back of my knee.

Moments before, I'd marveled at how little I can feel during work foreplay. I used to love being touched, especially in non-sexual ways, but I don't know that it matters to me anymore. Skin on skin is now unremarkable, even unoticeable. Quotidian, like cloth on skin or water spray on skin as you're nearing the end of your shower.

But I like him because he pays well and seems to have a sweetly monogamous streak when it comes to me as his prostitute. He also never gave me a hard time when he admitted he was a Republican and I made a face like I was repulsed. Our sex is always brief and follows a relatively predictable sequence. This time when he was done, he patted me on my flank, like you would a horse. I don't think he has any delusions about what we mean to each other.

At home, I curled on my stripped bare bed and cried that ugly, open-mouth, clown-faced cry, until the hair framing my face became slightly crusty with salt. I thought of Pema Chodron, her words along the lines of "We use our emotions. We use them." Meaning we blow them up, make them bigger and bigger until we're consumed.

I rolled over and took my hands away from my face and looked out my open window at higher windows on the other corner. A shadow was moving on the glass of my favorite apartment as though someone were shaking out and folding towels, or dancing. A light in the next room went off. The shadow slid away.

But I don't know what to do. That's always what I think in my most desperate moments, which are never clear dilemmas or important choices but rather crises over the simple circumstance of being alive.

I remembered more, something like, "What if instead of blaming and running away when we feel lonely or humiliated or sad, we just sat with it and had a little compassion for ourselves?" I thought of how wrong and cruel it would be to rush or dismiss a friend crying like this. I imagined Pema or someone telling me, *be with the fear of not knowing.* These thoughts were cascading and pulsing against one another, along with the parsing of how I'd once felt possibilities with my fear. Now the fear remained but there was no longer a sense of opportunity.

Amid all this, I had the certainty that someday, far removed, I would look back at these days with tender relief. Years earlier, I'd been drained of all the love, or what I thought was love, for the older man during our wretched break up. Now thinking of him—he who I slept with so many hours, laid with so many afternoons, came with and ate with and laughed with—is like thinking of a repugnant celebrity or politician, someone with whom you're vaguely familiar but don't personally know. Surely that gave me an unshakable faith in the temporary?

I thought of saying things I would not say aloud again, of how there's no longer anyone in my life I would trust with myself entirely, no single dear friend whose love is like a worn, strong safety net. Or how foolish my fear of being alone is since I'm alone all the time anyway. I thought of walking to the doorway and saying to my boyfriend, "we have no future together," or, "we don't love each other anymore."

On the mat days before, I pressed my face to my knees and of the skin under my lips thought, *this is yours, always*. Not always-always, of course, but at least for this always. And at dinner I'd reminded myself again, *I am all mine, I am enough*. Or rather, *I have to be enough. I will become enough. What alternative is there?*

Purity
December 18, 2009

Planned Parenthood called and left a message that I needed to come in about my test results. I returned the call and spoke with one of the clinicians.

"Can you come in now?" She said.

"No, I wouldn't get there before you close. It's really kind-of freaking me out that you called. I know you're not supposed to give out HIV results over the phone but can you tell me about the others?" I assumed it was about one of the others.

"Oh, let me see ... Ok, your gonorrhea, syphilis, chlamydia, and hepatitis were negative."

"Well, wait, so, what about HIV?"

"It was . . . unclear."

"So I have to take the test again?"

"Yes. I mean, you need to come in and talk with me about it."

"But that's . . . not uncommon? To get an inconclusive result? And I just come in tomorrow and take the test again?"

"Well, no, it's . . . it's very hard to talk about without explaining it all to you. Can you come in tomorrow?"

I called him because I had to tell someone.
"I just lost my breath," he said.

"I'm sorry. I didn't know whether to tell you now or tell you later or …"

"I think I'm going to be sick."

I called my best friend, the abortion midwife.

"What if it was positive? What if it was positive and she couldn't tell me on the phone so she tried to tell me something else?"

"No, that's not what would happen," AM said. Although she admitted later that she was thinking the same thing. "They're really not supposed to tell you anything at all over the phone. I can't believe she didn't follow protocol."

"Would you live with me if I was HIV-positive?"

"Yes. Do you want me to come with you in the morning?"

"Yes. But I can't keep having bad medical news just to get you to hang out with me."

We stayed on the line, googling together. *Indeterminate Western blot* was the only phrase in my mind, ugly and inarguable and official. *Seroconversion. Viral load. Indeterminate Western blot.*

I did what I always do when I don't know what to do with myself: yoga.

I felt deeply calm, a little scatterbrained on the surface but with certainty underneath. *Good, strong, sweet,* I whispered at my body. *You are so good, strong, sweet. Thank you. I'm sorry it took me so long to see it.* Towards the end of the long class, the teacher dimmed the lights and put us into a ten-minute paschimottanasana.

"I've had two profound moments in this pose," our teacher told us. "One was in a class taught by a teacher trainee who'd never taught before. And she told us she was brand new at the beginning of class, but she had a really beautiful, simple way of explaining how working with this pose was how she learned to forgive herself."

I saw then how the pose was entirely about forgiveness and maybe every pose is about forgiveness, even—especially—the celebratory ones. When I lifted my face from the blocks I'd been resting my head on, their foam faces were streaked with tears.

He was waiting for me at the apartment. He said some nasty things that were supposed to be jokes, and I just looked at him like, *ok. Whatever you need.*

"I assume our relationship is over now no matter what," I said. I was crying a little, and he tried to hug me and I pushed him away with my forearms, but he kept pushing into me.

"Let's be mature about this," I said, helplessly eating my tears. "Let's be adults. I don't think you'll ever get past this no matter what the result is."

"You could live with it, couldn't you?" He said, meaning I would keep living my life even if I had HIV.

"Yes," I replied. I knew he'd decided he couldn't. "You know it's possible that neither of us have it or both of us have it, but also that I have it and you don't. You might have to think about that."

"There's 100 percent chance if you have it, I have it."

"100 percent?"

"Well, not a hundred."

I tried to get him to read about indeterminate results online and I'd left a long message with everything I'd learned about ELISA and the Western blot on his voicemail. He admitted he didn't listen to it. He wouldn't look up anything about female to male transmission rates or interpreting test results. He wouldn't go get quick tested. He was acting like he wanted to hold on to this fantasy of death.

I gave up on trying to give him information and let him talk until he stopped. Then his shoulders slumped. He gestured for me to come hug him. We kissed.

I sat on the toilet seat with my knees under my chin and watched him through the glass as he showered.

"What will you do?" He asked. Meaning, if you're sick.

"Well I'd probably try to get a full time job for the health insurance. Then maybe move back to Philadelphia or stay here. Write and read, do yoga. Teach. I wouldn't tell my family until I had to."

"So many of the things I'd been living for wouldn't be possible anymore."

"Like what?"

"Like having a family," he said after a moment.

"That would make me sad, too," I said.

He stayed up late working while I lay on the couch. The cats took turns pushing their faces against mine or lying down in the backs of my knees. I fell asleep and woke up. I fell asleep again. When he was done, we went to bed and slept naked, pressed together.

The morning after the night of the full moon, I went to the city's HIV/AIDS clinic. I knew there was no way it would detect anything from that episode, but I wanted the piece of mind of being told then anyway.

The man who administered my test was small, turtle-ish looking and bald, like a Latino Wallace Shawn. Incredibly sweet. He'd given me a test years before and I told him so. I asked why they weren't doing the oral version anymore and he said it was giving them too many false positives.

"Wow, that's . . . so terrible," I said. "But I guess it's better than a real positive or a false negative."

While I was waiting for the results I looked at other people in the waiting room.

If I have HIV but could make one of these people have it instead, would I do it? I asked myself. Then: *of course not. Why am I thinking about this?* I lingered on their profiles like I was giving them blessings: *I wish you well, I hope you're well, I hope you're well.*

I'd felt entirely confident when I first came in. The results were a technicality; I already knew I was negative. But as I sat there, it started to feel very possible—even probable—that I was positive.

He called me back into his office and waited until I sat to tell me my test was negative.

"Oh, that's great," I said, breathing heavily with a smile. "I felt so sure I was when I came in but then while I was waiting . . . "

He nodded and smiled and said in his heavy accent, "Yes, everyone always says it's the longest twenty minutes of their life."

I was flooded with relief. I gave a donation, whatever cash I had in my wallet, but it didn't seem like enough.

The Friday of that week, I dropped off the envelope I'd been given during my morning appointment. And I hadn't been back since.

I saw the male half of the married couple earlier in the week.

"Do you like the outfit?" I'd asked, gesturing to my lingerie and stockings. "I went with a little Christmas theme because I figured no one else in your life would wear anything seasonal."

"You're right about that."

"It's sort-of like a Naughty Mrs. Claus thing . . . Oh no, I just remembered, I actually have a Naughty Mrs. Claus outfit! It's red velvet with white fur and tiny jingle bells on the tassels. Oh, I'm so sorry I didn't bring it."

"I am, too," he said. "Because that would have been really odd!"

"Well, not really odd. If you want it to be really odd then I'll wear it for you sometime next June."

He did the face touching again, touching my face with his fingertips like he's drawing it. I looked into his eyes while he did it. There was one moment when he was looking down, fingers at my slit, and he hadn't put on a condom yet. He was thinking very strongly but very calmly about something. I wondered if he was wondering what would happen if he just put his cock inside me, if I would yell or shout or just go with it, saying, "Ah, oh yes, that feels so good."

AM showed up early and we sat sleepily at the dining table, playing with the cats and rehashing the online information we uncovered the night before. Eventually we went to the corner and got a cab. Everyone in the office, including the security guard at the front door, said, "Oh yes, we're expecting you."

"That's a bad sign, isn't it?" I said.

"No," she said. But then later, "I'm nervous. Waiting makes me nervous."

A woman who'd prescribed birth control for me once came in wearing brown corduroy. She went through the door next to the front desk.

"Do you think that's her?" I said.

"No," AM said.

A moment later, the same woman gazed down at an open file in her hands and said to the front desk staff, "This might be short-lived."

Then she stepped to the side, opened the door and gestured for us.

"Did you hear that?" I whispered to AM. "Did you hear her say it would be short-lived? What does that mean?"

We sat in a triangle shape, in a room with a papered examining table.

My Western blot was negative. The ELISA was positive but the Western blot's supposed to confirm the ELISA and without the confirmation, the ELISA isn't considered valid. Although of course they recommended follow up to be sure. I told her about my risks and the negative test in July.

"Any shared cocaine?" She asked. "Were any of your partners West African? Had they been with someone from West Africa? Any traveling there?"

While I was checking out, she slid me a copy of the results. AM took it and began reading. The clinician asked a few questions about my insurance. She said goodbye and wished us happy holidays.

I angled my neck to look at the test results, too, and AM whipped out a copy of a pamphlet she'd grabbed from the waiting room that read "Abstinence: think about it." We both started laughing. I didn't say it, but I was thinking: *I love you.*

We took another taxi to the HIV/AIDs clinic. We wanted a second, more specialized opinion.

A young, cute guy in jeans took us back and asked what was up. There was a tiered bin of condoms on the desk near where he sat with labels that read: large, x-large (grande), regular, lube.

I told him. I handed him the papers and he frowned at them.

"This is really strange," he said. "Let me go ask someone with a little more experience."

He stepped out for only a moment, then returned. He said, "You're just one of those very rare few who gets a false positive. You can get another Western blot done in a few months just to make sure but, yeah, I'd say it's just one of those flukey things . . . really scary but better than the alternative."

False positive. What a strange phrase.

So AM and I walked to a café, and ordered breakfast, because what else was there to do other than eat, to keep my body strong for as long as I could.

N.B.

Sick People
December 20, 2009

A few years ago I dabbled with a Californian philanderer who worked at a local concert venue. He hit on me while we stood as strangers on a street corner: me, sweaty and irritated on my way to look at an apartment, and he on his way to deliver flowers to his girlfriend. We spent some confused evenings alone in his large house—his roommates never seemed to be home—and not much time in public together.

On one of these nights, with the streetlamp light barely prying through the blinds, our legs scissored together for a moment and I wriggled, and then he was inside me for the first time in a way that surprised us both. We disentangled but he seemed freaked out, and I didn't know how to manage the weirdness beyond assuring him I was safe. I told him we could go together to get tested, reasoning there was no way he could have contracted anything through mere seconds of contact.

It was terrible, and I kept saying I wanted to go home but his response was to grab me and hold me hard until I stopped.

Finally, he told me he'd gotten sick years ago, incredibly sick, and no one could figure out what was wrong with him. He lost weight at an alarming rate and had little energy. Eventually he ended up in the hospital, unable to support himself, and in an emergency room wheelchair—and here I know his race played a role—the doctor pronounced him HIV positive upon first sight. He wasn't, but the waiting period before the diagnosis was disproved left him permanently terrified.

"You didn't need to explain yourself," I said.

"I just don't want you to think it's you," he said. "I won't want you to think I'm the one man on the planet who doesn't want to fuck you." I remember that clearly, my sense that even in this moment his wooing instincts were in overdrive.

I sat on the side of the bed with my hand on his chest and my black dress back on because I was going to leave, but when I started to say something more about his being sick, he grabbed the back of my head and started kissing me crazily, pulling me on top and pushing my thighs until he could press my hips down over him. And for a moment we were both frozen like that, trembling a little, the intensity of that first moment magnified by his urgency until I lifted up and laid my head on his chest and said, "Is that really ok?"

"I don't know, I don't know," he said. And I was thinking, *ok, I'm just going to do that one more time*, he started it and then I did, and after another moment he pulled me up, gasping, "Oh baby, what am I supposed to do?" It was a tone of voice I'd never heard from him before: deep, desperate.

His girlfriend called and he stroked my legs while they were on the phone. I could hear her voice and how much she liked him. I could also hear the way he talked to her, which was entirely different than the way he talked to me. It was more mellow, gentle, moving towards warm. It did not make me feel good, and I took out my phone and started texting the other boy I was sleeping with at the time.

After he fell asleep, I let myself out and walked many blocks home in the sunrise while the bums tried to corner me and taxis ignored me. It was terrifically *Butterfield 8*, or any other movie where the trampy girl is shunned and then dies.

I think it's easy to despise stories of unprotected sex because it seems so uncivilized and brutish, déclassé. It's the same lack of bodily control that people sneer at when they see an obese person eating, the same revulsion disguised by protestations of self-respect and self-care. *How could someone value themselves so little?*

But irrationality or impulsiveness don't directly translate to immorality, unless you think every moment of passionate disregard is immoral. Unless you think there's something fundamentally evil in the human tendency to forget oneself and the rest of the world, and, for just a moment, be in unapologetic need.

In that moment with another girl's boyfriend, I wasn't feeling guilty or afraid, not wholly anyway. I felt exhilarated. I felt so excited to have access to a common, basic act so powerful that it can strip away a person's sensibilities and responsibilities and make them, yes, weak.

When I saw him months later at the venue, I was with AM, and he and I didn't speak to each other. We hadn't had contact in a long time although there were suspicions that he was the one sometimes knocking on my new door at two or three in the morning.

I pointed him out to AM and she said, "He has nice arms."

"Yeah, really nice arms," I replied. Then we were quiet for a minute and I said, "You know he looks really sexy from far away but up close he's not that hot."

"He looks really hot," AM said. She kept making comments about it for the rest of the night which managed to make me feel both pleased with myself and distressed. I had to keep in mind the stickiness of his perpetually unshowered skin, his corny/melodramatic West Coast ways, the filth castle he called a home.

AM left to go to the bathroom, then came back poking at me, pointing at something behind us. Finally she said, "Your boyfriend," and I saw him in the corner of my eye.

"You were standing looking at the stage and he was staring at you like—" She made illustrative eyes but I needed more, was it good or bad?

"Like you were prey, animalistic."

I paused. "Maybe he was looking at someone else."

She said, "There are three guys behind you."

I said, reminding myself, "He wears girl's jeans."

When AM and I were walking home from breakfast after the morning of my test results, she said, "This takes some of the glamor out of prostitution."

"I know," I said. "Although at first I felt like I could never work again and now I feel like it's not a big deal and I don't want to quit."

"But your work is so safe," she said. "Your behavior is much higher risk in your personal life."

Getting By
December 24, 2009

"Are you still upset about the test?" he asked, on top of me. He'd thrown me on the bed, clothed, and then thrown himself after.

"I don't know. It's kind of a big . . . thing to have happen."

"You're sure you don't have it, right?"

"But just the thought."

"Well if you want to talk about it, we can. I want to be there for you, you know, because I wasn't really for the abortion or your grandfather's death but this—"

"You called me an 'AIDS-giving whore.'"

"Oh, how convenient that you remembered my exact words!"

"AIDS-giving whore?" I repeated, incredulous. "It wasn't that hard to remember . . . I used a mnemonic."

Later he pushed himself in, bare. We said we'd use condoms until the second test. But the moment before, he'd said, "I miss being inside you," and I understood he meant feeling the inside of me, instead of feeling latex.

"Are you being irresponsible?" I asked him, legs spread. In our story, he's the one taking the risk. I cannot take risks; I already am the risk.

Did you ever see *Les Nuits Fauves*? I don't see much discussion about the romanticism of unprotected sex, the bizarre thrill of self-sacrifice in service of your love for or even mere attraction to another person.

"If I only had sex with you for the rest of my life, I'd be happy," he said. He's said it before but this time I knew it meant something different.

When I called and told him my results weren't clear, he was with a friend. I didn't know that at the time.

"I went totally white. He knew right away something was wrong."

"What did you say?"

"I couldn't think of anything to tell him so I just said you were pregnant again."

"Oh God, I wish you had just told him the truth. Saying I'm pregnant again makes me look so irresponsible."

He got the joke. And he laughed.

Ties
December 25, 2009

You must know there is much I don't tell. The worst of it stays unwritten, not out of any sense of propriety but because I don't want it here. Because I don't have the words to make it beautiful. Because I don't want the reconstructed memory lumbering in my head.

I don't know what other people's relationships are like but I know what this one has been like for me, and it's consisted of coming to know him most intimately through disappointment. I wonder if this is part of what makes it hard to tear away. A different, sticky type of love is woven from the knowledge of precisely how another person falls short of what you want or need. How can I explain it? Once you know their limits, you can perhaps forgive your own. And you can grant yourself permission to be private, to withhold the thoughts and feelings you know they would not handle carefully.

If you are something of a hermit, this has appeal. There is a great safety in not being known.

You learn a lot about yourself, though, in this recognition of all the ways you'll allow another person to fail you and how you respond to being failed. And then how responsible do you—do I—want to be for your expectations? What about the role of your inaction? If I alone am not sufficiently equipped to ease my pain, surely no one else can be.

I can't tell what aspects of this are valiant and which are cowardly but I suspect it is always a wrinkling dance of both.

After we both came and he laid his dark head on my pale clavicle, he said, "I love listening to your heart beat." He's said it before but only recently, maybe because he realizes this noise will not always be available to him and that such noise will not always exist.

If I were sick, would I cling to him? Or would I find the courage to be as alone in circumstance as I am inside?

I've done exercises that consist of sitting with a partner and following their breath, holding your hand above the crown of their head, their chest, their abdomen, caressing the eternal pulse. Afterward, I feel a connection, an intimacy that need not be discussed or returned to but hangs there in the air like mist—or more accurately, it surfaces like those car window finger tracks you only see when the temperature is right.

I've always thought it was possible to love anyone, literally anyone, no matter who you are and no matter who they are. All it takes is time.

That's not as romantic as immediate and passionate connection, but it's an option, and there's something truly good in it.

There are other forces, too: the granite weight of an established lifestyle, the comfort in the familiar, the sense of obligation. But as I said, those don't want recording.

The older man, the necessary mistake, once wrote something like, "I recognize the ways I've bound my life to yours."

So often when a binding is undone, the wound underneath is still gruesome and raw.

2010

Remembering
January 4, 2010

I've written a little about one client I trusted pulling me into his lap and sliding himself inside while I flayed with my useless arms. Didn't write about that laughable conversation during, me saying something terrified like, "You're in me!" while he murmured the equivalent of, "No, I'm not."

I had to start crying before he stopped, which once before (not at work) was also the way out. Tears mean no. Some men trust tears though they might not trust me.

He was Greek and he had a Greek pet name for me, something like "kookla," which he said was a term of endearment albeit not a traditional one. He would hold me and coo to me with that strange mix of menace and delight admirers bestow on helpless, cuddly things, readjusting my body against his and smoothing my hair with his hands, holding the halves of my face like a peach.

As soon as he released me, I ran to the bathroom and locked myself there. Outside the door he begged, "Kookla, please, come out."

I rocked on the soles of my feet and hid my sobbing face. I showered. I don't think I said anything. I may have told him to leave but that sounds like more force than I would have mustered. Probably I planned on hiding until he left. But he didn't leave, and I never worked for my lady pimp again.

How many times have I hoped that feathery hope, maybe the thing I want to happen will happen if I'm still and quiet?

Volcano
January 9, 2010

One of my biggest bruises when it comes to men is their sense of entitlement. I fear this above all else because I know it's the quality that causes them to lose sensibility and behave dangerously. And if I get even a whiff of that, any potential relationship is done. I will not engage with the man in question or I will engage very rarely to try to keep him calm. In my heart, whether I respond or not, there will be hate. You know the look in an animal's eyes when it's being backed into a corner and poked at, that sick mix of fear drowned out by the sheer violent will to protect the self?

You think I'm being hyperbolic. But I'm telling you what happens in the naked depths of my brain, not what gets filtered and fed through the surface. I'm telling you: that is my button. That's what happens when it's pushed. Sometimes I get emails that push it and my reaction is so powerful that I want to run from this blog forever. I want to abandon it and never look back.

What is it about simply reading someone else's words that would create such a sense of being owed something? How does that switch get thrown? What jump occurs from reading a stranger's words to somehow believing that same stranger owes you her attention and time and even more than that, owes you control of her behavior to some degree? It's weird. I know words are galvanizing, but still. Very weird. Very ugly.

I've had emailers tell me I'm not writing about my life in the right way, that I'm not being honest enough, that I should be ashamed, and underneath all that is the assumption that I owe them. That's what it keeps coming back to: entitlement. They deserve something I'm not giving. So far, they've all been guys.

Sometimes it's framed as, "I'm telling you this for your own good." As in, "you don't see what you need but I see what you need, and coincidentally, it's something I want. I, the person who knows nothing more than the stylized bits you've chosen to share."

I had a pregnancy scare recently. No period came during a week when it should have come, and eagerly at that, since I'd used birth control to skip the month before. But there was nothing. Not a single spot. And do you know what I thought? *Oh God, I can't write about another abortion. I can't. I can't tell that story again. It's going to be tedious and irritating. There's nothing new to be learned.*

Yet there was no possibility of not writing about it here. I have become a self-tattletale, trying to bite her tongue only when it comes to others.

One of my teachers says, "It's very interesting to have something important to say but to not say it." This doesn't mean that one should be silent in times of crisis but rather that sometimes it's ok to let the thought bake a little more. And it's ok to not cast yourself as the cosmic corrector. I should play with that practice more.

But I'm learning so much here about myself, and it's part of how I process my life. Everything now is grist for this mill.

Windows
January 19, 2010

Sometimes I lie in wait inside my body like a wild animal camouflaged by leaves. I step away and try to interpret the sensation, cast a bucket down into the well to see if I can dredge up a memory of pleasure, work to determine if this is what I recognize as pleasure now. Secret effort.

Recently I caught myself dragging my parted lips down a client's stomach, rolling my head on the stem of my neck so that my hair slithered over his skin while my hands worked his cock, my face a bleary smear of lust. *Wow*, I thought, *I'm so good at this.* "This" meaning going to a mindless place that has become nearly a pleasure-less place, or a place of pleasure that's sieved and muffled as through a curtain of gauze.

I can think of so few things that make me wet anymore. It's like my nerves have forgotten how to appreciate erotic touch. Everything either registers as unpleasant or soothing. There's no room for sexy. No matter where I am stroked, if it's done with any artfulness, my body collapses in a hammock of relief. I feel I'm being fed water after days without a drop. I think I need Temple Grandin to invent me a machine for this so I stay sane. I love to have hands laid on me, although I forget to seek it out as I once did. I used to demand it, not as foreplay but for reassurance and relaxation. It's been months since I asked someone to touch me.

And there used to be many motions that yielded wetness. Lips on my inner wrist. Being slowly cuffed into a spreader bar. The pressure of another's body on top of mine. If a man is intensely turned on, made weak and pliant by his arousal rather than angry or demanding, and if I am allowed to observe and sculpt this for a long time, yes, then it happens. Yet having control has never been my real fetish, at least not one of which I was ever made urgently aware.

We met at the hotel bar, which was nearly empty. He slid me a napkin that read "panty display."

I spread my legs but the skirt of my dress fell between them, so I lifted the hem and held it several inches above the stocking rim on my right thigh.

"Spread your legs," he said. "Stay that way."

There was a table of four men behind us who'd eyed me when I came in. I was the only woman in the restaurant. My back was to them. My client was across from me with his back to the wall.

"Do you know why I let you sit there?" He said. "I'm not worried about your embarrassment. But I don't want them to see. I want to be the only one." When we first met, he told me liked thinking of how I'd pass men in the lobby on my way out, and they might think something approving or lustful, but no one else in the hotel besides he would actually know what I looked like naked.

After several minutes, he slid me another napkin. On it, he'd written: "Go to room. Key inside."

"I'm not coming with you," he told me. "Say goodbye to me here."

He'd written a series of instructions and left them on the bed. They involved taking off all my clothes except my panties, putting on a blindfold and standing with my arms behind my back in front of the window, with the door's long locking piece swung open so the door stayed ajar. I was to think of something I'd never told anyone and be ready to tell it.

The eye mask wasn't tight and light seeped in through the gaps below my eyes. I watched the street, which I've done many times with impunity in various stages of undress. City people never look up.

A man approached his car, got in, started it, then idled. I could see the bluish glow of his phone's face through the sunroof. He darkened the screen and pulled away. Under the mask, I closed my eyes.

I alternated between searching for something to say and tuning into my body. I lifted and spread my toes. I pulled up my kneecaps and drew my shoulder blades down my back. I wondered if yoga had ruined any sexual charge I might get from these types of held positions. Or not ruined but removed. There's calmness now in being left inside my body, a confidence. Even discomfort feels familiar and manageable. And deeply internal. If I'm in a pose, I automatically forget other people.

But I had an assignment I couldn't forget. All the stories or thoughts that could pass for scandalous had already been shared, with partners or friends, or here. I tried to think of it in the form of a PostSecret. What line sounded revelatory and private? One of the possibilities was something I'd not verbalized before, but had been living with particularly intimately as of late: I'm afraid I'll only ever find sex sexy if it's with a total stranger. A real stranger, not a client, not even a new one. Not someone whose legal name and profession and tastes I've been told before we've met but someone entirely unknown who is not paying.

The other had less weight: Only one man has ever made me wet by kissing me and I didn't even let him fuck me. This is the one I chose.

The problem was that the night before I'd already told this man something I couldn't remember telling anyone else. He had me face the corner in this same position, with my panties pulled down just in line with the swelling split of my labia. He was adamant about not wanting to see my pussy.

"Tell me a fantasy you have that has never been realized," he said from across the room. "Loudly and clearly."

That was easy. There's only one fantasy for me, if I ever fantasize, which is different than clutching one brief image or phrase to get off. This one has eclipsed any others, if there ever were any others. I know there must have been but I remember nothing about them. And I hardly touch this one anymore.

"There's a man who I belong to. Not in a stylized way, just . . . I'm totally devoted to him. And he's older, very dignified, and a little cold, not because he's cruel but because he's so . . . collected."

"Distant. Aloof."

"Yes. And he has a huge house—this is so impossible—and he has other men come over, like, many men, and they're allowed to do whatever they want to me but the rule is that I can't come.

"These men aren't exactly cruel either. They just don't care about me. They're not violent, but they don't have any compassion, they don't really recognize me as a person."

"You're three holes for them to use."

"It's a game to them. So they do anything they can think of, using inanimate objects, a dog. And they know that if they make me come, I'll be upset. I'll be more upset than He will. And they manage it, they make me come. How isn't really important—a vibrator, their cocks, whatever. But it's forced out of me physically. I'm trying as hard as I can not to but I do, and he comes in at just the right moment so he sees it, and I'm looking at him while it happens, and crying, and I'm so ashamed. But he's angrier with them for breaking his rule than he is at me. And then for the first time, he's tender to me."

"And? That's it?"

"That's it."

He'd moved behind me at this point.

"I can feel the warmth from your body," he said, not touching me.

"I know," I said. "I can feel yours, too."

My telling him the fantasy on our first night was an exchange. He'd told me stories about his own experiences, which were rich with mind play and drama. Stories of arranging for a friend of his to suck off strangers as they drove around town in a limo, then for her to be at the mercy of two of his friends for days in a hotel. Or acting as a master to a submissive woman who'd wait in the position he instructed her for hours, pissing herself because she wasn't allowed to move, not wearing tampons for two years because he'd said her pussy was his and only he could dictate what went inside.

So for a moment when I heard someone enter the room I thought it might be one of the four men from the bar. But the breath told me it was him. He watched me for a while from far away. I reversed the cross of my forearms as I held my elbows behind my back. Otherwise I stayed still.

"What's your secret?" He said finally.

I told him about the boy.

"How old was he?"

"Twenty-four?"

"So this wasn't long ago."

"Oh no, it was. I was younger."

"How old were you?"

"Seventeen?"

"And he fucked you?"

"No. I wouldn't let him."

"Were you a virgin?"

"Yes."

"So it would have been terrible."

"It would have been the best sex of my life."

"You've fucked many men since then."

"Yes."

"But this one is the one you think about."

"I dream about finding him again."

"If it had been consummated, you wouldn't. Because it didn't happen, you've been thinking of him all these years."

"It's my greatest sexual regret."

Finally, he spoke again. "I don't want to enter you."

"You said last night you did." He'd told me that while he was reclining and masturbating, asking if I liked knowing he wanted to, and if I liked seeing men "hard because you're gorgeous." I already knew he wanted to be denied.

On the phone, he'd said, "I like seeing a woman sitting in a chair with her legs spread. But not if she's nude." He'd promised me he wouldn't come for a week, then pushed it to a month. "And I'll hire an escort in London, and Paris, and I might even fuck them but I won't come. Will you think of me during that time?"

Now he said, "you have a very lovely pussy but it's one dimensional. If I want a pussy, I just make a phone call. The rest of you is much more intriguing. You're too interesting to fuck."

I laughed in my blindfold. "If I have business cards, I'm getting that printed at the bottom."

"Well, you are. Fucking you would be missing the point. Have you been to Paris?"

"Of course."

"Have you seen the Mona Lisa?"

"Yes."

"It's smaller than you expected, wasn't it?"

"Yes! And far away because of the velvet ropes." I knew where he was going. Everything is tied together. The longer the view, the better you can see it. When I was fourteen and a typical American mall rat, the owner of the pizza place shouted, "Gioconda!" whenever I passed by. And here I am now, over a decade later, with another man calling me the same name.

"You know what she's most famous for her? Her smile. It's enigmatic. That's what you are. You play your cards close to your chest. And you're curious but also a little world-weary . . . I think your life is a distraction. I don't mean that it's unpleasant, but it's just a distraction. You know the word 'latent'?"

"Of course."

"Use it in a sentence."

"The postal worker had latent violent tendencies. It means dormant."

"Yes. I think there's something latent in you, but not violent tendencies. You have an aura of destiny. And the challenge for you will be recognizing your opportunity when it comes. I think a doorway will open and if you go through it, you'll be on your path to satisfaction."

"I hope you're right. That would be nice. To have a future."

"Everyone has a future."

"Of course. But I mean one that truly suits me."

"I'm sorry, but I don't think you're going to find the type of man you want. Because he'd have to be incredibly clever, even cleverer than you. He'd have to deal with what's between here"—he pressed his pointer finger on my temples, one after the other—"and I don't think I can do what I want with you."

"Which is?"

"Use my words to make you do something."

"Do what?"

"Anything. Something you think you don't want to do. Thank God I don't live here. It would frustrate the hell out of me, because you'd be such a handful. You would be an incredible challenge. And I'd be at a disadvantage, I'd have to work even harder because I'm not a young man. I don't have that young male power where I'm twenty-five and I have a hot body and an everhard cock and I can press it up against you and then take it away.

"Because you want to feel desired, intensely, you want to know a man wants to fuck you, but if he's too eager or makes himself too available, you lose interest. He has to be able to control his desire and use that to control you. You're saying, basically, give me all your attention while you're ignoring me."

I was laughing. I've been told this too many times to pin down. Is that my truest name? Difficult Woman?

When my laughter subsided, I said, "That's a bleak picture."

"Oblique?"

"A bleak. Because you're telling me you don't think I'll ever get what I want."

"The trouble is, he would have to walk such a fine line. And I think if you ever found the right man, it wouldn't be good for you."

"Why not?"

"Because if he succeeded, he would have so much power. He could really be cruel. And you don't mind a little applied cruelty, but you don't want—"

"It can't be a character trait."

"Yes."

"I see. It would be hard not to abuse me."

"And I don't think he could ever fuck you. Or if he did, it would have to be entirely clear he was just using you. Very detached. No talking. Abrupt . . . You like the way that sounds?"

"Yes."

"Let me try this. You meet a man, you feel his cock for a moment through his clothes and you know he wants to fuck you, you give him your number, and he doesn't call. But a week later you get an email with an instruction that says go here at this time, wear a skirt with no panties, spread your legs at midnight. And you do, and you wait, and eventually you leave because you don't see him anywhere. But he sends you another email saying only good girl. Just those two words. 'Good Girl'. And he has you do it again, and maybe again, and then the next time he shows himself to you and all he says is, 'I own you now.' And you say, 'Yes.' Is that about right?"

It had happened. My pussy sparked.

"What then?" he said. "I've told you a very nice story that you enjoyed, you run with it."

"But I don't know," I replied.

He sighed. "Ah yes. You really don't know. He'll have to figure out."

"No man's ever denied you an orgasm?" He asked during our second night.

"No."

"No one's ever just tied you up and teased you?"

"All the men who've tied me up think that forcing lots of orgasms is the more dominant thing to do. And that's boring."

"Oh God, men are so disappointing, aren't they? I'm so glad I don't have to date one. In fact, I'm sorry I showed you my penis last night. It changed the dynamic, didn't it?"

"If you hadn't, that would have been something new."

"I'm not happy with myself about that. I regret it . . . And now I know why you like denying men orgasms. You like making them pay."

I giggled here because I couldn't help it. "In many ways," I said.

"In many ways. Because they won't give you what you want. Because they won't deny you, you deny them."

When I plumb my mind in those moments at work, I'm blind and burrowing, delving into field upon textured field, through the crackly and the pliant. I finger and pass over the knotty grains where the mental fabric is eating itself, tangled up like the finest puddled gold chain. I'm looking for something to swim up with, some hot coal to hold. I don't find it.

There was something I wanted in my life, intently, for a long, long time. It was like a rough wind beating me to the edge of a cliff. It's not as though that quality of desiring can simply slacken off and stay low. It has to be satisfied or relinquished entirely. It cannot be contained, only extinguished or fully fed. And then nothing comes to replace it. You can't fill a void that large. The wanting pushed me to the brink, and I plummeted off.

The Master
January 20, 2010

My own name came to me like the sound of a bell. With a client's cock in my mouth and my freshly fucked pussy pointed to a window where other couples in the club watched: _____. I reached out and claimed it, pulling down what was floating by. *I'm _____*, I told myself. Not desperate or sad but a bit surprised. My whole life I've felt awkward saying my own name aloud. The sound seems unfamiliar, even in my head. It is only one of the words I answer to; sometimes I forget it is may be the truest word in me.

"It's possible that your distraction could become your dysfunction," the domination-inclined foreign man said. "Do you ever worry that might happen?"

"Yes," I said. Thinking of how I sometimes worry this will be the only work of my life, not by choice anymore but because I've refused all other options and burned all other bridges. "But not so much recently."

"You could be so distracted that you miss your chance. I don't want that to happen. It occurred to me last night that there must be some part of yourself you don't like, some aspect you don't think is worthy or lovable, something you're ashamed of in spite of your charm and intelligence and attractiveness . . . None of those qualities are protection against your inner demons, are they?"

"Well, that's true for everyone."

"Of course. But you're very good at engaging while being disengaged. You're friendly, you're open—you told me you've let a man piss in your mouth, my God, how much more open could you be? But I don't know anything about you." We were beginning the process of saying goodbye, and he was managing a feat no other man of his age has in this circumstance: offering me advice with a sincerity borne out of something larger than his ego.

He had me take off my panties, put them in my mouth, then tape my mouth shut. After I was tied on the bed, he pushed a large cyberskin dildo into me roughly.

"Cope," he said, his accent coming through with just the single word. We looked into each other's eyes.

"It's not even a struggle for you, is it?" he asked. "I mean, mentally."

I smiled against the tape and shook my head.

"Have you ever," he said slowly, "had a man slide his cock into your ass and then shove it into your mouth?"

I nodded.

"And what did you think of that?"

I shrugged.

He burst into laughter. "God, you're wonderful. How many women—let's say we have 100 women in the room and we ask all of them that same question. Five, maybe five will say 'that sounds amazingly sexy.' And the rest will all say 'ugh, God no, absolutely not.' And you're there saying 'ehh . . . ' That's why you're such a challenge. It's so hard to find your physical boundaries. That's why the only way to play with you is with your mind."

He moved beside me and put his hand over my nose, pinching it shut. "Let's try this for a moment. Are you going to test yourself for me?"

We waited until I had to jerk my head free. "Did you push yourself?" He asked. I made whatever face I could make.

"There are two times when that's nice to do to a woman. One is when she's close to orgasm. The other is when you're fucking her from behind, and then you cover her nose and mouth and tell her 'You're not allowed to breathe until you make my cock come. So you can either focus on not being able to breathe, and pass out, and I'll keep fucking you, or you can focus on using your pussy to get me off.' Maybe seven out of ten women will just start to panic. But I think you'd be one of the other three."

He said, "You know why I had you put the gag on? It's because your smile tells one story about you. But your eyes tell another."

This is something a tarot card reader told me. When she asked if she was right, I just smiled.

At the end, he came around to the other side of the mattress and said, "Lift your pretty head." He held the back of my skull with both hands and slid the tape away.

"Open your mouth." He removed the panties, which were soaked with saliva.

Then he kept his warm palms where they were and looked down into my eyes.

"Are you melancholy?" He asked.

"Yes," I said. "But it's ok. It's not too bad."

"Melancholy is my favorite emotion. Because you can still appreciate humor. You know one can be sad and it's just stupid, and you're thinking, 'Oh, get over it.' And then there's real sadness, like grief. And then there's something deeper than grief that has a real poignancy to it, that comes from recognizing the human condition. It took me a long time to realize this was the state I stayed in. One can only be as happy as you are sad. But most people don't realize that. They want to do away with all the sad and have only this happy wedge of the spectrum. They don't realize that all they're doing when they pare away the sadness is shaving down their happiness, too.

"I don't think you've quite done that with your emotions. But I think you're starting to do that with your actions. I want you to know that while you've become so good at deflection and distraction, and you've built up all this self-protection so you can hide the parts of yourself you don't like . . . What I'm saying is, don't be so damned good at it. Because it might cost you an opportunity. There's a dynamism in you that could be tremendous if applied in the right place. That's my wish for you, that you find that path."

He kept saying, "I'm never going to see you again," periodically throughout the several days, and I couldn't tell if he was being realistic or dramatic or both. Abruptly, just before I left, he asked, "Have you ever been to China?"

"No. I've never been there."

"Do you like to travel?"

"Yes."

"I wish I'd brought more money. It would be fun to take you with me. To sit next to you on a plane . . . You could have you own hotel room."

"But why?"

"Because being with you wouldn't be for sex. It would cost me a lot of time and money but let's say I pay you for a month and just keep you with me. To figure you out. To hope there's some moment where I can put my finger on it."

"The world's most expensive brain teaser," I said. "You can email me, you know."

"I won't contact you again unless I have some insight," he answered. "I'll send you a text if I get a brain wave."

Part of me was thinking at him, *don't go. I'll miss you.* But another part of me knew it was ok. Being left alone with a teaching is part of the teaching. And I felt so lucky to have had this unexpected man in my life.

When I walked out into the sun I felt the happiness shining out of my chest through the messy cloud of melancholy. The air was bright and clean and I lingered in it, face just barely tilted up.

I took the subway to the same café where AM and I had breakfast after the HIV results. I sat at the bar and ordered a soy hot chocolate, resting in the fact of the money and trying to decide how I felt about having made as much in one morning as some families make in a week. I'm finally starting to feel the responsibility of my income. Wondering how and when I should give it away, and to whom. Later, when I tucked the money in the safe, I had a vision of all of it gone—not used but destroyed somehow. I originally bought the safe to protect its contents not from theft but fire. *Oh God, what a waste*, I thought, *to have hoarded it all this time*. Another girl came in and ordered a mojito.

AM sent me a text message saying she wanted hippo-related art. She was making fun of me for my tumblr request to be pointed to art with foxes.

"Commission one from me." I replied. "I'll paint it with my boobs. It will be called *Mud Wallow*."

"I love you," she wrote.

"I love you, too," I replied. She is one of the few people in my life who knows my real name.

Chunks of Ash
January 29, 2010

The man from last year is getting married; he wrote to tell me. He said his only wish was to fuck me at least one last time before he did. He also said his fiancée would have to watch, emphasizing that she wouldn't have to be involved beyond the viewing. I thought about doing this, which is clearly not a good idea given the intensity of what little communication we've had. And a vision floated into my head of him on top of me while she sat watching near the wall, and him whispering in my hair that he was still in love with me. She's deaf. He wouldn't even have to whisper if his lips were hidden.

Because I am perversely drawn to intense emotional dynamics, part of me wanted to make this happen. I wanted to know what it would feel like to be in that position and see another person in this position of betraying a loved one in front of me, because of me. Perhaps I like seeing people—seeing men—in emotional extremes because I feel I exist there myself, and inciting it in them gives me the illusion of having control of it in myself. Or it's just sadism. Or are they one and the same?

And I liked the idea of bleeding from sex again. Probably because I like the drama of it, the sense that some price was paid. I like the red proof of having used my body in a type of consensual aggression. And the twinge of pain reminding me into the next day. Maybe that's how I most truly feel about sex, because that's how I feel about life, vengeful and passionate as a wild-eyed god: I want everyone to bleed. The foreign man said to me, keenly, "You're the type who, when she doesn't get what she thinks is right, makes sure the whole world's going to pay."

But this phrase kept rising up: sexual destruction. Do I want to continue to be sexually destructive? And I couldn't bring myself to meet him.

Of all ways I utilize sex—entertainment, investigation, validation—expressing love has to be one of the least common. This is not to say there's no tenderness or warmth that might be called love, even though my partner may be essentially a stranger. But sex is not on reserve. It's not in a special box on the highest shelf. It's a precise tool for delicate work, but I'm the one operating the tool, not the one being worked on. So I wield sex more than share it, although I try to wield it kindly most of the time.

These new impulses—giving away my money, restraining myself where I once would have run ahead—are hardly voluntary. It simply seems impossible to behave otherwise, even if another path has more allure. Two years ago I had to ask myself, could I become the type of wife who plugs her ears and closes her eyes and holds out her hand for the credit card so she can spend a day at the spa while her husband goes about the removed work of destroying futures, I thought the answer was no, but I didn't *know* the answer was no.

I still sometimes cling to thoughts of extravagant vacations, socially irresponsible clothing purchases, even the thick disregard for attempting a useful life. But now it's as though I'm being issued an invitation to touch an electrified jewel. (*Here, these are the things that could be yours.*) While my greed may still have a voice, the rest of me recoils. My whole body shrinks away like a cringing dog. I can scarcely reach out a hand without trembling.

Struggle With This
February 1, 2010

When he first told me, I began crying, smiling a little at the same time. Of my tears I was thinking a surprised version of "I guess I'll learn from this," or "this will take some thinking on," or "I didn't expect this of myself." Half laughing, half gasping at the gnarled sprig of pain sprouting buds in my heart.

He saw my wet face in the sliding light of the car and said, "Oh no," and reached out to touch me. "Oh no, Baby, I'm sorry."

"It's ok," I said, genuinely more shocked and inquisitive than suffering.

"Trust me, when you hear the details—there were so many funny things—"

"No!" I said. "No, don't say anything bad about her."

Gradually, as we rode through the night, it wasn't ok. I lost my hold on the hurt and it sank deeper, like a stone passing through pond water, settling sickly on the soft, murky floor.

I understand now the futility and desperation of wanting to be someone's Best Fuck when they may have been your worst or most forgettable, when you don't know how to come during sex or aren't interested in it because you're too eager to impress. A friend once told me about going back to a girl's house after their date, where she proceeded to get naked, put on a pair of black high heels, and give him an extravagant blowjob.

"That sounds sexy," I said.

"No, it was silly," he said. "I told her she didn't have to do all that."

"That must have embarrassed her," I said. But what else should he have done? The artifice was getting in the way. It didn't turn him on. Her idea of what would be sexy to him was wrong or she wasn't pulling it off well enough.

Other aspects are more important than a good pair of heels—sensitivity to the moment, real chemistry, confidence, the ability to improvise and respond. But those qualities aren't glamorous or sale-able, so instead we end up with thin landing strip pubic hair and "come on my face" as what's supposed to be the ultimate in erotic delight.

I'm talking about the idea that one's own sexuality can be so infinite as to satisfy all needs and desires—good-looking enough, willing enough, skillful enough, wild enough. That moronic media shock when a public figure cheats on a beautiful wife. If beauty isn't the unbreakable lariat, what is? If absolute sexual permissiveness—*ok, fuck me there, that way, videotape it, bring another girl*—still won't keep a man loyal to you, what will?

One of my friends once admitted to me that the only way she could come was alone with a vibrator, thinking about women; she never came with her boyfriend. The same boyfriend she was always taking nude pictures for, filming herself masturbating for, dying her hair and tanning and committing to new diets for. Sometimes I think we're all hollow dolls, cramming ourselves full of moldy straw.

"Maybe," I admitted to him, "not consciously at all—but maybe I was giving you one of those tests, trying to bait you to see if all of what you'd said before was true. Even encouraging you in the hope you would resist." The word for that wasn't coming to me at the time but it's here now: entrapment. I think my urging used to come from a sincere place, a place of play and curiosity that could afford to be reckless and expansive because we were newer with each other then and not living on all the silt layers of blame and hurt. I genuinely wanted to hear stories about what it was like when he was with other women. I'm the anthropologist, remember? Dedicated to her chosen work. But it's been years since I first exhorted him to fuck another woman and he's refused for years and the truth is probably that I'd become convinced he would never do it. So the shock was part of the pain.

I remembered an article I read once by Tori Amos in which she wrote about asking her husband to indulge some type of "perversion"—in my memory, it was tie her up and call her "whore." She had a history of sexual abuse, and that was how she dealt with it. But her husband said no, and she got angry with him, and he still said, "no, I'm not going to do that to you." And it was the right response.

Among the things he used to say to me—"I don't want to be with any other woman; if I only have sex with you for the rest of my life, I'll die happy"— one was specifically about commitment to himself, how he thought of himself and what he believed in, desire aside. "I want to be the man in your life who hasn't betrayed you," he said. And I know he was thinking of all the other refusals it entails: *I won't give you a reason to leave me. I won't excuse your behavior with my own.*

He said, "No matter how angry you are with me, believe me, I'm so much more disappointed in myself. It was like being in one of those POW camps where they make you choose which prisoner they're going to shoot."

Finally I became brave enough to ask to see her picture. He found one online from the school where she'd recently completed her masters program. She was blonde and very pretty.

"Do you want me to tell you about it?" he said.

"I already know everything there is to know about it," I replied, feeling flippant and safe again, dancing on a springboard ten feet above water. "You had anal. You came more than once."

"We didn't have anal sex," he said after a moment.

"Aha," I said, pretending to gloat but feeling fear-stricken. "So you came more than once."

He said nothing and maybe nodded.

"How many times?" I asked.

"Three," he said.

My face split open like it had been struck with a cleaver. He touched me gingerly on the bony peak of my shoulder. I kept crying, all the reasons to cry flapping down on one another like shuffled cards. I was figuring out new things about myself that changed the old things but the shadows of the old were still there. What had I said about the moment in the car? His fucking her highlighted all the ways I'd failed at something that I used to be deeply invested in but was beginning to let go. It was an unraveled part of me catching fire.

Once I thought I was going to be perfect. I was going to be sexually supreme, indispensable. But this is not something I achieved.

I thought of all the myths about naming and power, how when you claim the name of someone or something, you become its master. I knew I had to name the strange pain now to make it stop. I searched. Then I knew, and when it came to me I cried harder. It was humiliation. I told him this.

"Egos are stupid," I said. I'd been telling him repeatedly not to apologize, not to feel bad, I wasn't angry at him. Of course I saw the insanity of begrudging him something I'd been doing for years. How many times have I come with another man and what does that mean to me? Often it means nothing. But I kept thinking of a line I wrote some time ago: "heart and brain always stranded from one another, barely even glancing across the divide."

"That's how I felt when you started working even though you knew I didn't want you to. I felt small. I felt like I didn't matter."

"I'm sorry," I said. "But I don't want to live that way. I don't want to believe I'm worth less because you came three times with someone else. Why would that hurt me? It has nothing to do with me."

"It's human," he said. "That's just human, to feel hurt."

I know and have known for a long time what treacherous folly it is to sexually compare yourself to another. I like sex not because I've got it all figured out but precisely because I haven't figured it out and never will, because every new person is a new universe of desire. And a new universe of allure.

I once described a particular kiss from one man to another, and the other man then tried to approximate the kiss and it didn't work because it never works that way. You can't overlay the genius of another person's body over whoever is next in line. This man had his own way of kissing that turned me on, and his lips moved nothing like the other man's but it was unique and his own, and I liked them both. We are limitless in how we can experience pleasure. It doesn't need to look the same every time for us to recognize it. What kind of terrible life would that be if it did?

He told me all the details and the pain seeped away. I even felt a surge between my legs as I listened. I tried to defend her when he talked about the strange things she did that she seemed to think would be sexy but instead had made him want to laugh or caused physical pain. And again when he talked about some of the anxious ways she transparently sought his approval.

"She can't help it," I said. "Girls are always told we're not good enough."

He said he thought I'd managed to arrange the whole thing because of how much she bit him as they were making out, and I smiled.

"We have to go back to the restaurant and have her serve us," I decided. "I want to say 'I've heard a lot about you.'"

"Be nice," he said.

"Why would you think I'd be nice?" I said, meaning "why *wouldn't* you?"

"Freudian slip," he said.

"You know what I meant," I said. "I won't be cruel, I promise. I only want to see the look on her face."

Then he came in me three times and I came on him once, my thighs spread low around his hips and my hands clenching his ass to pull him as deeply inside me as I could.

Once I saw my married next-door neighbor kissing a woman not his wife outside our building. Two days later there was a commotion in the hall beyond my door. I waited for it to die down, then left to walk to a friend's party, pleased that I'd avoided the wife, who was cold and unlikable and unleashed her unbearable Chihuahuas in the elevators and halls—yet there the wife was, pacing on the corner across the street. We had never gotten along. But she looked beautiful that night. She looked so good and I wanted to tell her so.

"Hey, has that girl been coming around a lot?" She asked, flipping her cell phone closed as I came near, cornering me in the open air. There was a dazed and unusually convivial air about her.

"Pardon?" I said.

"I know he's seeing her! Has he been bringing her here?"

"I'm—no. No. I don't know." It came out meanly, like a judgment. I drew back, surprised by myself. Then I said, "I'm sorry. Are you ok?"

"I walked in on them together," she said. Then she laughed. "I think I'm in shock."

"I'm so sorry. Do you . . . do you need to talk about it somewhere?" I gestured back at the building, then, thinking better of it, off towards the bars. "Or do you want my number or something?"

"No. I'll be ok."

I didn't see her again until she brought a sexy and wary looking young man to help her move out her things, and we only passed each other in the hall. I had complained bitterly about her dogs; I fantasized about them dying until I realized she'd probably only replace them with others of the same size and temperament. But I wish I had let her know my allegiance lay with her, and that I was sorry. That her pain wasn't worth having the dogs gone.

Look Up
February 9, 2010

He broke his back in his early twenties. He lay for hours in the cold until someone found him, which he credited as a blessing since it allowed him immediate time alone to come to terms with his future as a paraplegic.

"Were you in a lot of pain?" I asked. "Or was there only numbness?"

"It was like someone had thrown a switch," he said. "There was no sensation at all."

He mentioned how cheerful and optimistic most people were in physical therapy, radiant with the relief of still being alive. He said it had given him a much deeper appreciation for life. I wondered if I would be like that.

When I first attempted to walk in the hospital after my surgery, I was too wrung out to feel much of anything besides a vague disbelief that standing on two feet was feasible. I managed to stagger between the two parallel poles and was quickly pushed to attempt crutches. I felt my breath going and said so, said, "I think I need to sit back down," the wheelchair sagging emptily at the side like a sweet hammock, but my mother was there, raw with anxiety, and she barked that I didn't, I needed to finish, so I fainted for my first and only time.

I have no idea how long I was out—ten, twenty, thirty seconds? I came to in front of the pinched faces of the nurse and my mother, a blissful stream of pure oxygen in my nostrils, and I didn't understand where I was. I wasn't sure if it was real. Because in the time I was out, I dreamed a decade-long smear of a dream. I saw years of my life ahead, not just saw but lived it, lived long periods as an adult in some other place while my sixteen year old collapsed form was being muscled back to the chair. I remember trying to speak as soon as I came back, feeling blessed, baffled, throbbing with realization, but I was shushed. In the noise and panic of revival, I forgot everything I'd learned.

One of my teachers talks about the idea that the Gods need humans to stay unenlightened because humans are their entertainment. ("Nobody wants to watch a show about somebody moral who has it all figured out," he says. "That's why Tony Soprano never stopped killing people.") But hiding enlightenment was a challenge, because humans are merely talking monkeys, turning over everything in their careless mania. So enlightenment was secreted away in the place they'd never look: inside themselves.

He had an amazing touch and I lay over his lap while he stroked me. I pinched clothespins on his nipples and pulled them off, sometimes slapping him, sometimes caressing him.

He asked me to masturbate and while I was doing so, with my legs splayed over him, he said, "Come for me," and I glanced at him for a moment with a smile until he said, "I mean really come for me." As in, don't fake it.

But I did. You can't take risks with someone who wants your orgasm that badly, can't gamble that your real come will be long enough or loud enough or quaking enough to convince him that it happened. I've been in that position many times, and there's nothing quite as deflating as learning that your orgasm disappointed another person because it wasn't theatric enough.

Near the end of our time together he asked if I wanted to watch him pee. It was nothing I'd expressed an interest in, so I gathered it was something he wanted. "Sure," I said. "I don't know when I'll get that offer again."

He took out a catheter from a bag he asked me to bring to him. "I've never peed in front of a woman before."

"How does it feel?" I asked, once he'd started. Although the only action it required from him was feeding the clear plastic tube down into his penis.

He nodded, relaxed. "I feel comfortable."

It reminded me of another relic of the accident, one I hadn't recalled in years. When I was taken out of the ambulance, one of the first things I whispered was that I had to pee. One nurse said I need a catheter. Probably because I couldn't move my legs into a good position, inserting it triggered but didn't capture the flow, and the cot beneath me grew wet and warm with urine. So I learned several things about the body's response to injury that day. One was that whatever cocktail of adrenaline and endorphins it released was excellent at suppressing the pain. The other was that it was equally excellent at suppressing the ego.

After our night together, I caught a train away from the snow, then a bus with an attendant whose forearm tattoo read in cursive: *one life, one chance*. Halfway through the ride, a man in front of me began pointing and craning his neck to look high out the window. He was so fascinated and excited that my blasé traveler mind gave way to curiosity, and I turned to see. At first I saw only a small stab of a rainbow, and I rolled my eyes. But then I looked for a moment longer, until I realized there was a giant faint circle of rainbow around the slightly blurred sun, another colored ray shooting off the top, like the outline of an eye, with slashes like punctuation through the nebulous clouds at the sides. Sky calligraphy. It was the most elaborate rainbow arrangement I've ever seen, so elaborate it hardly seemed possible. But it was there, it had happened and was happening. Nonchalantly, over the heads of many who would never look up.

Prewriting
February 21, 2010

A client and I once had a long discussion about tea in the afternoon at an Irish pub. You can talk about anything with a client, just like you can talk about anything with anybody. You can see who can name more African countries. You can cover politics, if you mostly agree. And you can do my favorite thing to do in any situation, which is create outlandish potential futures and flesh out the details of the resulting parallel universe. You can also speak about the uncomfortable, because sometimes it's unavoidable. A long time ago, at the end of one session, a client said, "I shouldn't come here anymore."

"Why?" I asked.

"It's not fair to my family," he said. "This money should be going towards my son's tuition fund."

"Well . . . " I said, "if it makes you feel any better, it's going towards mine."

And I never saw him again.

Recently I saw the man half of the married couple. I don't know that he's going to be married much longer. It's just a feeling I have. I haven't heard from his wife in a long time although she was the one who arranged for us to meet and I saw her alone a few times. Neither he nor I bring her up anymore. We don't even mention her name. At least once while we're naked he moves away from me a little bit to get a better look at my face, usually as he's kneeling and I'm on my back, then he'll stare at me for a bit. He'll have a look of concentration but it doesn't make me as uncomfortable as it might.

This time as we met and talked I took in his shortness and the way he was dressed and his mannerisms and I found it all sexy in one of the nicest ways: secretly. I mean the type that takes a bit longer to notice and feels much more rewarding for not being obvious. I realized it would not be impossible for me to date this man. I like how precise he is with his words.

He uses many words that most people would never think to incorporate into their spoken life.

I came out of the bathroom in a gold lingerie set while he was getting air on the balcony in spite of the chill, and when he noticed me he said, "Oh, the neighbors will complain," and rushed to close the curtains.

"Complain?!" I said. And then when we first laid together, he stroked my hip and said, "This is quite a prominent scar" although he's seen it plenty of times before.

"You're really charming me tonight," I said. "I don't know that I can take all this flattery."

"Your ass is so firm," he said as apology, hand gripping my cheek.

I laughed, shaking my head.

"Your teeth are so straight."

"I'm not buying a word of that. That's not even how you usually speak. You're a terrible liar."

He said he wanted to take me riding when the weather was warmer but he'd never been on a horse before, and I joked about making him feel bad with how good I was. We fell into that type of fantasizing I mentioned—maybe that's why I can imagine having some type of relationship with him—in which we'd be competing against each other in a pentathlon, which then progressed to a flat out manhunt.

"Have you ever even fired a gun before?" I said. "Because I have."

"My god, you're a dangerous dame," he replied. "You'd shoot me and ride right off into the sunset."

For the first time when writing about a client I thought, *how would he feel if he read this?* And I have no idea. Did I offend with the comment about his height? Or about the staring? If I could tell him something in conjunction with this, I would say: *I like you. I like spending time with you. Don't be freaked out because of what I said about dating. I don't expect us to start dating. I don't even necessarily want that, it's merely something I could see manifesting in one of the many parallel universes. I don't want your marriage to end, but I want you to keep seeing me.*

I understand something new about myself after last week. I see how I've replicated the experience with my big, big love in little microcosm relationships, encounters that are unexpected and intense and flare out with my disengagement. It's not all me; the universe is helping because it's providing me with these very exact men who compliment me in a certain way. It can't happen with just anybody, and it doesn't. It happens with these few when the craving wells up in me. Somehow the craving corresponds with the opportunity, or vice versa, like a surfer catching the right swell.

I can see myself plotting and daydreaming to try to make it happen again. It's exactly the right time. It only happens in this time, the first half of the year, before summer. Why can't I be calm? Why can't I read Thich Nhat Hanh and sit still, or go do paperwork at the AIDS clinic or simply write, for god's sake? I hurt a lot of people when I pursue this, including myself, although I suffer the least. Which makes it easy to repeat. I can see the outline of it like it's an actual cookie cutter, a hard metal shape I press down on my life. I see the progression, the beginning middle end, the attendant fears and exhilarations.

When I read a book like *The End of the Story*, I remember how much I need fiction to tell me how to be in my life. I am reminded that a writer's mind is uncannily predictable across bodies and ages.

"This was what happened," Lydia Davis writes, "so I had to look for another ending. I could have invented one, but I did not want to do that. I was not willing to invent much, though I'm not sure why: I could leave things out and I could rearrange things. I could let a thing be done earlier or later than it was done, but I could use only the elements of the actual story."

"You don't understand," I told my boyfriend. He was clearly unhappy about the idea of me going to see his waitress while she worked. He tried to keep me from figuring out the name of the restaurant but that was easy, and confirming it was easy, too. I only wanted to say the one thing to her: "I've heard a lot about you," and no more. I didn't want to insult her. I didn't want to drop something snide about what she does when she's turned on or what turns her on, as reported to me by him. I only wanted to float out this one sentence—"I've heard a lot about you"—while he was at my side, and see what it did. And if he would not come with me, I would go alone.

"You don't understand," I told him, "I need a story. I need an end to this story. Something more needs to happen. And then it will be over." But he was still unhappy and irritated, and I could see then the only way the story would end—and this would make it a better ending—is if I were to go alone and find her. Watch her at work and say nothing, or try to come on to her myself. Better yet would be to go where she works and sit at the bar and pick up a man there, and take him to my hotel room and fuck him, but only if the fucking were poignant or led to a poignant moment, either with him or by myself.

If you don't understand, there is no way I can make you.

When I went back to my old journal, I found things that surprised me there. Things about my boyfriend. I remembered professing often that I could never date him, but I found that in fact I had an entry in which I wrote "1) I realize I could date him."

I also found, several times, admission of his ability to make me come. Nobody had or has a better track record for making me come than he did while he was a client. Every single time I saw him, it would happen, and I saw him a lot. He would make it happen, even when I didn't want it to. "No matter what mood I'm in," I wrote. I have still never been with anyone who went down on me as well as he did. Of course when he was no longer my client, many things changed, for both of us.

Star Town
March 4, 2010

Most of the other women wore cocktail dresses, some very sparkly, and other women wore dresses over leggings or pants, which is not something I realized women still did. Several older men wore suits. I was one of the few women wearing simply jeans and boots, and it didn't matter. I was taller than almost all the others, carrying the nobility of tallness, the dignity of it, and enjoying it, which is rare.

We wandered through the clotted ring of bodies around the bar and into the emptier galleries of the second floor, taking in the ominous dancing nose and charcoal sketches of depressed men in suits, the paper cut outs and the gruesome animated clips playing in dark rooms. When the band began, Jacob spotted an empty corner with a clear view. From that vantage point, he nodded at a couple swaying off beat from each other and the music.

"Slow dancing," he said. And we began swinging our hips slowly and gyrating in a circle, dancing with each other but not touching each other, movements small and purposeful.

Back at my hotel, we lay on the couch and talked about yoga, then my work and the pictures I'd had taken that day.

"You look too innocent," he said.

"That's sort-of my thing," I replied. "When I was in high school, I could get away with anything. I could get trashed and puke on some guy's front lawn and then the next day he'd be like, 'man, Charlotte, things were crazy last night, you should have been there.' And I'd say, "I was there, I puked on your lawn!' I always thought I could have murdered someone in front of a crowd and no one would even remember it. They'd just tell the police, 'I think Charlotte was at home quilting that night.'"

He laughed. He played with my black leather and gold chain handcuffs cum bracelets.

"I'm locked in," he said. "Did you bring any other props?"

"I could have done the fake drinking out of something shot. But I've already done that. There was a picture of me with a teacup on my old site."

"A teacup?!"

"People loved it. I got men specifically mentioning that picture when they emailed me. I should have used a whole teapot this time and poured the hot water down my body."

"It's tea time with Charlotte!" he said.

I began laughing in the bathroom, washing off my makeup. "It's tea time!" I said. "That's my new site heading."

Then we talked about love and holding out, the idea of soul mates. I told him about BBL. I first saw him when we took the same literature class together. We didn't talk to each other but I thought about him. I thought things like, *that guy probably thinks he's so cute but he's not that cute.*

"And he thought, 'There's that girl who loves the library,'" Jacob said.

"Yeah. There's the president of the celibacy club, off to work on another book report."

"So what happened?"

"One day—I remember everything about it, the sun, where it happened, his face—he smiled at me. And I was like, 'Wow . . . ' My best friend was there. I kept talking about him to her, saying, 'Did you see that? Has he always looked that way? Is it just me or does he look amazing when he smiles?'"

Jacob wanted to spend the night. He was sleepy with vodka and flight fatigue.

"What time does your plane leave?"

"The car's coming to pick me up at six, so I should leave here at five."

"Ok," I got into bed while he peed in the bathroom. He left the door open.

"Where are you?" He said as he slid in between the sheets in the dark, scooting across the wide mattress to spoon me. I squeezed his hand and wrapped my feet around his. It felt like sleeping with my boyfriend. I closed my eyes and he took his hand away and tugged at the corner of the pillow between my legs.

"What's this?"

"I sleep this way. I have wide hips. I have to have some padding between my legs."

"Wide hips . . . ?" His hands started moving over my skin. One of them cupped my right hipbone, fingertips over the edge and pressed into the gap inside.

"I like this," he said of the sharp ridge.

"My handles?"

"Yes. Is this alright?"

"That you're touching me?"

"Yes."

"Yes."

His hands felt curious at first, friendly with a confused sleepiness, very high school. He tugged me like he wanted me to roll over and face him but I stayed on my side and he kept touching. The refusal to be deterred reminded me of high school as well. Then the tone of his touch changed.

I didn't say anything. I just held my human sized pillow and felt myself getting wet. He began to use his mouth to light up the lattice of nerves under the skin of my neck and its slope down to my shoulder. No part of me wanted it to stop.

"You like being kissed here?" He said, stroking that curve for a moment with the full flat of his palm.

"You're very good at it," I said. It was like nothing I'd ever felt—or at least nothing I remembered, and I'm sure I would remember something like that.

I rolled underneath him as he rolled over me, reaching back to unhook my bra as he pulled off his T-shirt. He pinned my wrists above my head and I got wetter. When I felt him working his way down my body on his way to lick me, I locked my thighs around his hips and stopped him. He moved back to my side and curled his fingers into the slick between my legs. I arched up against it with my breasts bare in the cool air and realized I could come like this, posing myself and writhing against him, but I wasn't sure I wanted to.

Finally I said, "We should stop."

"Sorry," he said, plunging his fingers inside me a few more times. He stopped, then did it again. Then he stopped and rolled onto his back. I lay on my side and reached an ankle back to hook around his calf. He flexed his foot at me, welcoming it there.

I thought of my boyfriend's penis, of how it can be not hard but is never flaccid, never hangs slack or flattened but sits on his balls in a friendly, perky way, brown foreskin wrinkling around the tip. And of his dense, dark pubic hair, which is woolier than white guy pubic hair and feels better on my skin and against my tongue.

Then I felt sad, and slutty, which is not an attitude towards myself I usually have. I thought, *I would sleep with anyone*, not as an insult but as a realization, and with that came the fear of being disrespected and misunderstood, of such availability leading to sex neither party wanted but that might feel inevitable or stupid to refuse, the way people almost always take what is free even if it's something they don't want or can't use. The way some men think a woman is stupid for having sex with a man who doesn't want to date her, especially when they themselves are that man.

Discernment, I thought to myself, *I have to discriminate between what I really want and what I don't*. But sometimes not *not* wanting it seems enough. Sometimes my wanting it would be canceled out by something nasty in the other person's mind, like the pride of taking something from me even though there's nothing to be taken, but I can't tell if it's actually there or if I'm only paranoid. I can't tell if I'm paranoid or if I'm naive and should be even more paranoid.

Lastly I felt a sudden concern that I will never be able to have a male friend again, not one who didn't assume we'd have sex, and wasn't intending to make it happen at the first opportunity. I wondered if Jacob would have acted as he did if he didn't know about my work. I wondered if this would ruin whatever seeds of friendship we had.

But in the morning he came around to my side to kiss my face goodbye, and I felt drool on my face and reached up with one hand to wipe away the saliva while I reached up with the other to stroke the back of his head. I was so appreciative, so relieved, that during it all he made no demands on me other than those of his hands. No attempts at narrating the moment, no "you're so wet," no continuous stream of smoke up my ass beyond his earliest comments on the softness of my skin.

"Even here," he'd said, with his fingers on my forearm. "You must use some type of oil."

The next morning I wore the same boots to my facial, and as the assistant wiped my face clean at the end, she asked, "Are you a model?"

"No," I replied, laughing.

"We get a lot of models here. You all look alike. You're not?"

"No."

"People don't give you numbers?"

"No."

"And you've never even tried?" She seemed upset now, a little distressed or personally offended.

"No. I'm too old to be a model. They're all in their teens."

"But you could still be . . . a star." She said this almost to herself, with the sudden quietness of personal conviction. And I thought of how no one believes in the American dream quite as fiercely as do non-American born people.

On the couch that night, I told Jacob I might be moving to Paris, and while it seemed an impossible opportunity to refuse, I most truly wanted to be in New York.

"You like this town?" He said, a little like a challenge. Not city but town, as though it were someplace small and unremarkable.

"I love it. Don't you?"

He nodded slowly. "Yeah. I think it's a good place to be."

Regression
March 13, 2010

Lately I've been fantasizing about Jacob and Mike, one fucking me from behind and pulling back my head so the other can come on my face. I don't usually use real people in my fantasies. Almost exclusively, I like daydreaming without touching myself about people I know, but for actually coming I rarely call a familiar body to my brain. So this occurrence is strange, and I veer towards the image but then back away, bring it close and then turn from it.

It's not strictly them in the physical sense, since I'm not attracted to either of them that way. The aforementioned scenario was first a dreary thought I had during the night with Jacob in my hotel room, a resigned vision of a future in which I'd somehow end up alone with the two of them in Mike's apartment, and we'd do some bong hits and restorative poses and then the next thing you know, I'd be fingercuffs. But they've always been mild men around me. Who knows where these ideas come from.

Jacob invited me to come to a famous person's house with him and Mike. I said no, thinking partially of what he expected and partially of the beautiful mean girl I often see him with and who I assumed would be there too. I didn't want to be around her, even if it meant passing up the chance to run wild in the empty many million-dollar mansion. I'm certain she's not remotely interested in him—she probably thinks the same mean things about him that she does about everyone else—and is most definitely so disdainful of me that I'm hardly worth one of her big open-jaw guffaws, but sometimes I'm certain of things like that and then I turn out to be wrong. But one thing I know unequivocally is that spending the night in a stranger's expensive home with people of questionable judgment is a hallmark of high school.

Sometimes I feel weary with the world's predictability. Sometimes I think seeing the future is the easiest ability, and it is not at all glamorous or shocking or spooky—it's only disappointing. This man will want this in this way. You'll be invited here and someone will arrive and someone else will leave and the night will grow older, no one will want to make the drive to take you where you should be sleeping. Then there will be that gap, the moment when what everyone pretended would happen has finally not happened, and now the part you were all expecting must begin, yet begin in a way that seems casual, so no one has to be responsible.

One of my favorite teachers said something very funny and sweet once as he channeled an imitation of those who invented asanas, prefacing it with the obvious statement that they didn't have TVs or iPods or even printed materials, and they were simply sitting around, looking at their hands and limbs. "Well," he said, studying his fingers, "Got this body. Let's see what I can do with that."

Yet that seems almost sinister at times: *well, I've got this body, I've got this impulse. Here are the pieces and they can be fitted into this shape. Even if the outcome isn't particularly desirable or desired, even if the actions aren't wise or good: I see this path, I know this path. Here we go.*

Another of my teachers gave the analogy of, every year, getting on an annual carnival's circular ride—you know, The Scrambler or The Blender or whatever. Of getting off feeling nauseated, thinking, never again. And yet finding yourself in line the next time the fair was in town, handing over your ticket.

That's something I'm working on: better recognizing those moments when I'm a buying a ticket for a ride that makes me sick.

Discretion and Valor
March 17, 2010

I reunited with one of my most eccentric clients not long ago. I'd love to tell you about him, not to ridicule or gawk at his tastes but simply because they're so wonderful. It's truly wonderful that human beings concoct the fetishes they do. His don't even fall into one easy category. It's a mash-up of several.

"Why?" He whimpered once. "Why do I like this so much?"

Then later he said, "You're seeing me this way and I'm supposed to be an important businessman." Just like that. Sometimes people are stunningly, perfectly self-aware, no metaphors or overwrought psychological analysis required. Sometimes we start speaking and we discover that we know ourselves better than we let on. That is essentially what happens with writing, for me.

When he said that, I thought, *nobody feels real*, musing on how we don't believe we're adults, that we're spouses or parents or whatever else, but later I realized it's the exact opposite. We feel too real—and by real, I mean complex beyond explanation, numinous—real beyond the quality of recognition we're afforded in the everyday circumstances of our lives. And we are beyond being known in the regular ways of the world.

That's where the friction comes from, and perhaps where the fetishes come in. I don't think I have any of my own but I like being part of others'. I even get turned on, not because of the particulars but because the erotic charge for the other person is so palpable. And after the sexual cruelty and aggression of webcam clients, these self-directed desires, the desires that hurt absolutely no one, seem dear.

"It's so embarrassing," he murmurs occasionally, shyly delighted by it. "It's so embarrassing for you to see me like this."

We had a pristine view of the White House and I don't mean that we could see it over other structures, in a clutter of office buildings and hotels. I mean we saw it straight on, blocked by nothing, the space between covered only in grass and trees, a road, a fence, then a lawn. On the park directly below, a couple lay on a blanket, making out.

My life is special, I thought as I watched this rich man go through his bizarre ritual. *My life makes me happy.* I'd thought that last part before even meeting him, when I was digging, half-dressed, through one of the big Tupperware bins in my closet, pushing aside the plastic-wrapped bulk orders of condoms, the vibrators and silk bags, as the kitten sat watching.

"Did I give you enough?" he asked as I prepared to leave. I don't think he even knows my actual rates. I think he only does the miraculous mental math of what the experience is worth to him. It is worth a lot. He'd bequeathed me with dense rubberbanded folds of twenties upon entering his room. ("You look like a drug dealer with these," I said. "I felt like a drug dealer," he replied. "That's why I wanted to get rid of them as soon as possible.")

"I didn't even feed you." He touched his hand to his hair. I could see the shapes of his session outfit under the t-shirt and flannel pajama bottoms he'd pulled on. I hoped he wouldn't forget and order room service like that.

"That's for the best," I said. "I'm like an animal when I eat."

"Really?"

"It's terrifying. You'd lose all faith in mankind. And you'd be charged for carpet cleaning."

We hugged goodbye and I felt those bizarre underclothes beneath but they seemed normal when worn by a warm human being.

He said, "Can I call you again?" and I said, "I hope you do."

Recently, my highest profile client wrote me an email that inspired tears. This may not be a feat in and of itself, as the right music and the right view from a train window can wet my eyes, but it was at the very least a testament to his considerably in-demand public speaking abilities. "I suppose, like most of us, you wonder if what you do makes a difference in the world," he wrote. "I can tell you that without a doubt you make a difference in my life."

His letter was merciful in its timing, coming as it did in the murky midst of my feeling profoundly worthless and confused. On that particular day I'd been simultaneously berating and mourning myself for my indecisiveness, my inactivity, my aimlessness: *The only thing I was put on this earth to do is to write, and I barely even do that.*

I tried to think of what I love doing, and how doing those things might stretch enough to fill the time when I'm waiting for the rest of my life to happen, when I'm not in a class or at a workshop or on a date or running an errand or working on a (non-sex) paying project. There's so much of that time! And when I'm faced with it, all the activities I yearn for when occupied with other jobs fly out of my head. I reminded myself that I would like to live forever not because I am scared of death or because I want to undertake some humanity-saving mission but because I need that time to read every book I want to read.

But I could not read for forty hours a week and feel good about myself. Nor could I do asana for forty hours a week or meditate or write.

N.B.

Even my devotion to daydreaming, to listening to music and floating off in my own mind, would stop sustaining me after a certain point. I need people, but I'm so well suited to solitude. I cancel plans with friends, dodge invitations to anything non-yoga related, and then I find myself dwelling over little exchanges, picking tiny slights into big dramas so I can feel connected in those moments when I don't. I should probably go back to teaching but I can't do that at the moment because of the imminent move.

And I am a bit scared to do it since it would hamper this other work. I suppose I feel this work is my life, my true life, and everything else is merely preparation, clearing the space and propping up the kindling. My boyfriend always says, "It's not like you *have* to do this." But yes, it is.

Because in many ways, it is everything: my source of amusement and diversion, my recreation, my sex, my identity, the most illuminating form of engagement, the most heightened form of contact. In the long moments when I'm not primping for, or in the middle of, or coming down from an appointment—yes, coming down, as with a drug—I feel I am merely awaiting instructions. Or waiting to figure out what else could possibly be as fascinating and worthwhile. Can you see that about it? Even when it's bad, even when I am uncomfortable or upset, it still seems worthwhile, because it defines my inner life.

I think it comes back to needing stories. That's why we all come to art, isn't it? We need a bright flag against the otherwise drab backdrop of our long and tedious lives.

This client also said in his email that I was the most beautiful woman he'd ever seen, which is akin to spending your entire life eating in the world's best restaurants, then sitting down for dinner at the Olive Garden and calling it the greatest meal you've ever had. I can't contest it, though. I mean, he deserves this fantasy that I am the most beautiful woman he's ever seen, if that is what he wants. That's part of the escape. That's how we daydream together.

It's art for him, too, after all. I don't even need to create it for him, just offer up the canvas and paint. And I would say that's become the hardest part of the job: not becoming freaked out by the compliments. Staying calm and reminding myself it's not something I have to live up to because, in his mind, it's something I've already done.

A different client and I reunited for the first time in months. He is intensely good and kind. Sometimes he ruminates on those who deny themselves sexual pleasure or disavow any sexual desires. "God made us to be so beautiful," he says, his smile like a hand trembling with pleasure. "The best way to praise Him is to appreciate that."

"Have you ever felt a caterpillar on your skin?" he asked me suddenly as we laid side by side.

"It's been a long time," I replied.

"Close your eyes," he said. And he began moving his fingertips over my thigh: together, apart. Together, apart.

Beacons
March 24, 2010

The married client emailed. We've been emailing daily, setting up one of our non-sex dates. It is clear to me now that I like him more than I should, but as long as he keeps seeing me, this is not a bad thing. I think that's one of the distinctions between an amateur and a pro: not that falling for clients stops happening but you learn to keep it to yourself and not make it his problem.

"I sometimes have a hard time bearing other people," he wrote me. "But it is easy to be with you." I know the first bit because he's told me as much before, while we were having breakfast and talking about misanthropy and Jonathan Swift. And his wife had told me as much, although she said people were frightened of/intimidated by him and that's what kept him at length. And my boyfriend told me as much, because my boyfriend has met him before. He's met a lot of my clients. They work in the same circles.

Once, one of his friends said to him, "I saw Charlotte leaving the X Hotel around midnight."

"That wasn't her," my boyfriend said, and changed the subject.

I am very cold him to him when he tries to tell me my work makes his life hard. In those moments, I am being unfair.

I had a date with a man I used to see when I worked for the agency.

"I've met you before!" I blurted the instant I saw his face. Being the discreet professional that I am. I was just excited to have found him again. We geeked out about books so intensely that the bouts of sex felt like a break from the main event, something we did when we needed a moment to let our brains rest.

And I had a date with a man I hadn't met before, in the city where I attended grad school but in which I hadn't spent a full hour in years.

"I hope you don't want dessert," he said at dinner after devouring his entree. "Because I can't wait any longer to touch you."

Oh boy, I thought, *this is going to be a lot of work.*

But he meant only that. We didn't have intercourse. He cried in the quiet, man way with his hands on my slack, scarred body. He was in a trance: *You're so beautiful. You're so fucking stunning.*

One of my favorite Bill Knott poems goes like this:

I am one man, I run my hands over
your body, I touch the secret vibes
of the earth. I breathe your
heartbeat, Naomi, and always
I am one man alone at night. I fill my hands
with your dark hair
and offer it to the hollows of your face. I am one man, searching
alone at night
like a beacon of ashes . . .

When You Don't Want It
March 28, 2010

I don't want to write here anymore. Can you tell that? I want to start keeping my stories to myself. Maybe I feel like I'm running out. My favorite, original teacher retired to go to yet more teacher training, saying she felt like she needed to be a student again. And then the favorite local teacher I found when the other left announced that she's scaling back as well because she's almost exhausted all the teaching techniques she knows. She said she felt like she was in a horserace and she was only a nose ahead when she wanted to be lengths.

When my boyfriend realized he knew one of my more eccentric clients, he said, "I wish I could tell (our mutual friend.) He would think it's hysterical."

"Don't do that," I said. "(My client's) so nice. He's so great."

"I know that. Everyone loves him. But he seems so straight-laced and normal, it would make everyone like him more."

"Promise me you will never do that. Never tell anyone."

"I wouldn't. I promise."

When we got home, I said very seriously, "Look, if we ever break up and you really want to hurt me, just hurt me. Don't bring any of my clients into it."

"I would never do that," he said.

I don't want to write here anymore. I feel like there is a Dream Song that ends: "I don't want to write anymore now I want to sleep." Something like that. Some poem, some line . . . My brain is full of those half-shaped clouds. This may be that or it may be another. It will pass by soon enough and who knows if I'll have gotten the lyric right or wrong.

This weekend, we somehow started talking about the waitress again and I felt myself getting upset. I let the discussion die away and then later in bed said, "Ok, clearly I have some insecurities around desirability. I start thinking that your friends who know about her will see me and think, *God, he could get someone really hot, what is he doing with Charlotte?*"

He said I was being crazy. Then he said the insecurity was because of my parents' divorce. I made fun of him for being an asshole. Then I said, "I need to take more international dates and then I'll know I'm really worth something!"

"Yes. Then it won't matter that Daddy didn't love you."

We were both joking, but not really.

It's funny that he likes to use the word "broken" for me. One thing I absolutely can't abide, that makes me lose all sensibility, is having my face slapped, and it's his greatest fantasy to fuck me while slapping my face. He wants me to come while he's doing it. It's how he wants to "break" me, and he's said as much before.

"Keep dreaming," I say whenever he brings it up. Either I'm not broken and probably invincible, or I'm already broken and therefore can't be broken again. What a relief.

When I feel like I don't want to write here, I make myself do it. On with the practices that are keeping me whole or keeping me in pieces.

Civilians
March 30, 2010

I met a new client who I didn't think I would get along with. His emails were bitter and off-putting, but I suspected I would be good for him. I realize that sounds arrogant and maybe it is. But I thought if I spent time with him I could soften him without hurting him, and in my estimation this was what he needed most. Far, far too much of his love life has been wrapped up in social climbing prostitutes, more than I even realized until meeting him, and I'm not actually one of those. I like touring higher floors, but I'm not trying to stay.

He was very easy to be with. He was much kinder and less demanding than I anticipated, and I properly enjoyed our time together. It's easy to be with most people when I'm working because the effort is primarily in making myself recede while being acutely present at the same time. My boyfriend always claims I like the work because, with a client, his attention is focused entirely on me, but I think the opposite is true.

If I'm doing my job well, he feels like we're starting a lifelong friendship even though he doesn't know anything about me. Anything. Can you imagine spending a whole day with me and not once hearing how obsessed I am with yoga? It's all about presenting myself as a sweet, open canvas, where there's no impression of baggage that might interfere with theirs. That's why we don't tell other people our truths very often, if ever, right? We're worried they won't understand, because their personality will be an obstacle to sympathizing with ours.

I also learned that he's been with a lot of porn stars, not just the blonde, boob-heavy types but the hipster touted indie types, too. One I was particularly surprised by because I wouldn't have suspected that she'd see clients in person. But why am I surprised by anything anymore? Frankly, I should start being more surprised when a woman hasn't worked as a prostitute at least once in her life. Not just porn stars but lawyers and grad students and dancers and mothers and basically everyone.

"I've had bad luck with women," he said at dinner.

"No you haven't!" I said. "I've been thinking about this. I thought you were unlucky, too, and that would be terrible. You can't do anything with bad luck. But good news. You just have bad—"

"Bad taste," he said.

"Yes," I said. "You have bad taste in women. That's not so hard to fix."

He stroked my hair very gently while we were in bed together. I remember once writing, "That's the problem with this city. Everyone's lonely, desperately lonely. They're all looking for something more than sex." Not true. Everyone everywhere is lonely. Moreover, this is not a problem. I've stolen that straight from Pema: "[The truth is] we are fundamentally alone, and there is nothing anywhere to hold on to. Moreover, this is not a problem."

Ok, I understand that. But I really wish this man would meet a woman who would say she loves him because she means it, and not because she wants to get something out of it. I'm not sure it will happen but I like to think that it will. The depth of his prosperity is directly proportional to the depth of emotional vacancy he has gone through. So maybe he would have to lose a little money first to keep his life in balance.

In the morning he mentioned he had a "city date."

"Do you know what means?" he asked. "It means a date with someone who's not an escort. I haven't had one of those in a long time."

I used the phrase a moment later and he gave me a puzzled look. "No, civvy date," he corrected. As in civilian. That made me think of how my father referred to our pajamas when my brother and I were growing up. "You wanna change into your skivvies?" he would say. And we would, and we'd bring down the sleeping bags that served as bed comforters and watch TV from the couch, eating slices of apple he'd cut straight from the fruit with a paring knife. Something about this man was making me think about my father anyway.

"My father only told me he loved me once," he said at dinner. I can't remember why that came up.

The Fortress
June 9, 2010

The pressure's off. Even with my favorite clients, the ones who are easy-going and pay the most. Expendable's too negative a word. They're not expendable as people, but they're expendable as my source. Not only my source of income but my source of . . . self-esteem? I've said before money was never the reason I worked. I think whatever the real reason was has begun to fade.

So I wasn't afraid to do a double for my especially eccentric client, even though the other woman joining us is so pretty and so good. He responded to her very well, better than I suspected, and I considered that he might stop seeing me for her. I was ok with it. If it made him happier, I wanted it to happen. If she was better at giving him what he wants, or just as good but cheaper, or just as good but different, or not as good as different—whatever he wants.

She left us to go to another date but I stayed with him.

"You liked her, didn't you?" I asked, smiling.

"I like you," he said. Then for the first time, while we were playing, he started calling me the "most beautiful" girl. I spend a lot of time looking into his eyes. I realized recently that's why so many of them say what they do about my face. They know me more by my eyes, not the whole of my features, and all that comes out is "beautiful" and it's not the right word. I know because I feel the same way about them. The word is not "beautiful." The word is "dear."

The next day, she and I met again with the same client, and I watched her with him from my seat. She was squatting, eyes following the movement of her own hands, in her pink single shoulder dress and heels, in her perfect jewelry, styled blonde hair resting on her tan back, and I felt happy that there are such impeccable people in the world. For most of my life I might have felt sad that I wasn't nearly as polished and feminine, like that state was fundamentally unavailable to me. And then later, I would have felt guilty and lazy for not working harder to become what I'm naturally not. There's not much of any that anymore. I only feel appreciative of her. Her elegance can exist in proximity to me without it being about me.

Like her bearing, her kindness seems constitutional. "I probably overextend myself," she admitted when we were talking about how she works. I've written about her before, about her fear of feeling guilty were she to charge more money. She gives her clients all of herself. The first time we worked together, she spoke extensively to that client about the man she was dating and about her ex-husband, and I was shocked. But when I sat her next to her and saw the freckles under the makeup on her nose, I understood. I like being around her because I realize why her clients are so devoted. I feel devoted to her and I don't even know her that well. The fact that she so clearly doesn't need devotion only makes me more ardent.

While I was looking at her in her crouch, struck by how perfect she is, I thought about her mother giving birth to her, her as a baby, about her not being the way she is now or somehow being that way always. Her death, too, was in my head. I don't know how to explain it. I was thinking of her formed and unformed, herself finite and infinite. In many ways, all at once.

"Thank you for this gig," she said when he was in the bathroom. "I got home last night, and it felt so nice to not have had sex."

I have a lot of clients I don't have sex with. One of my married clients once said, "You're my only real friend," and I knew it was true.

"The only thing I don't like about doubles," she said, "is when the other girl tries to make fun of the client."

"Right, you mean behind his back." Literally. Like while he's fucking one, the other is making faces and mouthing things over his shoulder.

"Yeah, you didn't do that. I like that you create a safe environment for them." That was just the way she put it.

She offered to drive him to the airport—that's how she is—and she dropped me off on the way. I sat in the backseat, hugged her goodbye from behind and leaned to give his sweet familiar face a kiss on the cheek. I felt like we were a family. I wanted it to stay that way.

The night before, when she'd been reading the script he typed for us, she repeated a line out loud with amused incredulity, eyes wide at me.

"I love our jobs!" she said, laughing. "Have you gone out with him before? Like for dinner?"

"Oh yeah."

"Have you ever talked to him just, normally, without any of this?"

"Yeah. For a long time, no, but then once I came over and that was all we did. And ever since then it's about half and half."

"Is he married?"

"Yes."

"With kids?"

"Yes."

"I really do love this job," she said, smoothing her stockings and shaking her head a little. Then she added, "But I'd hate to be one of the women on the other side."

The not having sex part. That's why I do the work now. Once it was for the sex because I wanted variety and newness, and to be tested and to be approved. Now sometimes I feel lost, like the body before me isn't a body anymore and maybe I know what I should be doing or how to do it but I can't plug into the sensations I want to create for him or what sensations should be arising for me. I was with another prized client recently and I said, after dismounting his face, "How did I ever make you come?" I started laughing: "Have you ever even come with me?"

"I'm not eighteen anymore," he said. "Other things matter to me now." He added, "I guess I come . . . when I want to come."

When I left his hotel there were no cabs at the stand. I told the doorman I'd go look for one myself, and I walked down the long street until I came to another street. The Capitol loomed like a full moon over the highway. The night was deserted except for the wind. My dress kept riding up and I wasn't wearing underwear. *This is how girls get killed,* I thought to myself. *But not really. I will not be killed tonight.*

I walked back to the hotel and asked the doorman to call me a taxi. I waited outside, staring down the alley of trees with their trunks wreathed in blue lights, to the white building rearing up at the end. The leaves of the trees in front of the hotel rustled in the light from the fixtures on the ground. It was trite, predictable—a little green circle designed to make an otherwise ugly complex seem less ugly. Either out of obligation or desire, human beings had planned to make this spot pretty, and it was. Even though the area was unreal and plotted, like a movie set or a model of the architect's plan, it managed to be appealing. I suppose one predictable path to beauty is through trees. Or touch.

No taxi came. The doorman himself drove me home.

Recently, I cancelled on a man I hadn't met before for an overnight. I did it without much notice, put off by something he said in an email although I knew in my gut that if I went I would be fine. We agreed to try again for a shorter period of time, and when I finally met him, I knew we were the right match. That happens a lot but not always. Sometimes it's only near perfect. It's been a long time since it's been outright wrong.

His wife was seriously ill with an eating disorder and always had been. I told him what I was like in high school. I said that anytime I had food in my stomach, I felt fat. We talked about how girls like that can't stand to be touched.

"But I would have my mom scratch my back," I said.

"My wife likes to have her back scratched, too," he said.

This man fucked me twice, or should I say I fucked him. Or should I say it doesn't matter. I was so wet. I wanted a third time but he said there wouldn't be one.

"I just had sex twice for the first time in years," he said. "I need to think about that. I need to find out how that makes me feel."

Riding the metro home, I thought of the first boy who ever carried my body, which would have been frail and light at the time, and he said as much to me when I protested—"you weigh nothing"—running me up and around the yard piggybacked on his gloriously solid and tall frame. This is the boy I should have lost my virginity to, who could have given me that first time story of "I loved him, he made it as good as he could for me. I was cared for." Because from the first moment I met him he was kind to me and made me feel special, made me laugh truly, gave me a type of attention I'd only read about it books and only dreamed about in my head, not even daring to write it down.

But the other boys in our group called him irritating, probably because he was confident and unselfconscious and good with some girls, though the queen bees sneered at him and he paid them no mind. Their disdain alone would not have kept me from him—of course I was shallow and swayable, but he was very special.

But something else happened that night in the dark by the water.

Teenagers are too good, they're too sensitive. They feel what's happening and can manipulate it with no coherent thought. No coherent thought is practically the only way they function. That boy had momentarily given me back my body and I was swept away in the joy of him. I was glowing. I had never felt so beautiful. And one of the other boys, the usual boys, complimented me, said I was skinny or he liked my jeans or said, "Hmm, for some reason tonight, you do look pretty." Whatever meaningless barb it was, it hooked me back to them and turned me cold to the kind outsider. What stupid and cruel mistakes I've made all my life.

I watched the sea of bodies detraining on the platforms and the crowds of men filled me with tenderness and something more muscular but still kind, a strength coming from the knowledge that so many of them need something they are not getting and I could give it to them, even if only for a few moments. *Come to me,* I think faintly sometimes, as I hold their faces in my gaze. Women are like that too, of course—unsatisfied, desirous, sad—but I'm not nearly as experienced in relieving them of their burdens. I think most of us figure it out for ourselves sooner or later, no assistance required. But the men? As they age, men seem to grow away from who they are while women wrap tighter and tighter, so in the end one is a fortress and the other is a fog.

I grew up with a script that said men are not kind, they are not decent, they do not want the right things, they do not do the right things. They are selfish, they are liars, and they are unworthy. But now I know the opposite is often true. I hope they know it, too.

City on The River
July 1, 2010

He gives often and without fanfare. It has always been this way. No wrapping, no ceremony. Everything like the diamonds sneaked in along the curve of a delicate pendant, almost tucked into the side. ("As long as they're non-conflict," I said uselessly. "Of course," he replied.)

I wore it as we rode on the river, gazing up at the buildings looming above. I hoped to see a naked woman very high up, pressed against one with a man behind her. I half expected to see myself hundreds of feet above, white and nude on the glass, another me living the life I expected. Of course still a whore, her days busy with go-here, do-that, go-home. That's what everyone everywhere does but it felt different in my mind.

It's hard to explain. It's nearly impossible to explain what I thought I would be when it's circumstantially no different than what I am—it's all in the tone. I thought this life would feel differently. I knew it would be cold in the spaces between the non-cold. I knew there would be many spaces. I thought that would make it glamorous.

All these structures—the man-made towers with rooms stacked over more rooms, ugly materials in uglier shapes—mean to me is loneliness, tied inextricably to commerce and profit, sadness perhaps ultimately the only motivating factor for capitalism. Dreams too. Yes, such buildings are full of hope but it's hope for diving back into the cycle of dissatisfaction. That's one definition of samsara: incessant activity and endless frustration.

Maybe I only ever envisioned myself grown and bathed in loneliness. That's what I wanted from a city, any city, and why I wanted to live in one: anonymity and painful quiet. It was what I expected; it was the most I could imagine. For my entire life I've been haunted by the conviction that the purest, most profound beauty is borne out of, and borne into, sadness. It seemed the only mode of being that would ever suit me.

Last Day of September
September 29, 2010

She went down on me and I faked coming as my client held and kissed me. I seized him with an intensity mimicking the tidal pull of an orgasm. He hugged me like we'd just shared something unspeakably pure, one arm around my back with a hand on my ribs and the other cupping the back of my head to hold my face next to his. He stayed that way for a long time and I felt bad for the other girl, but my first allegiance was to him, so I waited for him to break the grip.

"Charlotte has the ability . . . " he said to her, still squeezing me. I expected him to say something related to physicality or sexuality, but he finished with, "to make men think they're in love with her." Exactly like that. I "make" them. Not truly feel love but "think" they feel it.

After she left, he still marveled over her body. He pronounced her ass the best he'd ever seen and I was curiously unaffected by it all, noticing only my non-reaction. It was nice to feel happy with my body in spite of the insistent praise for another. Finally, I may be realizing the impossibility of having a different form than I do. She was very short, with the usual compact, ripe firmness that comes with petiteness, as though she were made of marzipan or clay, with baby grape nipples eternally taut. But I like my definition better, the almond shape of my muscles, the way the vastus medialis and vastus lateralis and adductors all rise into distinction when I bear weight on bent legs.

Finally his reverie segued into, "and you're a *fantastic* cocksucker." He lowered his voice to a whisper. He even went as far as to lean down near my ear, like she might be hovering outside the hotel room with a glass pressed against the door.

"I like it." I said. Meaning, at one time I liked it. Then my body acquired a habit and the pleasure could come or go without consequence.

"You have no gag reflex," he added.

"Well, I think that's genetic," I replied.

Earlier that week, visiting a new place, I prayed to see a fox. Only lightly, not fervently. I floated the idea out like a paper boat on a lake.

"Do you have foxes here?" I asked the taxi driver.

"Um, yeah, some," He said.

We passed a tree spotted incline and I said, "I think I saw some bears."

"You want to stop and go look?"

"Well, I don't want to keep you. You probably have other fares."

"No, I got nothing to do. Your call."

"Ok."

We both left the car and stood on the sidewalk with several other watchers, all of us straining to get an accurate count of how many cubs were behind the low pine branches.

One black bear was in the treetop. I put my hands in the pockets of my puffy vest. I wondered if I looked pretty, or if he'd just offered to linger together because he was nice. *He's being nice*, I told myself.

"Don't go down there," one woman said to us.

"Oh, I wouldn't," the driver laughed. He had a thin face, blue eyes and blonde hair. He wore a gray sweatshirt.

After my second ride, he offered me a discount.

"That's alright," I said, and paid the full fare.

On the fourth ride, he offered it again and I took it.

"Will you need a ride back?"

"Maybe." I said, although I knew I wouldn't. He looked about in his early thirties. While we were riding together, a song I'd never heard before came on the radio. It was upbeat, vaguely country, with lyrics along the lines of "I just want to light you up. I want to make you feel good." Obviously sexual but not really explicit. I kept meaning to check his hands for a wedding ring but I forgot.

There were no foxes. I've since tried to find out how common they are in the area, and the answer seems to be not very. In the process of searching, I read more about the scandalous killing of a friendly elk who made a habit of coming right up to people and also happened to be huge, which made him a good trophy. The dominant experience of the locals, regarding his death, was outrage. One person described his poaching as "an atrocity."

On the morning before I left, an elk ambled up the street and crossed as though he were a very slow car, puffing misty breath into the air as his antlers wagged up and down in time with his steps. I watched them disappear behind a donut shop. At sunrise, it looked like someone dragged a gold crayon around the mountains' outlines.

Someone said, "It's like that quote, 'Who you are is God's gift to you; who you become is your gift back to God.'" But I'd never heard that quote before and now I can't stop thinking about it.

Forgoing Titles
November 11, 2010

Incredible wetness. Brush against anything—his thighs, the sheets—and leave a trail wetness, with no relief. He won't touch me between my legs. His palms slide down but around and away, following the curve of my ass. I want to force his hand there with my own but I worry he has rules I don't understand, boundaries to assure him that he isn't cheating on his wife.

He says, "How much do you want me to fuck you?"

"Just feel how much," I say, my voice almost breaking with frustration.

He doesn't, he just puts on a condom and comes almost immediately when inside me. Maybe he doesn't hear me or thinks I don't mean it. Who can tell at times like these.

I've written about him before, about our nonnegotiable chemistry. Usually after a date I'll send an email saying, "Thank you for this and that, I had a good time, good luck with x, please let me know about y," and so on but I didn't do that to him. I didn't email him at all, because I knew he needed to think about what had happened. I waited for him to write me first, and when he did, I only replied, "I'm glad I met you. And I really wanted you to fuck me a third time."

"I liked that email," he told me at the restaurant. "I mean, I don't know if it was true or not."

"You're so skeptical. It's tricky with guys like you. Because if I try to convince you it's true, you'll just be more suspicious."

"Well, I appreciated it. It made me happy. I saved it. Sometimes I read it and it makes me feel good."

I told him it was not what I'd usually write but that I didn't want to interfere with his emotional process. "You're a good person," he said. I'm never as sure about that as other people seem to be.

He drank a little too much so that in his hotel room he was laughing at things that weren't funny, and saying things that he obviously thought were sexy but that I found trite. It depressed me and reminded me that drinking improves almost no one.

We take our time together each time, lots of grinding and kissing, and I stayed so turned on all night that he could touch almost anywhere on my body and I'd respond with writhing. I thought about masturbating in front of him, asking him if it was ok, because maybe he would think it was sexy. Or maybe it would make him feel inadequate.

"I've been married a long time, you know," he told me. "I haven't been with—I shouldn't tell you that."

"Tell me," I said.

"I haven't been with that many people," he said.

Another client mentioned numbers not long ago. "No one tells the truth on those surveys about sexual history," he said. "I mean, would you answer honestly about how many partners you've had?"

"I couldn't," I said. "I could only estimate."

This other client is handsome with a massive and, he feels, underappreciated cock. He asked about the worst client I've ever seen and I told him who came to mind, adding that I'd never been with anyone who seriously damaged me. Then I remembered that isn't true, and I said, "I did see someone who hurt me, and it didn't get better for a long time, and then finally I had to have surgery."

Hearing this description aloud, I realized it was outrageous, the most unacceptable, trashy situation, and I wanted to suck all my words out of the air because nothing I'd said conveyed how I felt about it, which was at peace. It was an accident, for one thing. I'm a vulnerable human body, for another. There are a lot of wounds to endure when you're in one of those. There are a lot of mistakes to absorb, for everyone. That's how it works.

In the morning, he kept saying, "thank you." But he was back in work mode and there was no hope for another fuck, no hope for touching his face with my face or my hands or my mouth beyond a kiss on the cheek. His wife is sick. It feels demented to share things he said about her here. Yet it feels crucial, so you can see who he is—not in the legal identity sense but in the way that matters.

I guess what stayed with me the most was that, when I asked him if he told her some of the things he told me, he arrived at a statement on the futility of trying to guilt someone out of an addiction.

I felt my mouth make a funny shape when he said that. I was remembering the times when my boyfriend talks about how ill with worry he is when I'm on an appointment, how he can't sleep or concentrate because he's so afraid something bad will happen to me. I actually laughed once, I couldn't help myself. I thought—think—his worry is hyperbolic and unnecessary. But hearing my client say that, I wondered if maybe I'm addicted to this work. I thought a little harder and decided my problem is more constitutional and that I'm immune to being guilted in any circumstance.

N.B.

After he said he was glad he'd had me stay the night, I said, "I hope so. I hope you don't regret it." We both looked away from each other. I was under an umbrella of tremendous sadness. As always, I couldn't think of anything to alleviate it so I tried to characterize it. It wasn't corrosive. It was like a wet sheet. It was a sadness that had no self-pity, was almost selfless. It felt borne out of the truth that this is a stupid, horrible world and it's the only one. That good people are often unhappy because they are so good.

At home, I wheeled my bag into my building behind a man walking a black Labrador. "I'm sorry," he said, of the dog's pace. Then, with love, "She's an old girl. She likes to take her time." And she turned to look at me and she was dying but she was glad to be with the man.

I'd taken an early train back because I thought I had to teach. I didn't, and as I walked home I fought back tears, resolving to stop teaching altogether, to quit this town and quit all pursuits save one. At home, I fell apart and sobbed with my hands over my face. I would give up almost every other aspect of my life before I would give up this work, and I don't know what that means or how I'm supposed to feel about it. It might be because I thought my life would be full of epic romance, epic love, but what usually marks love affairs as epic is their brevity as well as their passion. I like this man so much and there's no obvious reason why I should, but I think I could drink hours of his time and still be thirsty. Maybe what I want is that constant confirmation that real connection is possible. Maybe I don't want to let people too close to me even though I like being close to them.

While I was walking through the dead leaves, I thought about the idea that we're all part of this network of energy and we suffer because of our illusion of separation, but maybe the separation is not illusion, even though it is temporary. I don't buy the idea that everything temporary is by definition illusory. I like the philosophy that it's all real: your dreams, your fantasies, your waking life. But sometimes I doubt there are any merciful textures in the universe at all. Aren't we all trying? And yet none of us are saved.

Shit
November 21, 2010

This is what it was like: he was young-looking and young, tattooed with nearly shorn hair and boyish, slightly goofy. His body was knobby and tailored like all runners' but broad in the chest like a swimmer's, his obliques thick ropes sliding down inside his hip bones. I couldn't stop touching his stomach.

I said, "I can't stop touching your stomach."

He should have been in the military. I mentioned it to him and he said it was a big regret of his that he hadn't joined, that he decided to owe money instead of time when he went to medical school.

As we stood kissing, I squeezed his erection between my thighs and its head pressed out under the ledge of my ass. When I asked if his size had ever caused any problems, he replied, "That's nice of you to say."

I said, "You mean, never . . . "

"I've never had any feedback like that," he said.

And I just sort-of hit his stomach with incredulity, then relaxed my palm and fingers out over the muscle, biting a knuckle on my other hand. I was so turned on I thought I would come without being touched, and I trembled and tried to hold myself still against his chest so I could wait until he was inside. Once I did come, it was an orgasm with intentions to last forever, and my hand fell away and then came back, and then his hand replaced mine and after his cock was no longer hard he finally pulled out, reluctantly.

"Marry me," was the title of his email when he wrote me the next day. *That's funny*, I thought, and I appreciated its funniness. Because he is already married, among other considerations. But then several days later there was another email, this one saying he couldn't stop thinking of me and that he wanted us to be together in spite of all the obstacles.

It's easy for me to fall in love with a client but disastrous for them to fall in love with me. This is my unique privilege. I don't initiate our encounters. I don't have the responsibility of planning when to meet and where and for how long. That means I can—or hopefully, I have learned to—set that love aside, gently, and wait for a moment when I'm allowed to pick it up again. It means I can wander the city and savor daydreams of the future or memories of the past and ultimately I'm powerless, or I choose to be powerless, to actualize any of what I fantasize. But for them? They're the ones who make it happen. If they want to lie transparently or lie well to their wives, if they want to skip work, if they want to go by the bank and take out a stack of hundreds, I'm there waiting at the other end. They know I will show up. They can summon me.

The path of joy leads to sadness. All paths lead to sadness. I ached all day over that email.

Then I Would
December 1, 2010

The night I saw the client who won't touch me, I also saw Jacob. I'd sent him a message on the train saying that I would be in his town but wouldn't have time to visit. He badgered me a bit and finally I mentioned where we were meeting for dinner.

"I have to come by," he said.

"Ok," I agreed, "but don't do anything to freak him out. I really like this one."

I gave him instructions on what names he couldn't call me—not my real, not my work name. I knew how jumpy clients become if anything unplanned occurs.

When we entered the small restaurant, Jacob wasn't at the bar. I felt a little relieved and a little disappointed, and we carried on with our light meal, during which he said many wonderful things and I felt I was truly on a date. Then as we were leaving, we passed the bar and there was Jacob.

"Hey!" I said, drawing out the vowel as I laughed, genuinely surprised. We hugged and my right hand went to the nape of his neck, I don't know why, maybe because I was so happy and so turned on in anticipation of going back to the hotel with this other man—but also I was genuinely happy to see Jacob. His face plunged me into a sense of unconditional friendship and I felt overwhelmed, so I reached for the hair at the curve of his skull.

The softness of his hair shocked me and I reached back a second time, my fingers slowly swimming through his strands, and I felt sure that just that touch had given away everything, that my client now knew we'd slept together. So I said something about Jacob's work, something about calling him later, about it being great to see him, so on, who knows, and even though I feel completely accepted by Jacob, I couldn't help but wonder if he found my work appearance underwhelming. Sometimes I feel hot and posh but usually I suspect I don't look like anything special out on dates; worse, sometimes I'm almost certain that my make up is amateurish, and I look like someone who made an effort but that effort failed.

Recently, I was struck again with the thought that I could show up for most appointments in dirt-caked overalls with cow dung smeared on my face and the response would still be, "You're so beautiful, you're so beautiful," like a mantra in a foreign language, one the speaker likes the sound of but doesn't understand. I haven't figured it all out yet; there's some spell I cast and the man facing me can't see that.

Everyday people never say, "You're so beautiful," and truly beautiful women compel that from strangers. I know because I've been around truly beautiful women and I can't help but blurt it out. It's the offering you lay at their feet in awe, it's so obvious as to be obliterating and you can't form other thoughts. Normal people know I have an ordinary, even disappointing face. Wouldn't it be nice if my face were better? Or perhaps it would not matter in this realm at all.

But as for Jacob—yes, my seeing someone I knew did shake up the client a little. He murmured "what a small world," with disapproval, because how dare the world not accommodate this tormented adventure of his. I was terrified I'd fucked up and began rambling wildly, which I always do when I'm anxious about the consequences of something I've done. I launched into a horribly revealing, honest outline of how I knew Jacob and why. I even talked a little about Karyn and Mike and this friend of theirs who took my class and was sweet and quite cute. I joked with him when I saw him in the morning on his scooter, and then later I found out he's a model who's been on the cover of *Men's Health*.

The client seemed mollified. He even launched into his own

meditation on *Men's Health* as a ridiculous magazine, which of course made me feel more fondly toward him and you know the rest, the sad rest of that story.

While we were in bed together, my boyfriend asked, "Do you remember when we used to fall asleep at your work?" Meaning the agency incall.

"Yes I do," I said, with stillness in the words. "But I haven't thought of that in a long time." And I felt something I hardly ever feel with him, which is a faith in our thoughts being in exactly the same place with exactly the same tone, both of us remembering those pure, much younger selves and being touched by their newness and innocence and good intentions.

Sometimes I find myself mimicking our motions of tenderness with a client, and then I miss my boyfriend. I miss holding his hand to my face and then sliding it down my cheek to my mouth so I can kiss his palm. I miss the shape of his jaw and the texture of his hair.

Speaking of spells, I saw a truly infatuated client recently and it seemed unhappy for him. He played "Fake Plastic Trees" for me on his guitar and at the end his eyes were red with tears.

"I have a live version where Thom ends, 'If I could be who you wanted' with, 'then I would.'" I told him.

"I wish I'd thought to say that," he said, next to me and staring into my face like something there would save him.

When were lying together, he said, "I just hope whoever wins your love realizes he's the luckiest man on earth, and that he takes care of you and makes you happy every day."

"Do you have that?" I asked, knowing he wouldn't answer me and realizing he may even misunderstand and think I asked, "Do you have that to give to me?"

There was silence. Earlier he'd breathed, "Oh, Charlotte," crushing my hair in his hands, "my angel. You're so wet for me."

"Always," I replied, which was mostly true.

What a tremendous mindfuck to have these exchanges as part of a financial transaction. Or to have a financial transaction in the shadows of these exchanges. Whenever clients deliver a pained "if only we'd met a different way" line, I always think, "But we wouldn't have." This is the toll for our meeting; it takes place under these circumstances or it does not, would never, exist. At best, maybe some brushing of sleeves in the street, but certainly no connection with this intensity or this purity. The conditions allow and facilitate it but I've never been able to articulate that in any effective way.

And how many people take a mindfuck over no fuck at all.

Her Ribbon
December 28, 2010

There's a folktale I came across constantly as a child. A man becomes infatuated with a striking woman who wears a red velvet ribbon around her neck. He pursues her devoutly and she agrees to marry him, but cautions him that he must never question why she wears the ribbon. He agrees, because he would agree to anything to be with her. But his curiosity begins to consume him. And one night, when they're sleeping together in bed, as he stares at her fragile beauty in the moonlight, he is overcome with the impulse to break his promise. He reaches out and tugs at the tie, loosening the fabric until it pulls away from her skin. You already know what happens. As the velvet unwinds, her head falls off.

Obsession scares the shit out of me because I know that when someone's in it, they are incapable of talking themselves out. All they are capable of is rationalizing their obsession and the way they behave in service of it.

I've been there, a little. Part of why I loved Lydia Davis's *The End of the Story* was that her narrator did all the unacceptable things I'd done when I felt spurned by someone I loved, behaviors I told myself were harmless, like driving by his house at night. I didn't have any plans beyond just the driving. There was no logical progression of thought because I wasn't in a logical place. Nor was I in a violent place. I didn't want to hurt him or frighten him or even talk to him right at that moment. I wanted to be close to him, meaning I wanted him to want to be close to me, but that seemed impossible. I recognize (now and probably then without admitting it) such an act would be deeply unnerving to him no matter how unobtrusive I tried to be.

It's very scary to know that someone is intensely, undeterrably interested in you even though you're not expressing a similar interest and have not encouraged—may have even discouraged—theirs. I've written before about how much entitlement in a man scares me, and that's because obsession, in my experience as a target, is inextricably bound up in entitlement.

I saw it in action when I worked on webcam, and I felt it percolating in myself when I watched other girls on webcam, even if only for a few minutes, even if they didn't speak English. You ask this stranger a question and she doesn't answer. She fiddles with her bra, she adjusts her pillows. Someone else asks her a question and she answers. You ask her another question and she doesn't answer. *What a fucking bitch*, you start thinking. *She has my attention, I deserve hers.* Then comes the anger and the justification of the anger, the commitment to see that righteous anger through until she gives you the response you are owed. It starts getting ugly.

In three different ways have clients violated my privacy, that I'm aware of, anyway.

One was a man I barely knew, and he accidentally—it seemed accidental—made a comment that betrayed he had researched an aspect of my personal life. I tried not to react but I felt my face change, and I saw his face change. We changed the subject but the rest of the night was like swimming in cold oil. I did not see him again and he only requested that I do so once.

In the moment it was terrifying, yet I didn't feel as violated as I might. There was absolutely no connection between us. I'd only seen him once before and I could tell he liked me as much as he liked anyone else, bestowed as he was with that rather goofy, bounding dog energy, which was probably an act, a calculated appearance of indiscrimination to disguise a whirling mill of absolute judgment. Regardless, he was most definitely not a man obsessed. He was a man paranoid, which presents its own set of dangers, but more to his own well being than mine.

I still have no idea how he found out who I am but I don't make the mistake of assuming that the outcome is any less real simply because I don't understand the methods that allowed it.

My ex-boyfriend did some horrible things after our relationship ended. He was emotionally and mentally abusive but so what. Get stronger, be smarter. He stole money from me while we were together and then once again after we were apart but oh well, it's just money. Everyone told me it was worth thousands of dollars to be rid of him, and they were probably right. But I wasn't rid of him.

One day I received several calls on my cell phone from numbers I didn't recognize. There was a very strange, muffled voicemail that I couldn't make sense of. I called one of the numbers back and a man answered briefly before a woman took over and yelled, "Stop calling my husband!"

When I finished my walk home, I sat in my common room near the light of the window and dialed a different number. A different man answered.

"I got a call from this number," I said. "But I don't think I know anyone in this area code."

"Hmm," he said. "I don't think I know you either."

"There must be something wrong with my phone. I've gotten a bunch of strange calls recently. I'm sorry to have bothered you."

"It's ok," he said. "I'm driving through Vermont right now and the leaves are changing, and the light is so beautiful. There's no one else on the road. It feels nice to be sharing this with someone, in a way."

"Oh," I said, and we were both quiet for a moment. "Well, goodbye."

I'm slow sometimes. It took me at least ten minutes after hanging up to realize the man I was speaking with was a testicular cancer survivor who I'd spent a sex-free evening with near the waterfront. I checked an old email account and yes, there it was, a letter from a client saying, "Do you know anything about this?"

And below was a forwarded email from an anonymous account

with the address of my childhood home, the place where my family still lives and where I myself have not lived in years, my personal cell phone number, my legal name.

The second offending client began making requests that I spend unpaid time with him. Not physically intimate unpaid time, but unpaid time nonetheless. I mildly pointed out that I would join him for as long as he'd like and he knew my rates, but this was not the response he was looking for. Then he wrote me an email saying he'd seen me at the train station on a certain afternoon when I was having coffee with a different client. *Ok*, I thought, *it's just a coincidence.*

Then he wrote me an email discussing several recent projects I was working on in my personal life, offering his thoughts, offering his help. He ended with, "I realize I crossed a boundary and I apologize if that made you uncomfortable. But you are such an unusual person that I set aside my better judgment."

I did not reply. It was the first time anything like that had happened to me.

He kept writing. He realized he'd made a mistake, but he tried to downplay it with a sort-of "dear me, looks like I embarrassed myself!" attitude.

I wrote him a single line: "I think it would be best if we no longer saw one another," but of course that did not finish it.

He began inserting himself into my personal life, leaving notes. He wrote sporadic emails discussing his thoughts on my current activities, sometimes extensively. And finally one day I snapped. I did something I am not proud of: I threatened him. I insinuated that if he did not cease contact with me, forever, I would ruin his life. "Never write me again," I said. "That includes replying to tell me that you will never write me again."

So what's the moral of the folktale? I still can't figure it out. Is it that human beings are weak and at the mercy of their own urges? That curiosity destroys? That even in great love, it is impossible to refrain from harming others? I don't know. I recognize the truth of it but I could not articulate a lesson beyond that of the importance of respecting someone else's boundary, even if you don't understand why that boundary exists.

The third client, the married client with whom I shared so many sweet times, was once my favorite and I considered him a friend, but his trespass changed that. I wasn't angry so much as I was disappointed, sad for the friendship that was lost and frustrated with myself for not being more careful. I knew he was reaching a point of profound restlessness, that he was not happy with the limits in place, with his restrictions on knowing me, and that he was starting to sieve through every link I'd ever sent him, every passing comment, every allusion.

He was possessed with curiosity. He actually guessed my legal identity incorrectly at one point, but he did it in a clever enough way to not actually say, "Are you this person?" Still, he betrayed he was looking. So then I knew our time together was brief, but I was foolish enough to think he would not get it right, and then he did. He came to me with his revelation, dog-like, too, like a hunting dog with a bloodied fowl in his jowls, presenting it to me with an intention I cannot fathom, seemingly clueless about what had been ruined. I was most insulted that he lied about how he'd found out, that he concocted an implausible coincidence when I knew he had been digging.

I knew he would never hurt me, that he didn't want to use this information as a weapon, but our intentions so often don't matter. I could no longer be who I once was with him.

I know some clients think, "She knows who I am, she knows where I live, she knows where I work. Why can't I know her real name?" I understand why that would feel imbalanced. And some escorts are willing to make that trade with regulars, but I am not. My anonymity is my condition, almost the only condition. If you know my real name, I will fade away from you.

What's strange is that I do believe in ultimates, I believe in the untarnishable. I think some things cannot be damaged, but I believe they can go away. I mean, I'm not afraid of being outed. There's no fear, but there is a sort-of anticipatory regret. Something precious would be lost. Once the ribbon is pulled, you cannot tie it back on.

And if you believe yourself to be finely faceted; if you recognize and appreciate the many versions of yourself that are set free with certain other people and in certain situations; if you believe that you are all of those people all of the time, but that not every quality of you can be shining in equal measures at all times; you see how it is possible to have the door closed. You see how that "you" can be shut down or how someone else can be shut down to you.

It is an idea I rebel against yet I believe it may be true: if you accept the sacred, you also have to accept the desecration. I will never see that man again.

2011

Break
January 26, 2011

His kissing was repulsive. It pushed me to the point of forgetting, forgetting who I was or who I was pretending to be, which happens now and then—I become the child who wants something to stop, pushing or squirming away with whiny distress. I almost gagged while deep throating him, not because of the physicality but because of my revulsion. He bared my throat to the ceiling while I lay next to him, prying my neck open. If I reached out to touch him, he pinned my hands under my own body or under his. None of it hurt. It would have been sexy if it hadn't been with him, but with him it was horrible. I always fuck much harder when it's bad, in the hope of ending it sooner. I worried I would come.

Oh, so he wants a whore, I thought when I felt his hand in my hair, yanking my head from his mouth to his cock and back again. So many men of the men I see want to forget there's money involved.

I watched it while it was happening as best I could, all the overlapping reactions, the drumbeat of a nonverbal *no* underneath the knowledge that it's all only temporary. I grabbed the tissue-thin thought that he was almost certainly not being intentionally unpleasant. I brushed on how, in the morning, I would be talking to students about how to rotate this joint, where to place that hand. I thought of the marvelous things they say after class. I imagined them learning about this moment but I knew they wouldn't, that they didn't know about any of this, and then I felt safer.

Earlier in the month, I saw two men in one day, both regulars and both well liked. But for some reason the energy was low during the first appointment, and even his going down on me couldn't keep me wet. I don't know why I didn't bother to slip some lube against my slit but I didn't, and the condom dragged raw against my inner lips as we both halfheartedly bucked. He seemed sad; he's seemed sadder recently. He tortures himself with regret.

The doorman flirted with me as I entered the second hotel later, and I laughed gaily but hated it. The second client warned me there were private security men prowling his floor, and I saw one brusque body in a wide straddle at the top of his hall before I opened his door. I saw them again while I was leaving; long, black-clad legs and two sharp faces turning toward me.

We ended up wrestling and I kept laughing, kept struggling, because the struggle was fun. He was unexpectedly strong and I could barely maneuver. At one point my nose was pressed against his taint and I couldn't help but inhale the mostly clean but still salty smell, the type of scent that would make you say "ew" when you were younger but as an adult, it merely seems to be giving you information that's not necessarily good or bad.

Then he shoved a finger inside of me and my jaw fell open, my brain filled with one pure soprano note of pain. I was so abraded from the condoms earlier that I couldn't believe blood wasn't seeping through my labia, or that the tissue visibly pulpy and torn. I struggled a little, like an animal in a trap, and then I just gave way to it, grunting and puffing and allowing whatever anguished noises came out because so often noises of pain mimic the noises of sex. Finally, my fingers reached his and I pulled his hand away. I'd effectively faked an orgasm.

"You look amazing," he said as he sat back on his heels, sounding dazed. He is so likable. He would have been horrified if he knew.

I laughed and slapped at him like, "Give me a break," but then I went into his bathroom and I did look amazing. The pain must have suited me.

Where do we get our ideas of sexual fragility? I might know the answer to that, but I wonder why we all believe it without pause. Why are women assumed to be so sexually unstable as to be blown to bits by even one unpleasant encounter? The mind is strong. It doesn't have to be cowed by an ugly touch. Why would this ruin me? How can minutes or even hours of bad sex compare to something like the loss of a loved one? Why don't we talk as seriously and as often about the damage done by heartbreak? This is just a body. No, not "just"—"just" isn't fair. It's a miraculous body but it is temporal and it is not ultimate and it is capable of healing, capable of forgetting.

The wall rises up with certain people even though they're clean or otherwise attractive. My body's rejection is abrupt, visceral, complete. *No wonder your wife can't stand to fuck you,* I hissed once in my head while a client was over me. I didn't know that his wife wasn't sleeping with him;

he didn't talk about her much. Why would I think such a cruel thing? It haunted me until I realized that, locked away in my mind as it was, it couldn't hurt him. More importantly, it didn't change him. None of the nasty things I thought about him made him nasty or a bad lover or a bad person. That was a liberating concept. If other people are fundamentally untouched by the occasional mean judgments I pass against them, it means I am somehow so immune to any judgments others might pass against me.

The repulsive client lay calmly with me for a moment in the middle of our time together. We talked a little about his past. He said each of his parents used to beat him, and he got to a point as a young adult when he could not stand to be touched by anyone.

"It wasn't good," he said.

And he squinted in thought as he reminisced about the boys he went to college with in a country very far away. "I don't think most of them even enjoyed sex," he said. "I mean, to want it fifty times a day? How much can you be enjoying it when you have it if you only ever want more and more, with other people?"

"I have that edge in myself," he told me, when I teased him about his before-we-met, ridiculous suggestion that I try dominating him. "That's what worries me. I know that, so I don't put myself in positions where it will come out. If you were to hurt me, even accidentally . . . You know that movie *Fight Club*? It's true; you don't know who you are until you've been in a fight."

Then he began touching me just barely with his fingertips. He drew them over every inch of my skin over and over. He still pinned my hands and arms but I wasn't resisting. It was exquisite and it lasted a long time. I become a greedy root under such touching. I can soak in it forever.

"That was amazing," I said when he finally finished and drew me against him for a hug.

"I've never done that before," he replied, and I believed it.

N.B.

Nasty Business
February 15, 2011

He was insecure, impotent and quite overweight. Those are not necessarily ingredients for a bad date. I've had hot sex with someone heavy. I've come with someone impotent. And we're all insecure in certain areas.

But sometimes, insecurity is founded. There are men I wouldn't call insecure because their more prominent (most prominent) personality trait is simply "asshole," and this man had no meanness in him. Yet the time with him was interminable. I couldn't recall the last time I'd been with someone so boring, so interpersonally clueless, with such anxious body language. Clearly, he was sore with regret over the great inconvenience that was his presence in the world. He didn't tell one interesting story or reveal a single unusual detail, not even by accident.

I tried to remind myself that he has subjectivity just like me, just like everyone, rich mental and emotional processes that can never be conveyed to another. That he's a human being with the same desires as all others. But I just couldn't like him. I couldn't bring myself to enjoy or remember one moment of our time together. I couldn't even feel compassion for his self-doubt because it was true, he was an unremarkable person, and if I had been in control of my own time, I would have quit his company at the soonest opportunity. I tried to imagine the escort who might be a good fit for him and I couldn't. I could only think of other women who would tolerate him, be grateful for his money, or even not mind his personality so much. I couldn't think of anyone I knew who would actually enjoy him.

I did think, though, of a letter I wrote to God when I was about nine or ten. I wrote it during the summer, in the light of my bedroom window, and it was about seven pages long. After I realized God wouldn't teleport me off the planet and I was not cut out for suicide, I tore the letter into shreds and threw it away. It was very melodramatic and the gist of it was, "Why do people hurt each other? This world is too mean for me. Please take me back until it is better."

I had many pockets of despair as a child. And after.

I tried to diagnose this man's problem, and the best I could come up with was the environments he placed himself in, the people with whom he surrounded himself—they were all wrong. He was a Hummer trying to find a space in a compact car-only parking garage. Of course he was developing a complex. But there was a whole world out there with space for his Hummer. He could park it in a fucking field if he were ever to leave that one bad parking lot.

As for the physical interaction, it is rarely that wrong, but: when not a shred of attraction is present, when the sex is so awkward that someone watching might well assume it was a disastrous modern dance choreographed by the world's worst artistic director, when the intercourse is so bad that I call it "intercourse," the sullen child in me wants to say "may I be excused?" as soon as it's over, like I'm requesting to leave the table after a particularly nauseating meal. It is a great indignity to have to keep offering your genitals to someone who is clearly not qualified to handle them.

Replaceable
February 16, 2011

The uncanny client is finally feeling more comfortable with me.
"I'm melancholy after I see you," he said.
"I'm sorry," I said.
"I wonder why it can't be this way in my marriage," he replied, and I thought of saying that there was no reason why one pleasure should preclude the other but I stayed silent. When he held my body against his, standing, I imagined his wife finding out about me, screaming at him about "his whore", and I thought the possessive there was right. With many men I would be simply a whore, but I am in thrall to his body. I believe I could literally go down on him for hours and never want to rest.

"You look so beautiful in the mirror," he said. I could feel his head turned to watch. I kept my face to the safe side.

When he touched me with his delicious, inexplicably rough-skinned hands, I breathed wisps of memories of my telling the older man, "no one will ever touch me as well as you." If I were telling the truth, if I knew the truth then, what I would have said was: "Someday I will go long stretches of time without thinking of you and when I do, it will be bitter. Someday I will forget your touch entirely."

N.B.

Long Weekend
February 21, 2011

When he put his mouth to work between my legs on the first night, I'd felt repulsed. But, again, as it went on, as I prepared another plea for cessation and cried out, "it makes me want your cock," I came, the noise of my voice like weeping.

At dinner on the second night, I saw the most exquisite young girl. At first I thought she might be fifteen but I steadily downgraded her age the longer I watched her: fourteen, thirteen, twelve. She puffed out her upper lip and rested it on her straw, making faces at the boy across from her who may have been a relative. She had a sweetly tanned neck longer than her face, a wavy ponytail to her mid back, a flared, pink mouth. There was no denying her beauty but anyone who wanted to fuck her would have been disturbed in the extreme. She was so clearly presexual, so unashamed to have her mother stroke her hair in public.

A striking grown blonde entered, disrupting my line of vision as she crossed to the bar with a less attractive brunette friend. I made a silent wish that the young one would be nothing like this flinty older beauty who held her looks with angry arrogance, as though everyone who acknowledged her appeal disgusted her. And I wondered what it would be like for the preteen, growing up with such perfection.

On the last morning, seagulls assembled on the beach like a tiny white military. Elaine Scarry's palm trees flashed at alternate heights. I'd seen a bathing suit in his luggage the day before and felt a strange pang of—the indescribable. The horror of how vulnerable we are, how naked our hopes. I needed aspirin to calm the fever, and I'd forgotten to bring any but I knew he had some, so I went to the closet where he left his toiletries. The air inside smelled of his cologne, which I hated when it was freshly sprayed, but somehow now, smelling its stale echo, I felt endeared towards him.

At first I thought I was having fun but at the end I only felt like I'd carved away a slice of my life to be entirely lost, jettisoned from the people or routines that have meaning for me. And I felt another burden, the sense of having created a great crime by not writing more, every day, constantly, for all of my life. There was a touch of pride in that, almost like a child's sense of pleasure when he's being scolded for showing off. It's not that I think my writing is necessary for the rest of the world, but I have always known that it's the closest thing I will ever have to a purpose, the only task for which I could have been destined, if the idea of destiny is not completely useless.

Coming home to my boyfriend, I wanted to have sex with him because I felt grateful for him, either in his particulars or the mere fact of him or both, but as soon as I realized this on the plane as it taxied to the gate, I knew it would not happen or go wrong, the way it always does with us. And it did.

When the sadness finally became oppressive and heavy and I was incapable of damming it up, he noticed and called me to him. That's our dance. One pushes, one pulls, taking turns being the more affectionate or the more patient until we snap and withdraw and the other one takes over. There's something Sisyphean about it all. Rewardless. Exhausting. I'm afraid we—maybe I should say "I"—have only ever been happy when living in delusion. I realized he once wore the same cologne as the client; I'd first smelled it, and hated the smell, on him

He hugged me and I thought of the phrase that's been rattling in my head for a week or so now: *I tried to tell you but all I could say . . . I wanted to tell you but you never listen . . . I thought I could tell you but.* So finally I said, "I'm lonelier with you here."

The only way to assuage that loneliness is for me to be alone but he wouldn't leave. And so still I did not feel I'd told it all, or not told all of it right.

Prosperity
March 24, 2011

"I fail a lot but in my heart I'm trying," he wrote me. That was almost too sad to bear.

Days with a new client were unusually effortless. I didn't wear makeup at all.

"Nice shoes," one girl in the bathroom said of the gold Jimmy Choos a different client bought me.

"Nice hair," I said to her sincerely.

Someone tried to haul a jaguar on to a table.

"It's drugged," he said to me, as we watched the big cat slip to the floor in a heap. It had that look in its eyes like most mammals do at some point in their lives; a dampened half-hope for mercy.

Nothing bores me more than my own orgasms. I probably never expected to feel that way, or most of the ways I feel.

Fish in Water
March 25, 2011

When we were alone, he described her as "exquisitely gentle" and that was the perfect way to put it. At first I thought her near-whisper voice was an act, but the more time I spent around her, the more I realized she was simply kind. She washed me in the shower and I remembered that some women develop a sweet touch but you shouldn't take it personally because it's just their way. How confusing it must be for these men. Her delicate laugh shows beautiful white teeth.

At one point she began crying and my instinct was to hold her but when I'm upset, I don't want anyone to touch me. So I stopped myself, felt uncaring and useless, and later tried to explain.

She slipped in the snow and I held out a hand to take her things while she pushed herself up, but instead she put her hand in mine so she could rise.

"I like having you here," she said.

"It was a very costly lesson," she said at another time. It was warm inside and so cold outside. I wore a ratty old bra all day and my hair hung half curled like a common person's. The things you get away with.

Who knows how men get this money, where it comes from, why they spend it on me. All I know is that conversation, if you do it right, lasts far longer than any sex.

When times are good they are nonstop good. Good meaning profitable, busy. Before she went to bed one night she reached across his body for me. I squeezed her fingers.

Abandoning All Practices
April 11, 2011

There was one exquisitely wonderful client whose goodness was at times like a vice.

"You have very delicate features, don't you think so?" he asked, stroking my face. Often they will ask me to affirm their reactions but it is impossible. When I look at my own face I see my brother, my mother, my father, or I see no one. Once I caught my reflection in a door's mirror, my head dangling down the edge of the bed with a man standing above me and the angles and the colors of my face seemed completely foreign. I thought that if I were looking at a picture I would not have known who it was.

"You're very pretty," he persisted, adding, craftily, "I think you know that."

"Well, I'm glad you think so," I said.

"You are almost too beautiful," a dear Korean man told me once, staggeringly. He broke my heart recounting a debate with a classmate that ended with her telling him his English wasn't good enough for his education to count. I got so angry. I hoped this girl was full of regret and living a miserable life. How do I meet so many people who are so good? I did not know what to make of his emphasis on having finally slept with a white woman.

I am collecting these moments when I forget myself or when I can become someone else, and if those moments are too crowded together I puddle up like empty clothes. When I'm alone, I have nothing to hold on to.

Once I fell asleep in the arms of man who had been delighting me.

"This is all braggadocio," he said, pausing in the middle of his lovable holding forth, "but you're not stopping me."

He talked about his childhood, I asked if he ever had a pet crow.

"Oh, well, everyone wants a pet crow!" he replied.

He talked about tarantula hawks. He wore coke bottle glasses and described his style as "Larry David." He called me conservative and brazen and sweetheart.

When we were eating lunch, he looked at the broccoli on my plate and said, "A cauliflower is a fractal."

I reached across the table and put my hand on his. He had won me.

I slipped off while he was showing me pictures on his phone and came to at his words about a picnic.

"A picnic!" I said as I awoke.

He Touched Me
April 22, 2011

It was last minute. I opened the door wearing only lingerie. The quality of his touch was different or I imagined it was different. He still never reaches between my legs but his hands hinted that this time he would. I'd forgotten that he gets so close. I let myself anticipate his fingers there. I assumed his fingers there so flagrantly that I imagined writing about it, my thoughts streaming by like silver needles of light while his heat moved away.

After he came, so quickly, we lay next to each other and I looked at his face while he didn't look at mine. I rested my gaze on every feature, cherishing the wrinkles around his eyes, the pores of his skin, the tilt of the bridge of his nose. It is as though his face fits somewhere inside me, like his face is a type of key. I can imagine other women finding him ugly. I can imagine other women not noticing him at all. This is the type of connection that doesn't make sense and is probably one-sided. The only thing you can do is live with it.

He told me about what happened at home, or rather what was happening. He cried. I positioned myself so I couldn't watch him and stroked his torso. I waited and let the noise be background while I focused on how my skin passed over his. Somehow the idea entered me to make a transfer, to offer him all the goodness I feel for him, to lift away all his pain. I wanted to give the most tender blowjob any human being has given another one. I thought I would tell him this way, with my mouth.

It was a misunderstanding. I tried as best as I could and managed nothing. He did not recognize my intentions. He finally said he didn't think it would happen another time and I was sure then that he saw me only working to get him hard so I could get him off, get him out. I realized whatever happens to me when I see him would stay unspoken and unsayable, and my wanting him to understand was selfish. He showered and I felt cramped, like my body had no place in that room.

Finally I apologized as he was putting on his shoes.

I said, "I'm really sorry if anything I did made you feel worse."

He seemed surprised, assured me that wasn't so. Or maybe I only remember it that way to placate myself.

I thought something big was going to happen between us. I thought I would be writing about a different moment.

One Door Among Many
June 27, 2011

I dreamed so furiously I woke up exhausted, morning after morning. Dreams of excoriating my father. Dreams of heartache that stayed all day.

I stood in a dimly lit room looking out at Chicago's water and tower. I stood in a New York room, four men later, looking out at the waning day. In Versailles, it stayed light until ten p.m. and we were at it again, lingering in the antique jewelry shop, pretending a proposal would ever make sense, then sitting on the ground in new clothes laying dreamily against each other in the cold.

I wanted to write badly about the one who wasn't paying me, about our pale flirtations and how I clung to them for weeks. But I didn't want it enough to do it. A grotesque man said, "I could tell you were submissive" and his hand left trailing bruises like comet tails, like lashes from a whip.

One client gutted himself in front of me, saying, "I've never talked like this with anyone else," and I forgot all the details. Nothing seemed worth remembering. No one seemed to notice what I left behind.

I met the celebrity and he barely touched me but had me swelling wet. Isn't that always the way. He came so quickly. We hardly talked. He asked, "Was it like you thought it'd be?"

I frowned, I paused. I opened my mouth to speak before I spoke.

"Yes," I said, disappointing him. He smelled strongly of his own frightened sweat.

I said, "It feels like I keep being rewarded for making the wrong choices." Wrong meaning easy. But if it happens so naturally, why do I object? A canceled flight becomes a cheaper flight, becomes being paid more generously than I anticipated. It's somehow ominous. The better I am at making money, the more I make and the less it matters. Then the better I become. It can't stop.

The more time I spend shaping my body, the less I am inside my body. I can't talk or teach about it anymore. I don't even want to be there. I stop talking to the people who care. The first fox I saw in a year was dead in daylight at the edge of the road.

In dreams there is always the car without brakes. I never die but that's the punishment: I have to keep driving.

Unreliable Narrators
July 5, 2011

He bound my hair in his fist and swiveled my skull slowly in front of his face like he was examining a piece of merchandise.

"Gorgeous," he said to himself, his grip tugging at my roots.

Our fucking would be intensely painful. The night before I'd been with another hung man and I was sure the sensation would make me pass out. I graded it an eight on a scale of one to ten, not knowing what a ten would be. It was the type of pain that lifts you out of a world where pain is not possible. Surrender pain. It would be two days before I'd get to my gynecologist. I had to ride it out.

Moments before, he compared me to a friend I'd introduced him to: "She's very sweet, authentic. Not as calculating and guarded as you."

"That's why she needs me in her life," I said, with a laugh like a blade.

He'd gone on about what a difficult woman I would be to date, how impossible it must be for me to have any romantic relationships.

"Well, it's a good thing you're not trying to date me then, isn't it?" I replied.

"You're just a overly cerebral princess who thinks she special," he said, like that would hurt me.

I don't know how to take that assessment seriously from someone who pays to spend time with me. It doesn't mean anything for him to insult me. Doesn't hating the person you're having sex with just mean you hate yourself?

"Oh, that's a spirited blow job," he said as he sat on the couch. "There's some spirit! This is better than last time. You're feeling competitive."

I've never had an inferiority complex about my oral abilities but I'd seen my friend quite literally suck the come out of men in under ninety seconds from first contact to final pull off.

"She gives head like a stripper," he confirmed. "They get really good at doing it quick. She's a tornado."

By the end of the day I actually liked him. He passed through vile to whatever comes after. Recognizable? I caught myself actually caring about what he was saying, about his equally horrible rich friends and the stupid girls who fuck him for free or for the dangled carrot of some new clothes and a paid-for flight to wherever he happens to be.

The photographer was the one who flirted. I'd never met him before until he took my pictures, and they were not very good so he promised me a second set and I actually got wet while he shot me the first time, which is such a cliché. I'd only worked with women or friends before, so I wasn't used to someone murmuring, "God, that's sexy," when I piked my ass in the air for the camera.

I hadn't expected him to be attractive. There was something almost doggish about the lines around his mouth and somehow this slight resemblance to a pit bull worked with his gentleness. He dressed well. I trusted two things: 1) that he flattered most women shamelessly and 2) he still usually meant what he said.

The second time was at his home and I don't think he kissed me then though he did the first. We sat side by side as his kitchen table.

"When was the last time you had a boyfriend?" He asked.

And I said, "I don't know how to answer that," which was both honest and not honest, the only way I know how to be.

He emailed me later about the two of us going to see "Sleep No More" and I experienced a desire I didn't think I would allow myself to satisfy, and it felt so sweet and so cruel. For a brief time, he felt like my secret, like a portrait in a heart locket against the bones of my chest. He was something to daydream on. I came more than once imagining him treating me meanly, in a way I doubt he ever would. I didn't tell him my real name.

I finally decided I had to do something with my money.

At my first bank, the man asked, "What are you saving this for, a house or . . . ?" and I felt my body coil back a little as I snapped, "It's just money I don't need to spend right now."

I was unnecessarily angry at the mindset that money is meant to be spent. Of course it is but I somehow think of accruing as a value in itself. Gold for the gates of Heaven.

At the second bank, the woman beamed at me.

"Good girl," she kept saying. "Good girl. Keep saving."

She thought I was so responsible.

The Cipher
July 11, 2011

A man in a suit greeted us immediately outside of the gate and pushed us impatiently through an empty "UN official" customs line.

"From America," he told various airport security members near-giddily.

"How do they feel about Obama here?" Someone asked at lunch.

The former ambassador shook his head a bit and made a strange face: "They loved Bush." We could not believe it.

"Because of how he handled Syria," he added.

Only one person actually looked at my passport from the moment I stepped off the plane until the moment I got back on.

From around his cigar, an American man spoke to me.

"I don't know Arabic," I said and his inscrutable sunglassed face stared back. He lost interest immediately, almost robotically, like he'd mentally deleted a file.

A different American demanded to know where I was from with false joviality, laying back in his chair with his expansive, soft torso on display. I hated him from the first moment I heard his voice, no matter how hard he tried to spark a conversation. He reminded me too much of a certain client.

I held the hand of who I'd come with and kept asking if he wanted any food, although I could only summon the wait staff to get it. It was scandal if we even tried to fetch our own soda from the refrigerator, in this home we'd slept in the night before. I felt angry at everyone and intimidated by the handsome men at the far table. Only one other woman was in attendance, heavy-set and at least twenty years older than I. It was too hot outside of the shade.

"How are you feeling?" the bodyguard asked from his spot in what had become the guard's alcove, making a move to stand when I came inside.

"Fine, I'm fine."

"I can come back and get you in the morning," he offered.

"We'll see," I said. "I think he's better. Did you eat?" I doubted he was allowed.

When we left, I saw security scattered around the gleaming cars and SUVS downstairs, some with coiled wire laying by their necks and down their collars, and a strange air of eagerness and anxiousness in the daylight. I imagined the feeling: you almost want something to happen because your entire being is prepared for it happen, and yet for something to happen would be hell.

When our car pulled out, Mr. X smacked the back like it were the ass of a woman. He crossed the street to escort someone else to their ride, and we waved.

"You see, we are not in Hezbollah land now," Mr. X said proudly the afternoon before as a gold girl in a silver bikini strutted past our table, twice. I tried not to eye her ass but it was very hard. Comparing, always comparing.

The pool DJ played Latin pop and young people stumbled out of the water and onto the terrace where they all knew Mr. X. "Everyone knows Mr. X," we were told, and shown, many times. The women, with their beautiful hair ruined by chlorine and sun, smiled with self-satisfaction when introduced to us as though they were holding court. The radio promised them "ninety seconds to orgasm" in the latest *In Style* magazine and posters by the highway offered maternity lingerie. "Fuck me, I'm famous," read fliers handed out near the airport door.

In international thrillers, in action movies, at least as I remember from the few I've watched recently and those I saw growing up, there's always a scene where the "bad guys" relax with their wives or mistresses or larger harems of female entertainment, useless bodyguards nearby, as "the good guys" spy on them and coordinate their attack. (They used those phrases there, "bad guys" and "good guys," unironically: "We have to support Mr. X because he is a good guy.")

I had this thought a year ago, maybe longer, while I was reading an article in *Harpers* about oil barons or arms dealers or some type of shady cash lenders who met two nameless Russian beauties at a café where they (the men) were interviewed by the journalist. It was a thought for the ciphers, for those story-less female bodies that end up in proximity to dangerous power because of how they look, and whose eventual loss is less than a casualty, the equivalence of destroyed furniture or perhaps a wrecked Porsche. They don't always die, but they never have futures.

I know I am not like those women. Perversely, there is a shame in not being like them, in being almost poised to play the part but not endowed with whatever sad gifts make it fully possible.

"Do you like your driver?" Mr. X asked. Craftiness crept over him when we answered in the affirmative. "He's a bodyguard. Former military."

"But he's so gentle," I said, remembering how aware and kind he'd been at the ruins. It was not the right thing to say.

Before midnight the three of us were almost alone.
"We're full," we protested as more and more food arrived.
"Just taste it," Mr. X said.
"You're indulgent," he would tell my guy when I went to the restroom

to wash my hands, referring to the meat and cheese I snuck from his plates to feed the scrawny cat.

When Mr. X caught me doing it, I'd asked, "Am I embarrassing you?" Of course I was. Even though we had the huge, open-air space to ourselves, with only a few staff members nearby.

It was the happiest I was for the entire trip, though, there in the fuzzy dark with the quiet and the hungry cat, staccato lights on the slopes. Mr. X insisted on bringing several of his own sweaters for me in case I got cold there on the mountain.

"This one's blue," he said in a nod to what I was already wearing.

During our last dinner, he said, "You look very elegant tonight, my madam."

In many ways, it was an unforgettable country.

The Last Words On August
August 25, 2011

I woke when he got out of bed. Through the windows, morning broke on the skyscrapers, the visible clouds rimmed in coral and rose. I pretended to sleep for five minutes more, playing with my breath, moving the parts of my body he couldn't see: my ankle deep under the comforter, my wrist dangling off the mattress's edge. After those moments passed, I glanced out the window and the pink scallops were gone, it was just an ordinary sky struggling into day.

The night before he said, "I've never kissed the backs of a woman's knees before," and I wondered how someone went through more than half a century of life without it happening, not even accidentally. It may be simply that different bodies speak to a partner in different ways. I remember when I was still new to all this and a man flipped me on my stomach and then held himself in a plank above me, dragging his erection over the skin of my back. Every sex manual I've ever seen is an insult.

From his first line of description about the book he'd chosen as a gift, I knew who'd written it and that I already owned it, but I had to wait. I had to suppress the desire to say so. I wouldn't know how to teach that, the skill of the right amount of restraint. You're supposed to show them you're smart but probably not smarter than them. You want to surprise and impress but you can't do it at their ego's expense. You're a supplement. You're not the star.

"You're almost intimidatingly good-looking," one man told me after we shared our first kiss.

"No," I said, laughing. But I thought about it later and maybe. The trappings matter so much: right haircut, color, style; right make-up (the lighter the better; it's less strange in the morning,) the right shoes, the right dress, the eye contact. I look in the mirror and I see me, working, which is different than myself. Their desire makes me a different person. I think it's not so hard to shape myself that way. I intuit what they like to see and try to create the conditions for them to see it. He only said "almost."

Summer is predictably slow for everyone in this business but this month was not slow for me. I feel more singular now than I remember feeling ever before, strong but hollow. When I get upset about something in my "real" life, I comfort myself by thinking, *I don't need this. I have that.* Then when something upsets me in my sex life—not just sex that I sell, because sex that I sell is the only sex I have anymore—I think, *I can stop this whenever I want to. I never have to do it again.* So one life is the back up but I haven't yet decided which.

Before I went to sleep I scribbled, "obliterated" in my notebook. I'd been fantasizing of a release from being present during sex, or at least a particular type of present—present enough to get going, like a top, and then present enough to choose to disappear. Lately I've not been drawn away and out of myself, I've chosen to leave. Or it happens automatically and not through compulsion.

I leafed through men in my mind, the ones I'd had the best sex with. Some of them I'd never come with. I like that better; I like just writhing for hours. They all have so much in common: A lean, broad body. A certain sweetness. A hefty cock. A wife.

I thought of emailing each one of them, suggesting we meet—for free if they were clients, in secret if they weren't. But I didn't. All four of them had expressed fear, not that they would characterize it as such, but I don't know what else to call it. It was a fear of infatuation, fear of the mindless passion that is instructive as any addiction as to how little other parts of your life matter.

So many of the men I meet send their daughters or their sons or their wives to rehab. I never would have guessed.

A different client and I laughed over dinner about the time he accidentally bought a six-figure blazer. He is often villainized in the media and it pains me. I think, sincerely, "If you could only know him like I do."

No one understands how this world works.

Wedding Rings
September 29, 2011

Some keep them on. Some take them off. I wonder where the ring goes when it's no longer on the hand, what places a man keeps it so it's not lost or forgotten over a day or a full weekend or even a few hours. Many married men have hired me on their birthdays.

Married or not, many enjoy talking about their sons, if they have them. They do not soon tire of describing how handsome and smart and accomplished he is. On occasion, the handsome part is true. If there are two sons, one will be the clear favorite.

"Show me a picture," I said once, after listening for some time about this miracle of a boy.

"I'm not showing you a picture of my son," he said.

I kept looking at him. "Oh, alright," he said, and reached for his phone.

Weeks before, I took some sniffs of something that hurt and for a time the night was wonderful. A sober man I'd known but not known for years met me in a bar, and then later we went to my hotel room and he laid his clear head in my lap while I stroked his hair in a trance on the bed. After my friend left us, he asked if he could masturbate and he came quickly while I touched him. There may have been some unspoken pact that neither of us would write about it. Or maybe he forgot it even happened.

I am still capable of feeling used. I am still capable of having a sexual experience that makes me feel like my entire life has been a mean joke.

The date went pretty wrong with one father client, a man I'd seen several times before and remembered fondly. It started out so promising.

"You're a witch!" he cried early on in our reunion. He'd repeat it again now and then, ducking his head afterward like a boy hiding from something that embarrasses him.

It crumpled later and I wanted to blame him but it might have been all my fault. I felt like a statue with a human being buried inside. Everything was muffled: the sadness, the anger. I just tried to hold still.

Before I left, I stood in the Sunday light of his hotel room, holding the image of his son.

"You wouldn't stand a chance with him," he said, like that would hurt me.

Emptying My Pockets
December 7, 2011

When it's good, you don't feel the time passing. That's something you want in personal sex, too, isn't it? Saying it that way seems sad—why wouldn't you want to feel every minute?—but it's not. Or rather it's no more or less sad than any other way of life.

I remember talking with one client about his brother, who had taken a radically different path.

"Do you think he's jealous of you?" I asked.

"In the same way I'm jealous of him," he responded. I don't know a single word for that, the tragedy inherent in every choice.

I had to apologize to him later for the blood, my legs trembling. That's the curious effect I never get used to when I'm with endowed men, the way an oversized cock sets my whole body quivering. It's more diffuse than an orgasm, more satisfying because it involves no satisfaction. There's brutality, there's writhing. Writhing is the sexiest verb I know. It's so full of suffering.

I still dream about it, no matter how much I'm getting. I let my mind at night tell me when I might be horny since it's hardly a feeling that comes over me anymore. But I know something is happening if I dream about almost coming. I know some sunken part of me still wants it. A lost anchor shifting in the sand.

"Do you ever start having feelings for any of your clients?" He asked me. "Have you ever had to stop seeing someone?"

He was frustrated by my answers, partly because I was being a little obtuse, partly because he wasn't asking me what he really wanted to know.

I don't think many people are sadder than the American men who start seeing prostitutes in their thirties. They often have erectile problems. They seem completely baffled by the circumstances of their life and the world at large. They're ineffectual; they read political blogs and have impotent political opinions they hide from their colleagues who may or may not do the same. They make money in jobs they don't care about, doing work they outright despise, married to women they don't talk to. No judgment. It just isn't sexy. Usually they're good people but only in the easy ways—that goes for most of us, I guess.

That's how I see it in my meaner moments, anyway, and if it's mean, it might not be true. One of my most frequent dates has a gruffness about him when we're in public. It may be nerves but it comes out towards me oppressively, with a touch of disrespect. I found myself thinking something cruel about the way he walked as I followed him down the hall to his room.

Be nice to him, I admonished myself. *You've* had sex *with this man.*

He thinks about everything with the same intensity that I do, but with a different mind. I like that about him.

Once he recalled asking me if I were comfortable while going down on him.

And according to him, I said, "Oh yes, this is very sustainable."

"I did not!" I shouted, laughing, appalled, as he recounted this. "I did not say that!"

"You did." He said. "I thought it was wonderful."

"I want to be your best client," he used to tell me.

Then finally, he told me he already was. I probably laughed at that, too.

"I'll tell you why I'm your best client," he went on. "Because I don't want you to be anyone other than who you are. I'm sure most people you meet want you to be different. But I don't desire or hope or expect for anything more from you than what you are It's all a gift. The way you reveal yourself and the way you don't reveal yourself. It's all a gift."

He says things like this often. I lose track of them. I hold them, I let them go. I keep them in a pocket with loose seams. There are so many things I've forgotten over the past few months, all the moments I didn't want to write down or maybe didn't want to remember.

It's only through working that I've met the sort who like to check in. They'll ask, "Are you ok?" right in the middle. Usually, confused, I will return the question to them.

Once when this happened, when I asked a man how he was doing, he said, "I'm an old man on top of a young woman, with good intentions," and rolled to the side. I've been carrying that one for a while.

It was our first date and he invented a reason to know my real name.

"Let's let it be a surprise," I said, knowing he was wrong about the imagined scenario. I think that hurt him but it couldn't be helped.

"You make me feel like I'm home," he said as he lay sprawled out after. He reached for my hand. "It's not a quality that can be taught."

Which is not the same as a quality that can't be learned.

Melting
December 28, 2011

"Open your eyes," he instructed. "Open your eyes. Look at me." He held my face in his hands as I rocked over him. "You're the most beautiful woman I've ever fucked."

I don't know how he expected me to respond, but I had the distinct impression he was saying it primarily to elicit a reaction. He told me the same thing earlier too, when he wasn't inside of me.

The elegant way to deflect these lines is to turn them into a compliment for the giver rather than a put down of yourself.

"Oh, I find that hard to believe," I said then. "I'm sure you've been with lots of attractive women." Thinking to myself, with rude pleasure, that I was referring to other women he'd paid.

"I don't think you understand how attractive you are," he replied, like he was really on to something, like he'd stumbled upon a secret I wanted to keep hidden. All of this made me lose respect for him—that he was underestimating me enough to think I would enjoy or be flattered by this game. So it was strange later when he said, "You keep your intellect in a cage because otherwise it would scare away men like me. Thank you. Thank you for humoring me."

But he had his cute moments.

"If you ever feel like something isn't working out right just tell me, 'Baby, you left me hanging,' and I'll say, 'Baby, I'll take care of it! Tell me what I need to do!'" He was talking about money. He wanted to know if I'd been with someone else earlier that morning and was hoping I had. More and more, the men I meet savor my sluttishness.

I knew he wanted something to make him feel dirty, so I told him the truth, about laying in bed for an hour and fantasizing about a man I hadn't seen in years while I got very wet, and that I was saving that wetness for him because our date was only a few hours away.

"What happened?" he asked. "Why don't you see each other anymore?"

"He begged me not to reply to his emails. So I didn't. He wrote me a few times and I never wrote back. He told me whenever we corresponded he couldn't function—" I stopped myself. It sounded too dramatic. "He couldn't think about anything else except us being together, and he was supposed to be married soon."

"Because you're haunting," my client said immediately. "You know that, right? He was haunted by you. You're hard to forget. I bet that happens a lot."

"It's happened like that one other time," I admitted, though it's happened more than once. There's nothing to be proud about.

"Thank you for giving me the best fuck of my life," he said. We were doing it over and over again. Sex somersaults—in various positions so he could get the best views in the wall mirror. Me on my knees and tilting my pussy so he could see it while I went down on him. I suggested he come on my face, which is safer to do if it's their second or third time. He wouldn't quit.

"My god, you're so beautiful. Look at you." Pulling my hair back from my face and gazing rapturously. Working so hard to convince at least one of us.

That night I got back into bed and stared at my reflection in the wall mirror while I ate, watching my face as I chewed. It felt like having a staring contest with another person, but a curious one rather than an angry one. And there was no winner.

Before he left he said, "You're looking into a fogged mirror. You might sometimes think 'oh I look skinny, I look cute'—you have no idea. And my job is to wipe it"—he made a motion like swiping glass with his sleeve—"clean."

I scrawled it down afterward. Seeing words on paper helps me decide if they mean anything. It still feels hollow.

"No one appreciates you like me," he said, and that made me a little angry. He has no idea the competition he's up against. He doesn't know this is something other men say and he doesn't know how things men say run together like rivulets in melting ice.

"I remember this from last time," he said while I was on top, half curled up on him like a child. I didn't. Whose benefit all these declarations are for—that's usually transparent.

Over Christmas my father, the rabid conservative, laughed about being approached by prostitutes in Vegas and declared it should be legal. I love him but not in the way I've ever loved anyone else and it's so cluttered up I don't know what to do with it. I want us to be able to spend time with each other but I don't want to have to talk about the past or excavate our anger, and I don't know how it will be possible otherwise.

He made me come upstairs and he played a song for me on his guitar and asked if I remembered being a child, laughing when I first heard the line about the fire engine being a clean machine. Of course I remembered. It's the first thing I think of when I think of us, though he played it on the piano then.

I'd never been confronted with his love like that, never had an offering that naked. There was no way to respond, no plug for connecting with each other in any way more than an uncomfortable smile and, "Yeah,

I remember." We're not supposed to be so explicit in this family. We don't cry in front of each other. We don't touch.

I don't know if everyone else ricochets like this. I've always had it in me, though, that complete coldness. If people demand too much, I'll get rid of them. One of my friends mentioned that she felt she couldn't defend taking the money of married men. Usually it seems to me an action that needs no defending.

I realized I primarily only experience guilt if I've impacted another in a way in which I have no stake. I mean, if I stood up someone for lunch because I confused the date, I would feel terrible. But if I bailed out last minute for lunch because there was something else I wanted to do, I would feel nothing. And if my lunch date became angry with me, I would come back at them ten times angrier, thinking, *I sent you a text a half hour before, how much more do you want from me?*

2012

Incomplete
January 10, 2012

All of it will sound strange because it was. He dressed as though he were going to help a friend paint. He wore huge, ridiculous black gloves, like something he'd found in someone else's house, and one front tooth was slightly chipped, a different color than the rest. He asked if I had change for the parking meter. It shouldn't have been a big deal but it was.

Once we sat down, I asked him about his sheaf of papers, and as I was asking I saw under the torn corner of one, my foot. He'd printed out my pictures.

"You don't look happy," he said.

"I don't think . . . I think I . . . "

To his credit, he understood. We shook hands and he got in his car and drove away, while I stood on the street corner trying not to cry, waiting for a cab to approach.

You have to realize, it never starts like that. The men I see are gentlemen. They at least have the air of having lived and functioned in the world for a long time. He'd cashed in a bunch of stocks, he told me that much. I won't even say what type of car he drove. I'm never this much of a snob. I never have to be.

"I am experiencing regret," he texted me. He called, but I didn't answer. He sent me an email. ("What was it? I went home and I had everything ready and I really wanted to be with you.")

It occurred to me that maybe he knew who I was—I mean that he knew about this blog. He had that way about him, a writer's way: sincere, awkward, caught up in his own scattered brain.

I wanted the year to be over.

I agreed to meet him again and it was horrible. The restaurant was crowded, which was a surprise.

"Do you have the envelope?" I asked him, when I started to sense the rapid slide downhill. I never have to ask that.

"It's a bank envelope," he said.

"Ok, well, you can still slide it over to me." Not giving a fuck. Angry. I have an anger in me. It's rare that I let it come out around clients.

N.B.

"It's _____ dollars," he said. I just kept looking at him. "Do you want it?"

I flashed my eyes at him. Who cared. Let him see my greed. "Yes."

"Then are you going to come back with me?" He whisper-hissed, leaning towards me.

"No," I said. "Not today."

"But maybe later?"

"I'll think about it . . . " Meaning no.

We'd been together for ten minutes and he said he was going to leave. I said he should do whatever makes him comfortable, which I knew was ambivalent enough to keep him seated. He said I wasn't being open to him. We fought about what had gone wrong, misunderstanding each other.

Finally I couldn't help it, I started thinking about the table of tourists next to us, and how obvious our conversation was, how obvious our arrangement. I started smiling and he thought it was for something he'd said.

"That's the first smile you've ever given me," he said.

"That's not true," I said. "I was really trying yesterday."

"You're a hard woman," he said. "A hard fucking woman. I won't lie. It's kind of hot."

We started smiling at each other, laughing a little at ourselves.

"I'll give you all the money to come back to my place right now for one hour," he said.

And his house was just like it would be, of course—wood paneling, an old family home. His family's old home. Great cold spaces because no one but him had been inside for some time. Full of emptiness. It felt almost abandoned, like a mausoleum holding the bedroom of a friend from my adolescence.

I took off my underwear and tights in the bathroom and stood before him on the rust colored carpet. We kissed. I got wet. I usually get wet with a first time. But this was very wet. He felt me with his fingers and laid me down on his bed. I clung to him.

"I don't want to come," he said.

"Don't," I said, clinging like a barnacle, like a monkey to its mother. I didn't want either of us to come. I wanted it to last and last.

He repositioned me with pillows underneath. He pressed my face flat to the side with his palm full on my cheek. He wrapped his arms completely around me while I lay on my stomach, saying things I didn't hear into my hair. It was so good. Luminous. Inexplicable. One thick gold smear. His stomach was firm with give, full but lean. I noticed his body when he got up to adjust the floor heater. Unintentional. Just right.

He tried to distract himself, to stall by talking to me while inside me. "When was the last time you cried?" was one of his questions.

I didn't want to admit it had been the day before, so I said, "Recently."

We saw each other the following week. It was much like it had been before but not as good. That's predictable. It's too hard to recreate a very good first time on the second time though it might be better than the first by the fourth or fifth. Still, I was incredibly wet and I still wanted it to last, and when he came I wanted him to fuck me a second time—I'd never come with him, I was saving it like it was a battery that needed to be charged more, and I'd been so close many times—but he didn't, maybe to try to prove some point about what he wanted me there for.

The second time, when he was driving me to the metro, he said something to me and there was a pause, and I asked him about his truck.

"You don't have to talk," he said. " I like your silences."

I saw someone else later that night, a nice someone with whom I have much in common. He was candid and engaging. I think he almost cried for a moment, but it's hard to tell with men. I think their faces slip towards tears sometimes without them even realizing. I laughed at dinner when a snap pea fell from my chopsticks before it could reach my mouth.

"I'm not watching you eat," he said, interrupting himself.

"That's too bad," I said. "Because I'm making it interesting."

He told me he wanted to make sure I enjoyed myself, that my enjoyment was more important than anything else and I knew it was true, for him. I felt so guilty then about this cruel thought I'd had about his wife.

When googling him, I learned something personal about her, something very personal that she'd made very public, and I thought, *no wonder he wants to see prostitutes.* That was so heartless. Maybe it was true, but still so mean. There's no reason to lay a relationship bare like that, even in your own head, not based on skeletal knowledge, especially not when it's about people you don't love. I felt ashamed.

It seemed to me he'd had too much to drink. The sex wasn't very good, and I thought about texting the writer and telling him I wanted to come over. It felt unfinished between us—the moment, the sex, something. And I knew he would let me come over after midnight, not because I have some power over him but because we have power over each other, or rather there's a power acting on both of us that we can be spun up in.

I'm not trying to deny responsibility. I'm actually more careful with someone when I can tell it could be out of our control. If you've felt it before, you know. There's no right word. It's a link that required no forging. It's like finding a worn path in woods no one has walked. It can only be uncovered. It is already there.

But the un-ended quality was what defined it. So I didn't send him a message.

I almost started crying in a bookstore a few days after the second time I saw the writer. It was such a beautiful day, the most perfect weather, and there were lots of people mingling around the shelves. Books move me, just the feeling of them in my hands. I was thinking of how I could never stand to have a job that wouldn't allow browsing in a bookstore on a weekday afternoon with nowhere to go and no one to answer to. I have a really good life and I'm so bad at being happy.

All I can think to say about 2011 was that I made more money than I probably ever thought I would make, double what I made the year before. I'm not sure I feel richer but I do feel older.

Shabby Love
February 4, 2012

One city is quietly special for me. It's the place where I first truly committed to doing this, to arranging a life of men and travel and money. I already had those things but it wasn't enough. I wanted more. I still want more.

It matters that I made the decision while I was in a place I'd never been before, alone in a hotel room, like I was pushing pause on that moment, sustaining "alone in a hotel room" across a long field of time.

I continue to have trouble feeling love across distances yet I don't stay at home. When I'm away, I forget about people who are supposed to matter to me and I feel forgotten by them.

Though I've never been a romantic, never fantasized about weddings or marriages or having children, I've realized I want one man to love me behind everything else. I want his love to be my scenery while I do whatever I want on the stage. I suppose this is what a father is supposed to do, but mine can't, or I wouldn't ask him to now. There were moments in my childhood when he managed, maybe, but ultimately I pushed it away. His love was poor so I thought I'd rather not have it at all. Let the stage be empty until something better fills the background.

I guess that's too much to ask from most people. I've been told it's too hard. What would I be like if I were an easy person to love? Hardly myself: easy to become infatuated with, impossible to partner.

"Do you think you'll ever turn yourself over to one man?" a client once asked.

I laughed. "Turn myself over," I said. "Like he's a sheriff."

He told me it was the defining question of his own life, whether he could subvert the unsatisfied aspects of himself, could quiet or erase them in order to please another. He acted as though I might not know he was married, so I played along. Finally he admitted that once during a romantic dinner at a vacation spot, his wife told him, "I had a dream that you were paying for sex."

And he leaned across the table and said, "At least I was buying something worth paying for."

"She doesn't realize that the ooey-gooey stuff isn't enough for me," he said, meaning the emotional intimacy or rather the illusion of it, the platonic massages, the flattery he dispenses so relentlessly. "But, it's like no, Honey. I need my cock sucked. And I need my cocked sucked like Charlotte sucks my cock."

I smirked. Moments earlier, I'd knelt before him and he drew my head back using my hair as a handle, pulling my face perfectly parallel to catch all of his come. "Oh, baby," he gasped the first time I ever put my mouth on him, eventually yanking me away by the ponytail in his fist to kiss me. "I love the way you take care of me."

My most generous client is an astoundingly tall man who I first met while I was high, or at least I was at the point where all the symptoms of feeling high bled into the symptoms of having been up for a long time without sleeping or eating. I was in a good mood and probably even more expressive than usual. When, after less than two hours, he left the suite he'd reserved for us, I knew not to take it personally. Occasionally men have to be businesslike about sex, practical, either because that's their dominant mode and it's too hard to shake, or because they're making an effort to keep the encounter elemental.

It's not that he's spent more on me than any other person but that he leaves exorbitant amounts given that we won't be together for very long. It seems all he usually wants to do is go down on me and fill me with his massive fingers.

I saw him again in another city, and then again. Sometimes it doesn't take much for me to feel attached. Sometimes tenderness can bloom even more readily without the long dinners and the shows. When I saw him most recently there was something unusually warm in how he treated me. We hugged goodbye for a long breath while the sun was setting. I had the impression that we meant something to each other, and it was terrible to be left by myself.

I sat on the bed in the robe pouching around me like a deflated gown, my iPod still playing on the room's stereo system. Expansive loneliness seeped out to fill the corners of the room. I could barely move. I felt sad enough to shatter.

It could be that I'm good enough to trick even myself. I thought of how other girls I know sometimes say they can't stand to think of any part of the man's genitals touching their own, and they try to keep his strokes shallow so he doesn't press in past the rim of the condom. That never even occurs to me. I always go for depth. I always touch their faces or at least the necks' smooth slope to the base of the skull. I lay my head on their chests uninvited.

"I wish we'd met under different circumstances," one client said recently. "Not because the circumstances under which we met are wrong. But because I'd like to know you personally." It was preoccupying him. It was all he could talk about while we laid together, how he wanted to be my friend.

I didn't ask him why—I barely spoke at all—but he told me, "I think you're special. I think you're incredibly intelligent. You might even be frighteningly brilliant."

I laughed. "You have no evidence of that."

"I know X," he said. "I know Y."

I just shook my head.

"I'd like to go out to dinner with you and have you talk. Just talk." He stared into my eyes and I remember his next words exactly. "It would be a blessing to listen to you."

When we'd met for the first time in a different city, he was describing his day without saying exactly where he'd been, but it was obvious. I made a casual mention of the cafeteria the company's space is known for, and he admitted that was where he'd been.

"They have so much money there," he said. "Silly money—so much money that they don't know what to do with it all. And do you know what all of them want?"

I smiled because of course I knew. "More money."

"More money," he whispered.

Gradually I've come to see how often good people can be behind bad things. Once I saw a client hours before he was to speak at Pat Robertson's university. And he was nice. He wrote me an email afterward calling me an angel, enchanting. It's so easy to be angry with broad strokes. It's too easy to hate people because of how they look on paper but then you meet them and they're not so bad. The truth is not most of us are not trying as hard as we could. And maybe most of us don't deserve kindness or forgiveness but what other options are there.

March
April 30, 2012

"Do I smell like my car?" He said. "Do I smell like [what I transport in my truck]?"

"Yes."

"Oh. Do you want me to take a shower?"

"You can if you want to. You don't have to."

"Ok, well, I will if you want me to. But I don't want to." He peered at me like I was going to challenge him. "I just want to make it clear that I will."

"If you're going to be preoccupied by it, you should. Do whatever makes you comfortable."

"I can't even smell it."

"I know, because you're used to it. I'll get used to it too."

"Just tell me if you want me to."

"If you want to take one, take one."

"I'm not going to take a shower," he said, leaning back into the couch.

"We've established that." I said. My body language was slightly combative. I angled myself to face him fully and moved further away in the process. "You said in your email you had something you wanted to tell me."

He sighed. "Well yeah but I thought we were going to be cuddled up, under the covers. Not like this."

"It never gets easier with me," I told him. We weren't fighting exactly. We were tussling, feeling each other out.

"Really? Why would you say that? Why? Why are you like that?" Our conversation overlaps like someone shuffling cards. I can't remember it all because it goes so fast at first. He teases out every one of his reactions at once. Somehow that makes it harder to be evasive. Maybe it confuses me.

I laughed, a short laugh. "I don't know why, that's just how it is."

"People have told you that?" He either asked or I was already thinking it or both. The older man said, "I have to start over with you, every time." That was either when I first noticed it, or it could have been with him that I first developed it.

"Yeah, people have told me. I'm telling you what people have told me."

"It's cause you're a hard woman. I think you're a bit of a seductress, though." He said it as though he were talking to himself. "But you're a seductress." Shuffling his sentences, too, repeating words as he refined his thoughts.

I was dressed in a black strappy tank top and my hair was in my face. I hadn't shaved because he asked me not to.

I said, "What's up with the aversion to showers, like you're a little kid?"

I don't treat him like he's my client but he doesn't act like he is. He almost acts like he's been sent to deal with me, not against his will, but there's an inevitability when we're together that lets me show him my edge. I know what I can get away with; I know the hostility is provocative, maybe necessary. I think he's a man who needs to be challenged. Our chemistry is already there, it's not something we have to create, so my coldness can't threaten it.

I can't remember how we ended up in bed. I remember him pulling back the covers and me asking, "In our jeans?"

And he said yes but then we both took ours off. Undressed ungracefully on opposite sides of the bed, like adversaries or spouses.

Up close, with my nose at his neck, he smelled good. I couldn't even notice the car smell anymore. I meant to tell him that but I didn't.

His lips are so soft and he kisses conservatively. It makes me wonder if he doesn't like the way I'm kissing him, and I almost don't mind if he doesn't. Whatever the cause, it's such a relief to not have my mouth violated by an unwelcome tongue.

"So you said you're seeing someone," I asked him, only curious. But he pulled away.

"Alright, let's set the table here," he said. I laughed at him for that and repeated it later: *let's set the table.*

"Do you really think we have amazing sex or is that something you tell everyone?"

"I don't think I've ever told anyone that before," I said. I meant that I'd never said it to a client but I may have never said it to anyone. He was quoting an email I wrote him, when I teased him about my needing to find someone else to do it with.

"Ok. So am I just like any other client to you? Because if I am, it's fine, I'll keep seeing you and paying you."

"And if you're not?" I asked.

"I'll . . . probably keep paying you."

I laughed because he was right and I loved that he had the presence of mind to know it.

I wish I could ask him how he would write this. I can't remember it nearly as well as I wish I could. The exact words with which he asked me to tell him he was special—they escape me.

"We have an uncommon . . . " I said it with hesitancy, trying to find the right words. I can't remember what I said or if I said anything more at all.

"I want you naked and on top of me," he whispered.

"That can happen," I said.

He rolled us over. "But I want to be patient."

It's redundant to mention the wetness. He breathed something to me that I couldn't completely hear: "Last time, when you were on top of me, I came because you . . . "

I don't know that I want to come with him at all but I wish our fucking lasted longer, or that it would happen again and again. I can't tell if he only goes once out of some idea of respect, or because he's sated. I don't know if he thinks I have an orgasm, or if he's not sure and doesn't care, or not sure and feels embarrassed asking. He's only a few years older than me but in a lot of ways it feels like he's younger.

Once I searched my boyfriend's suitcase for condoms while we were away on a trip together. He'd threatened to sleep with another woman and I thought if I found them, I'd know how serious he was. I didn't, and it felt like the meaningless information it was.

Later, he told me he fucked her, then went on court and blamed his loss on still being angry at me. The fact that I was the undercurrent in his mind even while he was with her made the act irrelevant. You get smarter at seeing how true power manifests. And it's not about limiting someone's actions.

I have complete control over my orgasms now, which comes with age for a lot of people, I think. It happens when I want it to happen or not at all. My control over the orgasms of the men I'm with is not bad, either. Usually it's in the eyes. Underneath one of my more demanding clients— one of those men who is insistent upon my enjoying it as much as he does—I let a thrill of pleasure fall over my face, a small, dirty smile with my mouth open, my eyelids giving one slow-motion flutter, and I felt him get harder inside of me, and a breath later he came.

I'm not sure how I feel about being this disconnected from arousal. It doesn't make me unhappy, at least not directly. I can feel some motion of a man's turning me on and I simply make it stop. I cut it off. Not what he's doing but what I'm feeling.

I don't know why I can't afford to give more orgasms away. I don't feel closer to someone after I come. But I feel covetous of climax, though it has no meaning. I think I want someone to earn it through an extraordinary summoning of pleasure, not just through repetitious and mechanical movements.

The last time I came with a client, it was a single father of two who cried when he spoke about his sons. We did a father-daughter role play and I felt my own wetness at the top of my inner thighs before he'd even touched me. I wiped some of it away with the back of my hand as discreetly as I could, embarrassed, not sure he would believe it was real.

In every fantasy I can remember having since I've been an adult, there is more than one man and they speak, particularly to each other, but I never do. I might moan or whine or whimper, but I never even try to form a word. It's a dream of being used completely.

The distance isn't something I need because my work is so horrible. The distance is probably something I want, because it's as close as I can come to disappearing.

"I don't want you to move somewhere I don't know about, where I have no way of finding you," my mom said recently. She's said this so often I've forgotten if it's an unfounded fear of hers or something I've actually done in the past.

"You were on top of me, and the way the light was coming in through the window—you looked like a goddess," a client told me. "I began thinking of how you sat across me at the restaurant, clothed, conversing, just hours before. And now here you were . . . and how utterly the same and yet not the same you were at that moment."

That used to be the type of thought that snagged me, too, but I don't dwell there anymore.

One man dressed me in a giant, worn T-shirt of his and taught me how to blend oil paint on the canvas and I felt like a child again from the delight. One man drenched me in chocolate sauce, bottle after bottle of it, pouring it down my pants, into my underwear, over my hair. He shuddered in ecstasy while he rubbed the viscous liquid over my skin and I couldn't stop smiling, tasting its false sweetness on my mouth.

"Don't forget the pockets," I told him, as I held them open at my hips. I slid my hands in afterward and the substance was cold, silky, thick. I laughed.

I sucked his chocolate-covered cock while I was wet with myself and sticky with the rest of it, kneeling in an oily brown bathtub. I lay back in his arms and we soaked in it afterward as the warm water diluted the mess.

"You're beautiful," he said over and over, my hair matted into heavy dreads, my eyelashes even coated, as he looked me full in the face. You could fall in love with someone after an hour or two as pure as that.

I thought, *whoever would take me would have to take my bitterness.* My sleep became ragged if my sleep came at all. I tried to write someone an email about something that took a long time. "It costs forever," I found myself typing.

Quick Canal
June 20, 2012

Though I was quite young when watching films like *Mannequin* and *Tootsie*, the 1980s' take on urban women's lives was what I grew up holding on to. I imagined that once I was of age I would live alone in a city, enveloped in that 80s coldness as I dated and stopped dating, had friends with whom I was not particularly intimate, wore masculine, loud fashion. Suits especially—and I have never once owned or worn a suit.

While I never suspected I would be a whore, I probably knew better than to believe I would work any conventional nine to five job, so in many ways this particular dream of the future was a dream of being someone else. But a gentle dream, a writer's dream born out of curiosity and not unhappiness, although I do sometimes feel vaguely cheated that this life is not to be had. I allow myself a momentary bow to that child's idea of what life will be like in the future.

Sometimes I look at a stranger while I'm out in public and try to summon a sense of the depth of their life, to fathom the sheer number of incidents that have hurt and delighted, ruined and remade. The little things, too, because they are just as important: the cheap thefts, the funny confusions, the moments that seemed to have no consequence beyond leaving a mental image. It's staggering to think about all these histories being dragged about by every living thing. It seems nearly impossible. My own is so detailed and vast that I can recall only a small fraction.

Recently I thought for the first time in years of childhood church services in the summer, when Sunday mornings took place outside by the thin river in town and my father and some of his friends led the services through song. The sermonizing was brief and informal, and my brother and I sat in the sun or whatever sparse shade we could find, squinting, playing with ants, singing. The stack of sheet music that sat at home on the kitchen table until this day was now pinned flat in the wind. How well I recall the swell of "How Great Thou Art," that triumphant crescendo of "then sings my soul." It can prick tears today, although at the time I probably sang the words absently, with my head down or tilted up, gaze half-full of sky, half-full of trees.

It doesn't matter if I forget this again for years or for forever, because it will always be sitting somewhere inside me and I will react a certain way or say a certain thing, unwittingly, responding to all those times I sat on the scratchy ground and watched my father play guitar as the water moved behind him.

I mean, everyone is this way. Everyone.

Myth
July 30, 2012

It started in a familiar city I'd not visited for years. Dinner and then fucking. Then a show and more fucking in his room, where he told me that his wife never gave him blow jobs and hated to have even his pre-come make contact with her skin. Which I should have already guessed given what our time consists of.

He is a kept man, and when he told me about his days of orchestrating a seamless life for another person, I became almost jealous. I'd googled his wife before and I knew about her outlandish income. But his regard for his young son is nearly nonexistent or profoundly inaccessible to me. Sometimes I feel at ease with him and at other times he seems too alien for me to understand. He's generous with praise, he lavishes compliments on his life and his wife, but I can't figure out what matters to him or what he thinks he's accomplishing.

I know he believes we share unusual commonalities, and that's probably right. I too have felt like I'm winning a race no one's watching, a race with no prize and perhaps without end. He pressed me to talk more about my work, why I do it. He said many flattering things, including one about how abundance keeps coming to me because I'm willing to give it away. But I'm not asked to give it away, and I haven't.

He said something about my mystery, as they all do. Is my mystery his mystery? It could be the two of us circle the other's deep-seeming shallow, glimpsing a reflection, confounded from seeing more. He's a former professional dancer with a thick head of hair. He curled his feet for me as proof.

It was nothing like that in the mountains. A different client greeted me there with one of his lean hugs, trembling less this time than the times before though no less excited.

"I can't believe you're really here," he said. He's excellent at hugging, and we clung to each other for a long time. It was maybe an hour later that another hug turned into more, and when I swallowed his come on my knees in his kitchen, I glanced to the left and saw my face in the broad side of his toaster, as though the appliance had been placed at exactly that angle for exactly that purpose.

He said he wanted to make a movie together but I had to write the screenplay.

"I can't write it," I said, though I thought maybe I could. We ate corn on the cob and made out. He smeared me with so many things—pieces of pies, copious amounts of custard—and then we washed it away. I came only once, rubbing myself against his erection with our hips pressed together and our torsos apart, side by side on the bed. It had been building up for hours. By that time it was dark and I didn't want to move, I couldn't think of any of the normal actions I might perform before falling asleep. I couldn't think of anything more that needed to be done.

Every day blue unfolded beyond the windows and the home was full of light. Every morning I rolled over him and made him come with my mouth.

"I haven't had this much sex in twenty-five years," he said, and we laughed.

He played his keyboard upstairs while I listened to it downstairs, sorting my things. On the first night, without flourish, he gathered my hair in his hands and held it to his nose. And when we notched our bodies together before sleep, he kissed my shoulder quickly and lightly many times, the kiss of a man overwhelmed with sweetness, cherishing the feeling of being full. It's almost audible, that swell of emotion, the wave that seizes up everything nearby. He did it just as my boyfriend does on nights when he loves me the most, so I thought of my boyfriend and I simultaneously thought of him, the man I was with, and whether I should feel torn or guilty or awkward were considerations that melted before they could surface. It was a deep sleep, a sleep that felt necessary.

Months before all that, I'd been in the hills of a different coast, alone for the first time with a client I'd passed several days with in the even more distant past—but always with other paid women there too. He told me I looked younger and thinner now, which made me cross. We sat in his hot tub at night and picked food from his garden during the day, and when I wrapped a scarf around my head to keep away the flies, he said I looked like I was from "Magic City". Then he had to tell me what that was.

I tried to write something after that visit but this was all I could manage:

The mountains broke all things open. In the dream of myself, there is only future, no past. The mountains are pulses of my younger selves, wholly separate and completely beyond explaining.

I also wrote, "It's so easy, when you're happy, to swear you'll never give in to suffering again."

One man asked me why I kept doing this work and I gestured to what was around us, the mostly empty restaurant, the waterfall behind the glass. I tried to explain that it was about the adventure, about experiences

I would never otherwise have. I didn't tell him that collecting these moments seems like the only point of being alive.

The next day I drove up a winding mountain path and a different he was at the end of it.

The last leg of the long trip was with two people, a man and another girl for hire. Her skin may have been even paler than mine—"I like your color," the mountain man said to me one day in the car—though she had several exquisite tattoos. She and I wrung out every moment alone together, like in the public bathroom before the movie, desperate to be candid with one another. We'd never met before, but I came shortly after we did, while straddling his face. Even when I know another woman's noises are fake, they'll turn me on.

"He's so sweaty," she whispered to me while he was in the shower. "I felt bad when he was lying on top of you. Like, 'Give her some space!'"

Some working women I've been with try to fetishize the other woman's body ("Doesn't Ashley have the best ass you've ever seen?") but when I said something to him about how soft her skin was and how beautiful her tattoos, she didn't respond in kind.

She faked sleep masterfully in the morning. I was fooled until he got up to use the bathroom and I heard her shifting to her side. I turned on my own and we looked into each other's wide eyes.

"I have morning breath," she said, making a face.

"Me too," I whispered. "I hate that. It doesn't make any sense. I brush my teeth right before bed every time."

We lied quiet for a beat, listening for him. The previous day, he found us giggling, and asked something like, "What are you two saying about me?"

When he was taking turns fucking us, she was underneath him and I was lying next to them, and she reached out for my hand. I wasn't sure if she knew it was me, or if she was aware of what she was doing or if her work body was taking over, touching any skin it brushed against, but I closed my fingers around hers. It felt like an honor. I don't like holding hands with men but there is something unspeakably special about holding hands with another woman.

"You're so pretty in the morning, it's not fair, you're not even wearing make-up," she said in a half-bitter, half-wistful rush, and I felt like I should say something self-effacing but I could only giggle, and then so did she. We laughed in the morning light, hiding our bad breath behind our hands, rolling closer towards each other across the space where his body had been.

Being Happy
October 7, 2012

After one particular stretch of days with a client whose presence curdles me, I was even more eager to see my favorite. I imagined leaping on him when he opened the door, locking my legs around his waist, but it didn't happen like that. In person he's nowhere near as perfect as I remember, yet in some ways he's more perfect because he's real, and the ways in which we're not suited to one another are a gift. We have independent lives to preserve, after all. I'm continually impressed by the simplicity of his sincerity, how he can say something like, "It's heaven to wake up to you," and it doesn't sound clichéd.

In the mountains again, he sat before the keyboard as his coffee brewed and he played two verses of "Close To You." I stood in the kitchen perhaps fifteen feet away with the morning spilling through the doors and windows, in a long cotton dress down to my feet that I'd bought only to wear there. He asked me questions I couldn't answer, though not for my lack of trying. I asked him nothing although there's much that I wonder, especially about his wife.

When he clung to me at night, I had the memory of a similarly built man from years before, the one who woke me with penetration, who came and fell asleep with his heavy cock still stretching me as I lay awake around the thickness and fullness, semen leaking between my legs. It had never happened that way before nor happened that way since. I have dreams about it and once woke up in desperation with my heart screaming, *I would give away anything to be with him like that again.* I never will be, which is right and as it should be, the pain the price of a singular experience.

I can admit now that sometimes my work makes me sad but more reliably the mere fact of living makes me sad. I work to deny the diffuse sadness, I use distraction and sharper sadnesses to set small fires in the place that's always dark. At one time I thought I could make a trade, could make an exchange as smoothly as a con artist's hand passes one card in place of another, and that a relationship or some other diversion might offer the same relief so I could step away. But it's too much of a risk. I won't abandon a patch of calm water to swim through the waves toward the shore.

The most perceptive client knew it, and my mother knows it. She's lived all her life watching it take shape in me, unable to explain it though she understands.

"I thought it was because you were so smart. You wanted so much of the world, you didn't know what to do. So you turned all that energy in on yourself," she told me, speaking of my girlhood, and I had nothing to say.

The parental blessing of "whatever makes you happy" always sounded hopeless when it came from her to me, fully meant and futile. Whatever makes it bearable. Whatever keeps you treading water. Whatever moments bob your head about the surface so you can see the wide horizon and grab a breath of cold, bracing air.

By The Time You Read This
November 20, 2012

He says what they all say, "Either you're the greatest actress or . . ." *Or this is who you are, this is real, how I feel with you is real.* Though you'd think it would mean something different coming from him.

"I can't work with an actress unless I'm attracted to her," he said, and I lost some respect for him. I think I was limiting his attraction to physical and predictable, like all the times he's called me beautiful when my breasts look too heavy and my face is smeared with something strange, mean nothing.

He told me thought he'd only do "this" once or twice, to "get it out" of his system. "I didn't expect to like you so much," he said, and we grinned goofily across the table at one another.

He's my favorite. I don't know what else to say.

He started in about writing a screenplay again and I couldn't hear it. "What's the point?" I demanded.

He said something about challenging misconceptions and showing people what it's actually like. I said people don't want to know, there's plenty material already, but they're happier with their ignorant meanness and small, nasty fantasies. One movie wouldn't change anything; people would say I was a fluke and a freak and glamorizing it.

It seemed hopeless, and every piece of media and art seemed trivial and useless to me then. I kept pressing him on the point.

"Because it's fun," he said, most convincingly yet. "Making a movie is fun."

I went quiet. I was becoming strongly angry, teenage angry, even, like I'd been personally slighted. It was almost out of my control when I blurted, "It doesn't interest me."

"What doesn't?" He said, and that made me angry too, because I thought he should have been there with me, thinking like I was thinking.

"Rehashing my life. Telling 'my story.' I would have to talk about how I got started and . . . It doesn't interest me at all. I can't think of anything more boring." I could barely speak for all the anger gathering inside me. Sick of the suggestion that I should purposefully spread out my tired history, which I know so well, for palatable consumption and probably sick too of knowing it all the time, the way everyone knows their own history in every waking moment, like a scent you think you've gotten used to just before you catch a whiff of it again.

I wanted to be an actress once, when I was in college. I am an actress now.

After dinner, he started a fire and I lied against him.

"You made a fire," I said. "That's so manly. And you cook. You play the piano."

"I'm good at husband stuff," he said. "Except for this."

I assume one day he'll read what I've written here and that sometime before or shortly after we'll be entirely out of each other's lives.

On a plane I sat next to a woman who told me her mother had just died. She apologized for ruining my flight and got drunk while she asked if I were religious. She made me take a black rosary her mother brought back from Italy. We laughed not infrequently. I fed her my chocolate. She asked at least five times how her hair looked, if she should wear it up or down. She clutched me in grief, sobbing into my shoulder after I took hold of her hand.

"You're so beautiful," she told me when she pulled away. "You're special, I can tell. Oh, look at your teeth."

In a way, it took a lot for me to grasp her hand but in another way there is nothing more natural in the world for me than to physically comfort a stranger.

You are a deck of cards. Someone pulls a card. Someone else pulls another. "Oh, you're the jack of spades," he says. "No, you're the five of diamonds."

Pull and show: the three of hearts, the ten of clubs, the joker. Yes. Yes I am the five of diamonds, I am the ace of clubs, I am the queen of hearts, I am, I am, I am.

2013

One Wing
March 11, 2013

I saw the mountain client in a city, and he asked, "Did you have another gig this morning before me?"

I laughed and repeated him ("a gig") and then there was a moment of quiet before I asked, "You really want to know?"

"Well . . . yeah," he said, and made an exhalation almost like a laugh.

I had, so I told him the truth.

He still got hard and came, however much that matters.

In the shower he said "Will you take me in your mouth again?" and he finished like that.

There was a moment earlier when he corrected me about something and I corrected him back and he said, "I don't want to argue with you," in a worn, disappointed tone, like we were two exes trading off the kids.

I've seen him in different cities, different hotels, and no matter the place he always smells the same.

The gig that morning had been my first virgin, a tall, skinny guy who looked like he could be sixteen but brought his work badge and talked about his graduate degree.

He told me immediately it was his first time. I asked what he'd like and he said he didn't know. He kept backing away from me so that I felt like I was chasing him around the room, but we were both laughing.

"Let's just hug," I offered, but even then he let his arms hang by his side.

I kissed him and he said, "I don't know how to kiss."

"Nobody does," I said. I think he thought I was being flippant to reassure him, but I meant it.

I kissed his unmoving lips twice more, and he said "thank you."

We spent more than an hour talking about philosophy, about life. I said I couldn't manage to believe in God but I hoped there was something more for us than biological, terminal life, and that out of all the infinite possibilities of what could occur, it seemed more likely something would happen after death than nothing.

"That's correct," he said.

He was on a quest to experience everything he never had. He'd smoked pot for the first time the week before.

More and more, what it requires is blurring myself, being the right amount of inside and outside. Lately I've begun feeling not quite distressed but simply too much aware of what's happening and how little I like it. I wasn't getting the balance right. So I started concentrating on my right hip bone, the skin over the crest, the protruding ridge. Sometimes I would look with my eyes, sometimes it was all internal. Whenever I felt even the slightest possibility of panic, it was back to the quiet right hip bone, still and strong. The rule is that it's the only thing I can think of.

I had to do it once when a client flexed the muscles around his cock while he was inside me, showing off, maybe trying to be funny. *Only my boyfriend does that in me,* I thought, wounded, but erased that with my right hipbone, my right hipbone.

Years ago, when I babysat, a family told me to sing "You Are My Sunshine" to their daughter before bed, as they did with her each night. But when I started, she stopped me.

"You can't sing that song!" she said, obviously disturbed. I was glad; I'd felt weird about it anyway.

I love the smell of laundry coming up from basements in cities where I don't live. It reminds me of the first few cities I was ever in, and how when I smelled that in them, I realized I really could live there someday.

I've lived in cities for years but that smell still carries that sense of possibility, the promise of a jailbreak into a different future, a different life, a different self. Sometime when I'm walking home on a brisk night with the wind blowing, I remember being lost and crying in London at eighteen, feeling heartbroken but also ok, calmed by the purposeful bodies around me, the people who lived and worked in that place. It seems important to recall periodically how preoccupied and mystified I was that anyone ever got on with their adult lives without making it out to be a big deal. And now I'm one of those people doing it, maybe.

In the shower, he hugged me low and I could see his bald spot, which is considerable, the curls around it flattened to his skull where the skin is splotched with sun marks and age. I thought, *one day he'll die, but he'll have had this.* And then turned it on myself: *One die I'll die, but I'll have had this.*

Not "had" because it was so meaningful a thing to cling to. It wasn't. But "had" because we were both doing it, we'd done it—whatever this "it" was—and it was a part of us and a part of our pasts forever now, like all the mundane and wild experiences: the chicken pox, the first dead pet, the best ice cream sundae. It happened and who will it ever matter to besides us? In a way it lasts forever and in another way it evaporates as it occurs. Who can doubt how entirely we will all be erased.

One of my clients invented a game in which we take turns telling the other one false thing and one true thing about ourselves, stories of our past experiences. We both love it—of course we do. It's picking pennies out of a fountain, remembering what the wishes were and then dropping them back into the water to continue their business of being forgotten.

He's my best client, in every sense of the word, which makes him the hardest to write about. He's the one who said once, "If the other men you see don't appreciate you as much as I do, they're a bunch of rotten fools."

With the cock-flexing client, I'd felt precarious the whole time it was happening. From the moment he laid back and made it clear I was to straddle him, I wanted to go completely away. Instead I gripped the tightly pleated curtain above the headboard with my fingers still wet from lube and felt almost pleased at making it dirty, which is unlike me. But immediately I felt I could picture all the other paid women before me who'd touched this fabric with their slippery hands, in this storied hotel in this massive city, women who'd liked it or not liked it and who eventually left the hotel room and then left the building, and gone home to their lives, and I felt so close to them that it lifted me. I don't think I've ever used the phrase before, but it lifted me up, it lifted me out. It sustained me for as long as it could in a tolerable place.

When I think of the man's house in the mountains, I realize how much the home is inside me now: the sense of the empty space inside the largest room, the way the light enters and leaves, even the contents of the pantry. How little it seems tied to the man who brought me there. It almost feels like only mine.

**Cathedral
May 29, 2013**

I knew he had money and I knew he was good-looking so I grudgingly allowed the date even though it was last minute and I was tired. The situation was so much worse than I'd thought: former military, PhD, beautiful wide shoulders, unforgettable jaw.

He asked me if I'd ever been in the Pentagon and I announced proudly, "I've had sex in the Pentagon."

He reminded me of a man who's important in the self-made mythology of my life, and I'd been thinking of that other man so much recently, the timing was uncanny. I'd hoped, with a small hope, that if I put the anguish of missing him into the world, we'd find each other again. Or maybe I would get someone close to him, a 2.0. Why don't I just call him who he is? Patrick. His name was Patrick.

As we stripped away the layers of clothing, the thought grew stronger in my head like an approaching drumbeat: *how could any woman not want to have sex with this man?* If I could have spared a moment, I might have lingered with the curiosity of what his wife is like.

He pinned my arm in a certain way while his hand moved between my legs and I was almost too amazed to appreciate it. I'd wanted something, someone, like this for so long, but I'd forgotten what it was like to keep wanting it in the moment, to be compelled to slide my face and my tongue and my abdomen over every part of him, to lick his cock until we were both delirious.

I bet I'll never see him again, I realized while letting my mouth linger on his neck and shoulders. I was fucking up and I couldn't stop it. I couldn't work and I couldn't be only myself; I was too confused by my need. He and I shouldn't have been meeting like this.

I kissed him everywhere I could. It used to comfort me to know that the moment was temporary, that the connection could last as a potent, bittersweet memory but the bitterness was too hard to endure this time.

It hurt so much. I used to be able to take it but now somehow couldn't get beyond it. He wanted me to come and we took turns rubbing with our hands but all I could feel was the pain, the blameless pain of his size. I'd been so richly wet after sucking him but then the condom scrubbed it all away and I tried to fantasize, to conjure up something that would help me get there for him, but my mind kept falling short. It was like trying to jump without letting my feet leave the ground.

And underneath the clutter of almost thoughts and the thick sawing sensation was a dread like the low, constant drone of a guitar. A panic of not being good enough. A sense of sheer futility, in this moment and beyond, in everything. I thought of all the ugly men I've come with, men I didn't particularly like or respect, who were balding and in bad shape. I felt how I was failing him and failing myself. I knew it might not matter anyway if it was already decided that we'd never meet again. But who makes the decisions? In my stupid, craven heart, I still believe in fate.

We fell apart. Neither of us had come but he said, "Thank you."

"You're not allowed to say that," I replied. We joined together again.

"Well, I did anyway," he said, with my head on his chest.

And then, "That was amazing," and though it didn't sound like an attempt to reassure me in the face of the opposite truth, the possibility that it could be a lie made it terrible to hear.

I stayed mostly quiet and touched him all over. It hadn't been romantic but it had been intimate. I wasn't sure if I'd enjoyed any of it and I knew he should have left almost an hour ago but I needed to wash him in tenderness for as long as I could.

He'd asked me why I was such a champion of a much-maligned city and I replied, "You know when something important happens to you somewhere, that city becomes important to you?"

And he asked me what had happened to me in that city and I said, "I fell in love."

I was so sloppy. Embarrassing myself, my soul spilling out like a drink in a drunk's swaying hand.

"You seem like a special person," I finally said. This is a hedged version of what clients tell me, and I detest hearing it and have never said it to anyone else. He asked me why I said that, or maybe he asked what it meant, but either way I said, "I don't know."

Now I do; I was trying to say he had become special to me, immediately, within the first moment of meeting. A key in a lock. Yet I was so full of that mounting desire, as most of my clients are, the desire that builds for months and cascades into desperation for a powerful connection, for dissolution into the reverie of what another person could mean to you in the most perfect world. Maybe he was only the nearest vessel for that outpouring and everything else is irrelevant.

Or it's the shadow of that—I had a crater of loneliness, and he fell inside.

He said he hoped he hadn't hurt me and I said he hadn't.

Then, thinking of his ego, I said, "Ask me tomorrow."

VOLUME
11

The nice thing about talking to someone famous is that his face is familiar, so you're not necessarily nervous. It's a little like running into someone from your high school, someone you never spent any time with but who you still recognize now and feel some affinity for.

I think I am still as clueless as I was in high school. If the front man in a band tells you the back of your jaw is sexy and asks where you got such "beautiful ivory skin" and where you got your dress, and your boots, and sits with you for hours and tells you where the band is staying but then just says, "It was a pleasure meeting you," at the end of the night, is this your cue to show up at the hotel naked? Does he just not want, as a married man, to ask you to come back and fuck him in front of his band mates? Would band mates care about that? Is he free with compliments because it doesn't matter how sexy your jaw is, he's who he is and there's no way you will ever feel superior?

I am worthless after an evening of flirting, if everything remains coy and implied. I just want a man to tell me what he wants so I can give it to him. Or not.

I saw a client today who likes wrestling, which means I was paid exorbitantly to sit on him while wearing a pair of short shorts and a sports bra. His favorite move is the schoolgirl pin, and he asks me execute this as close to his face as possible so that I'm ultimately straddling his throat. When he swallowed, I felt his Adam's apple roll against my pussy lips. His expression remained one of rapturous relaxation. He never takes off any of his clothes and when I ask him how he liked a particular move he normally just nods, smiling, and says, "Yeah . . . that was a good one."

How can I feel one moment like my mistakes are limitless and irreparable, then, in the next, as though I'm luckier than I could ever deserve? I suppose both can be true at once, and probably are.

N.B.

The wife was nervous. All the wives I've met have been, as are many of the men. I know that signals anticipation, investment. Some type of desire. The husband loved hair, not body hair but head hair, and the attendant grooming: combing, cutting, blowing dry. His wife would dial his number as she sat through a styling consultation and what he overheard drove him to hide in the bathroom at work, masturbating. He mentioned the youthful shame, now dissolved, and the ways in which his wife wore wigs, taunted during sex that she would get her hair cut without him, blew out his hair while he touched himself. She smiled. She was wonderful.

He was not the first man I've met with this proclivity. For an old client, I used to pretend to cut my hair, or wore a wig and cut that instead.

This work has its unpleasant moments, and even its outright terrible moments. But nothing—not the hours reading or writing poetry, not the nights curled against a man's burning body, not the heart-stretching sight of a still-foreign place bleeding larger and larger across the ground as the plane ascends—has so thoroughly instructed me in this truth: the world is ceaseless in its delights.

A year ago, I saw a pompous Persian author who became abusive when I refused to drink alcohol and partake sufficiently in his mediocre pot. (It was a serious screening failure, a moment of "I know better, but...")

Before he drove recklessly through the city while I boiled in my own venomous veneer of civility, before I was naked and squirting on his face, before he made his Bataille-esque proposal that I spend the summer in Monte Carlo seducing and debasing his wife — "She hates whores; they disgust her. She thinks she's better than you all. I want you to reduce her to depravity, and then we'll tell her what you are" — he reminisced about Madame Claude.

Inexcusably and inexplicably, I had never heard of Claude before. According to him, she worked as an agent during WWII, and eventually groomed other beautiful young woman to do the same. (They slept with officials to gather information to share with the Resistance.) After the war was over, she realized she could turn her endeavor into a proper prostitution ring and so she did, with unimaginable success. Movie stars worked for her — while they were stars, not before. He mentioned Sophia Loren specifically, and I've forgotten the others.

My client first found out about Claude's when he lived in Paris and regularly spent his nights out with one particular friend. This friend always had stunning women in tow, but my client never managed to get lucky with any of them. When he expressed his frustration, his friend replied, "Of course you don't. You don't pay them!"

My client was offended. He was young and charming. Surely he did not need to pay any woman for sex. But one morning, when he was leaving a hotel after partying all night with his friend, he saw Paul Newman in the lobby with his arm around one of their own (sometimes) party girls. "I said to myself right then," he told me, "if Paul Newman pays for it, then, dammit, I do too."

This man is also the one said that America would be a third world country within ten years. He had a very strong opinion as to the best brand of televisions. It was at least not a boring night.

There was a sweaty sheen of sunlight on his back as we laid in our warm bed. He told me he would give up ever having an orgasm again in exchange for giving me mine. But life is kind; it doesn't work that way.

A few weeks ago, I saw an unusually striking woman. She wore a fitted sheath, a short jacket, and fine mesh fishnets with Mary Jane heels. Everything—her clothing, her shoulder bag, her severe bob—was matte black. She looked at no one as she strode through the subway station straight to a taxi.

I'm not sure why I assume every fiercely attractive and confident woman I see is a sex worker. It may be wishful thinking (is that what I look like before a session?) or it could be that the recognition of sexual certainty otherwise confuses me. It's a quality I can't seem to retain outside of that particular realm. But other women probably come by their power more honestly, and it's contingent upon nothing but their own incontestable beauty.

There are only two times in my life when I feel invincible: going to and coming from an appointment.

I first listened to Gillian Welch when a friend in grad school made me a CD of her songs. This friend is an articulate artist who now works on the films of an old and well-respected director. She trafficked in all media even then: words, images, sound. We met because of poetry. It was what we both believed in at the time, though after school we drifted away from it through fear or anger or irresponsibility, or some combination. We were deeply unhappy at our particular institution, and we wandered the cold campus together pledging to leave if the other would.

On my first night out with her, she swayed dreamily to the opening act for Peaches (Electrocute, I can't believe I remember.) and asked if I'd ever dated a girl. I'd climb up the fire escape into her luminous bedroom, and she'd fret about not having vaginal orgasms with her long-distance boyfriend, or her high school girlfriend dating an older woman. Near the time of our graduation, we took a walk together. I acted like a bratty shit for the duration, but when we got home, she sat on the steps and hugged me. I refused attempts at mentoring from the poet who made her cry. She took pictures of me with an old camera that I eventually bought from her. I never used it and this summer I finally gave it away.

She told me sometimes when she sat down to write, all that came out were pieces of the lyrics to "I Dream A Highway." But the song's melody was so much more like her than were the song's lyrics.

We were halfway through the lobby before I noticed a table was overturned. I stared at it. I couldn't stop staring at it. I thought, *Couldn't that start a fire? Why hasn't someone rightened the lamp?* Then I realized there was no one at the check-in desk. There was no one anywhere. I didn't see bullet holes. I didn't see blood. There must have been blood. And bodies? I couldn't stop staring at the lamp.

I said aloud, "This is creepy." We were holding hands. I had nothing on me but jewelry and clothes. "It's like an apocalypse movie. Where is everyone?"

The young, thin Russian in the elevator with us said, "Um . . . " and tapped his watch. "Ten, ten minutes ago? Bom," he said. "Bomb?" we repeated, confused. He was asking us something we couldn't answer. I looked ahead through the doors. There was no one at the entrance, either.

We went outside and there were people standing back who gestured to us. There was a man in a purple shirt, a civilian, saying, "Come away from there!" ushering us into the street. I didn't understand, but he was speaking English. We said, "We need a taxi."

You're thinking: what morons. We laughed about it later, when we needed to laugh about something, anything: "They must have thought we were so stupid. Stupid Americans." But why would we think the truth? The reality is not what you imagine.

The man in the purple shirt said there had been a gunman. He said, "Didn't you hear the explosion?" We thought the first blast was a thunderclap, and I'd gone out to the balcony and thought, *but it's not raining*. The hotel security man, in his turban and tourist-pleasing tunic, said, "Just wait here," and "here" meant across the street.

My companion wasn't wearing his glasses. He didn't see the men with machine guns crouching feet away, running, looking at the facade. I turned, and turned him, and said, "Ok," and took his hand and began to walk towards the Gateway.

He said, "What?" He could barely see.

We made it to the rim. People stood on their boats in the sea, watching. A haggard German woman in a floral wrap dress clutched her elbows. A handsome local translated for us as people came back and forth. We sat on the stone bench and a gaunt, happy boy rubbed his arms and said something. "He says it's cold," the local told us. We smiled and agreed.

We heard an explosion to the right, far away and deeper into the city. There was nowhere to go. To the left was more of the Taj. And who knew what was to the right, on the darker side streets, except more chaos.

Civilians stood back, watching, or stood close and watched. Anyone could stand anywhere. There was a man in a red shirt taking pictures. After thirty minutes, more guests came running out. An Indian woman in pink was crying. I gingerly rubbed her back. She and her husband were waiting for a taxi when the shots started, and she thought he was running behind her but he wasn't. She hid in the bookstore with the others who had just come out. She mistook me for another girl, saying ". . . and then you came in."

A Japanese man let her use his phone. She called and called and found out her husband had been shot, and he was being taken to a hospital. An inexplicably jolly British man who also hid in the bookshop said he saw the glass panels shatter and thought, "oh, they're doing construction."

Minutes later, I thought I heard gunfire so I drew him off the bench to the ground, with our backs against the stone. I could tell he was irritated with me, he thought I was being stupid. But then there was another blast from the hotel and I put my arms around him, my hands over his eyes. Birds flew off the tower like pieces of debris, then settled back on the roof. There was another explosion inside. Glass sprayed out. We were all frozen, then we were all running. I was shaking. I couldn't help it.

Our local was still near us. My companion told him, "Please, we need to get here, where can we get a taxi?"

The happy boy was with us. "Be careful," I told him. I knew he didn't understand. "Someone tell him to be careful." I said to nobody. "You're just a little boy," to him.

The local man said he would take us, and we began walking through the side streets. "You have to give him money," I whispered to the man with me.

There were no cars. The homeless were sleeping, or awake and lying down, and people inside were gathered around TVs, metal gateways drawn down in front of shop doors. I tried to smile at the people sitting on the sidewalk. They all stared as we walked past. I didn't know what to do. I was wearing a black sweater, my skin so white it seemed fluorescent. I felt like everything was my fault.

He handed the local man money and the local man said nothing, put it in his pocket, then quietly drew it out again and fanned the bills so he could see the amount. Then he put it away.

Outside, there was a clot of people in white waiter uniforms. We gave them the name several times before they'd let us through. We invited the local man with us. I was still shaking. Upstairs, there was hugging and I almost collapsed. People kept offering me alcohol. They were laughing, oblivious. I sat down. A smiling man started talking to me about where I live back home. My muscles relaxed. Hours later, no one left was laughing. We turned off the lights and someone brought up projector. We watched the news without sound and passed around phones.

I began bleeding because I didn't have my birth control. Our crisis sex was a blowjob in a child's bed. What I want most now is chapstick and my laptop. We are possession-less and safe in Mumbai.

The best thing is finding something you've forgotten writing. There's a (possibly long) moment of did I *write* that? if it's good, or if it's very bad, . . . *did I write* that?

My laptop came back to me from Colaba still in sleep mode, just as it was left charging in the room. This was what was written in the open text edit window:

desperation of lonely men in airports; first class and business class almost always all men, faces lined from the wrinkles in packaged blankets pulled below their chins—

is it possible I want to be unhappy, or have I just grown to feel safety in it. If I can't feel anything else, shouldn't it be familiar? Should I welcome it?

And then this directly below, about having sex in the backseat of a car with a man whose cock was so big I bled for a day:

child's pose feeling him move in and out and I was making that ugly noise in my throat that comes on unbidden but then I start to enjoy it, enjoy the rasp and I start mimicking myself, squirming. (People passing nearby close enough so we could hear their laughter, even their conversation, lights coming and passing and staying, staying still, him, and him coming at me lips first, curving his spine like a silent film star, drawing me back under.)

Last night I had sex with a couple. They were both tan, dyed blond, with bland and predictable tattoos. Completely shaved, of course. He was tall with the corresponding big cock, lanky and fit. Just before we went to the bedroom, I recognized him from yoga class months ago. He practiced next to me once or twice, and I thought he was hot but we were/are of two very different aesthetics, so I didn't dwell on it. I'd forgotten how much "not my type" can be a turn on.

She was curvy and petite, with small pink nipples and an amazing ass. She had her hair in a ponytail the entire time. I loved her body. He obviously loved her body, too, but now there was some pale black-haired witch to bury his cock inside. And he did, over and over again. There was a very particular type of energy when he grabbed my hips, when he went from my cunt to my mouth. That charge of something new.

No matter what one might think of his overly cultivated physical appearance, holding out for three hours with two women is nothing to sneer at.

The blonde couple wants a repeat, or at least the man does. But I don't think it's going to happen. The look the girl gave me over his thigh after I deep-throated him was not a "hope you can join us again" look. He actually told me that people used to call him Ken Doll before he had facial hair.

When the three of us were sitting on the couch in our underwear, he picked up one of his two cats. There were lit candles, an empty bottle of red wine, and a box of animal crackers on the table in front of us. "How awesome is this cat?" He said, holding it upright under its armpits like it were a stuffed animal. It returned his gaze in a pained, tolerant way. He answered himself: "Pretty fucking awesome."

He started laughing immediately after he came, as always. My head was on his shoulder. I'd been sucking his right nipple.

"That's how I know it's really good." He said. "I didn't do that with the dancer."

"Well, thank you. I laugh too sometimes. Sometimes I cry."

"Yeah . . . I've never cried. That seems like more of a girl thing."

"I guess." I rolled onto my back and lifted my head so he could slide his arm underneath. Then, thinking aloud, "I've seen men cry after they come."

"Huh. The gay ones."

"Alright, Mr. Pot-Calling-The-Kettle, I think actually fucking another guy in the ass makes you slightly more gay than crying after you come."

He smiled, shook his head, muttering in the dark. "Gay."

We lay together. I had my palm on his neck, which was muscled and warm. I slid it up to his jaw, his solid fighting-dog face. Eight years in the Marines. I never would have known if he hadn't told me.

When I was three years old, my parents began their divorce. My brother and I became the core family unit because we were the only ones always together. I don't remember any of what it was like for all of us to live in the same house, only what it was like to be breaking apart, to sit confused in the car when my dad drove us home, James Taylor's cover of "Everyday" in the tape deck and me crying, telling my dad, "I hate the roller-coaster song." I actually wanted him to stay with us then. I wanted to be with him all the time.

It's easy to remember his wrong moments, things he said that should not have been said, what should have been said but wasn't. The good moments are packed aside until something sly pulls them out, like a song. He played records constantly, like CSN's "Our House," in the house he eventually bought after living with his mother for two years. I couldn't, as a little girl, understand what that would do a man's self-esteem, or how that would make him regard the people who were supposed to be his home.

And he played the piano when a record wasn't on. "Penny Lane" was my favorite because of "It's a clean machine." How could a line like that be in a song for grown ups? He put electric candles in the windows during Christmas time and he let us keep the cat who followed us home on the Halloween of our last minute hobo costumes, even though he was allergic.

Years after I moved away, on Valentine's Day, she died while at the vet's office for an operation. He likes telling the story of driving home with her body in a box in the passenger seat, sobbing, crying more than he did when his own mother passed away. He likes telling all sorts of stories, even ones that other people might not want to hear. He laughs about it now, incredulous: "I was so broken up about that cat."

I began sleeping with two ex-military men before I knew of their past. They look nothing alike but have some things in common: their attitude towards sex, maturity that's solid without seeming weary, a good sense of humor. That general air of trustworthiness. When I first worked at an agency I saw a very young enlistee several times. He was unfailing polite, milk-white and short, with a muscled, vulnerable body. I remember finding his orgasms incredibly sweet. He was within a year of my age and sometimes called me "Ma'am."

I never thought I would fetishize the armed forces—I'm too liberal, too unapologetically, tree hugging-ly liberal—and yet I ask to see old pictures, ask questions about rankings and boot camp. I see now what draws some women to those men besides the uniforms and discipline. I assumed that for most women being with some type of serviceman meant "this man is capable because he can hurt things. He will protect me by hurting the things that would hurt me."

But that's not it at all, at least not for me. Instead, I feel incredibly tender towards each of them, even maternal. *What a strange world you've been in, what strange things have been asked of you. I know you're strong but let's rest for a while.* They're not missing limbs or having night terrors, I know they weren't wounded in any obvious way, but it still seems to me that such a history of severity can be answered only with softness.

On the plane, in *Harper's*, I came across a transcript of the Mumbai terrorists' phone conversations. "We have three foreigners, including women from Singapore and China" one of the men said.

"Kill them," said the man on the other end.

This was in the hotel we stayed at during our first trip to India. When I first said, "I want to live here." And we walked by it in November with our friends and the beggar children following, fighting one another, cartwheeling and shoving in that muggy Mumbai air while the garish, metal-plated carriages passed by, bright green and red bulbs flashing, slow horses showing their ribs. My hands were covered in occasion-less mehendi. The sea was black and quiet. We caught a cab back to the Taj, and the next night the Taj was all destruction, but the mehendi lasted for weeks.

It was strange to be yanked back into that place of breath-holding, watching the news as much as our host family would tolerate, listening to the children celebrate their day off of school, crying at night, crying and not wanting to be touched. When I got home I showed the magazine to him, after he'd spanked me and held my mouth on his cock and came inside of me. I pulled on a sweatshirt and squatted at my suitcase, unpacking, leaking onto the hardwood floor while he read. I watched him from the corner of my eye. He winced just barely when he read the calls from Nariman House:

"Don't saddle yourself with the burden of the hostages. Immediately kill them."

"Yes, we shall do so, God willing."

Several years ago, a man paid to dominate me for four hours. It was an uncommon request. When he originally contacted me I was to be in charge, but somewhere in our correspondence he changed his mind. He paid for a pre-session a week in advance, during which we sat clothed in his apartment, chatting. He was in his late fifties and wore all black.

On the day of the long appointment, he fastened a beautiful wide fur-lined collar around my neck the moment after I stepped through the door. It was attached to a leash, and he held the leash high, near where it fastened to the collar, so it took minimal effort to pull my face forward. What followed involved a TENS unit, icy-hot, dildos, a paddle, tape, and a back massager. I don't think I cried, but I did fume. I came too many times to count, but it was meaningless. Like someone rattling a cage. Afterward, he insisted I eat some almond butter and drink carrot juice. It was the first time I'd had either.

I agreed to the session mostly to test myself, to see how I would handle the circumstances. I don't like pain and if someone is inflicting it upon me, I get incredibly angry. Even spanking was a learned taste, and it still has the potential to enrage me. Face slapping I abide only on request. My request.

As someone who grew up with a brother and spent years in high school thick in a clique of wild boys, I grew to fear the snap: that moment in men when what they'd begun in jest suddenly passed into something beyond reason or self-control. I'd provoked it accidentally during playful wrestling, seen others bring it about while drunk or pissed off and reckless. I realized my snap comes almost immediately after being hurt—pain need not be sustained or repeated—and while mine's not as intense as a man's, it lasts longer.

But, it's ok sometimes to be hurt by someone skilled. If they are confident and calm, you realize you won't truly be damaged. Their authority helps you admit the temporal nature of sensation. It's entirely different whether pain comes because someone doesn't realize how much they're hurting you, or knows but just doesn't care

---

It started when I shyly told the older man that I regularly peed in the shower. (I was shy about everything then.) Since we often showered together, it didn't take very long for us to pee on each other's legs as we stood together, and eventually he asked me to do it on his chest while he lay underneath me. It wasn't sexy to me, just playful and funny. But play made me curious, and later, with another man, I wanted to know what it tasted like. This curiosity came after he pissed on my face and some of it seeped through my closed lips. I was shocked, because what reached my tongue was like broth. It tasted good.

So one day this other man grabbed the back of my head and dragged me to the bathtub where he pushed me to my knees in front of him. We were both naked. He forced my mouth down on his cock and I sucked until he stopped me, before he was fully hard. He began pissing in my face and I laughed. So he yanked my head and angled the stream into my open mouth, but it just made me laugh harder. I couldn't stop laughing. I choked and coughed it up, then laughed and sputtered more as it kept coming. When he was finished, he drew my mouth back to his cock. My eyes were burning. Finally he pulled me up from my knees and made a move like he was about to kiss me. We swayed our faces inches away as though they were magnets of the same polarization or flowers dowsing at the sun.

"You can't do it, can you?" I said, triumphant. I could feel how unevenly wet my hair was, matted in parts, could smell the rivulets down my chest and stomach. It was sticky and half dry on my face.

"I can't do it!" He replied. He was laughing by then too.

One of the ex-military men told me he had no place in his life for me because I wasn't willing to date him. ("It may just be the new medication," he wrote, trying to bait me into calling him. Or it could be that he misunderstood our frequent fucking of other people to somehow be a sign of impending commitment to each other.) The not-a-Valentine's-Day-present was a Hermes bracelet. He told me not to lose it, which is just proof that he doesn't know me very well. I never misplace things.

I've been reluctant to schedule appointments and canceling some of the ones I have scheduled. When things are going well in other areas of my life, I feel less frenzied to bounce into that safety net. I want more time alone or alone in groups of people, working in the private way. I walked home in the dark from yoga, in a head kerchief and galoshes, ready to drink rain from the branches.

In practical terms, I want for nothing and owe no one my time or energy. I can't tell if that's a type of emptiness or a type of weightlessness. But the difference matters.

"It's braille," he said, fingertips on my raised nipple. "It says yes."
"Read it all," I said, pressing my breasts together.
He drew his finger over each peak. "Yes. Yes."

The single most astounding aspect of watching men with other working women is their degree of gullibility. My friend was not faking in an over-the-top, porn-style screaming way. But she was amping up to orgasms very quickly and then not doing much shaking or trembling to indicate coming. She'd simply say, "Wow, did you feel me come?" or let her preceding "You're going to make me come" do the work for her. She also did a funny thing that I've only seen from blondes: swear to indicate her pleasure's intensity. I don't mean that she was dirty talking, simply that she was saying, "Oh fuck," or "Fuck yeah," to encourage him, in an affected voice. Simpering, not whimpering, which would be hot.

But she's very hot. The mother of two children, though you would never guess from her body. She met her soon-to-be-ex-husband in church. She said sex was "a big deal" to her for a while, that she didn't even want to have it for a year of her life. She thought this actually made it easier for her to work now.

"They're just sticking this condom-covered . . . thing inside you and—I don't know." She was driving me home. Her eyelashes extensions were stark in the streetlights. "It's so sensation-less, you know? It's like I don't even feel anything."

I'd never thought to articulate it that way but there are times when my body dies down. There's no pleasure or pain, just a type of absence. I know some people want this admission to act as proof of trauma but it doesn't. It's more like distraction. Like your body isn't paying attention because it isn't all that interested.

She loves the work. I love my work. Sensation-less isn't bad. How many employees let their minds go blank during the work day, while standing in front of a copier or listening to a boss? It's ok that your body sometimes goes blank. "But with my boyfriend," she said, "I feel everything."

Most amusing of all was her dismounting line: "I can't believe how many times you just made me came!" Well. No other woman in the room can believe it, either.

I feel worn out. My mistakes are also often a test for those around me. That's the child's way, isn't it? By any means necessary, it will have what it wants: attention, excitement. My best friend described it perfectly once, the long view you have when doing something ultimately bad for you: "I'm about to make a really big mistake. Here I go . . . I'm gonna do it . . . Uh oh, I'm doing it!"

I ate nothing all day and walked around the city until I was exhausted. Took a class where the teacher ground down around the crunchy muscles of my neck and said, "A lot of stuff in here, my friend." I could only laugh at the pain. And laugh at the realization that again, resistance has melted into acceptance. I like this city now. I like the trees and confusing streets. I like all the men in suits. I like the frequency with which whole downtown blocks are shut down in the middle of the night and there will never be any news on why this occurred. I like Secret Service stopping pedestrians on the sidewalk to escort bland looking people I don't recognize into black limos.

I was thinking a lot about my favorite instructor, who was devastated by the death of her father. This is transparent in every mention of him. She's so cheerful but even her body holds this sorrow. I kept thinking of her to tell myself, this is not devastation. Or it could be a type of devastation, but not that of someone dying.

Devastation, I floated the word, pushed it out in my brain, while stomping along in the sunlight. *Opportunity*, I offered instead, looking down into a blooming flowerbed. The sun shone all day long.

When I'm most in need, I feel deeply alone. Even more than alone, I feel abandoned. I feel the people who should be there for me are unavailable or unwilling to listen or offer advice. Of course, I'm the one who should be there for me. I'm the one failing. We're taught that other people should take care of our hearts, but it's no one else's job. That whole romantic trope of, "I'm giving you my heart, take good care of it please," is so destructive. Your heart shouldn't be a burden to those you love. You should show them your strong heart to make them stronger.

On Sunday, I did an hour-long group meditation with a man who instructed us to picture ourselves in a library of our own self-image with a fire in the center. My room had no door, was made of dark wood and all the books in it were old hardcovers, pre-dust jackets, blue and red like encyclopedias. Many were slim but some were thick. None of them had titles on the spines. I tried to think of what they each would be. "Impatient?" "Loyal?"

"Pull some of the negative ones," he said. "And put them in the fire."

I was hesitant. I wondered if putting them in the fire meant not working to change them. I thought "selfish" shouldn't be discarded if it's accurate. It should be burned away the hard, long, earnest way, like being baked to a crisp in the sun. Through effort. But I wasn't getting it. What is the highest life worth to you? What are you willing to give up?

"Now pull some of the positive ones," he said. I kept my eyes closed. I felt like I could keep my eyes closed forever. "Put those in the fire, too."

N.B.

After the double, as usually happens when I spend time touching a naked girl, I kept thinking about the extraordinary quality of my friend's skin. Even though her body is tight and toned (no cellulite, no love handles, but not ropey or aggressively athletic) there was a give to the surface. A plumpness, actually, like that of tree fruit. And she was dressed impeccably in a pearls and a black bandage dress. I'm so easily fascinated by seamless femininity. For whatever reason—my impatience, ignorance, insecurity—I can't fathom having the skills or wherewithal to look that flawless.

I don't know how any client couldn't love her, even as she spoke transparently about her boyfriend or paused during her pelvic rocking to try to remember the name of a movie. At one point, while I was working a glass dildo in and out of her, she said, "Oh, we forgot all about this little guy. He's just hanging out here, like 'hel-lo,'" and she tapped the man's half limp penis on her arm as if it were knocking at a door.

When I was younger, after a particularly irresponsible and binge-y month, my mother threatened to kick me out of the house. This wasn't a dramatic, howling encounter. Just more of a "get it together" wake-up call. It entailed her expounding on where she might have failed in providing me with whatever parenting renders a daughter disinterested in cocaine.

At one point she said, "I realized I never tell you or your brother that I'm proud of you. Growing up in the Midwest, that wasn't something we said to each other. It would never feel right to me to say I'm proud of you because your accomplishments are your own. You can be proud of you, but . . . I shouldn't be taking credit."

I started crying almost immediately. It wasn't a gambit for forgiveness or tenderness. I hated her seeing me cry and we were never tender with each other. It was unintentional and abrupt, a kick and a seize, the same experience as that of reaching the last moment in a poem in which the lines latch together to make something perfect and complete and sensible. And you never saw it coming.

I've been thinking through the effects of ending a long-term relationship. I try to imagine what it would be like to be apart, to become strangers, to someday feel nothing for each other. I wonder if we'd manage to stay friends—he says, no—and in my daydreamy way I recently imagined him still offering me a particular opportunity with the explanation, "I believe in you." Not in the context of this specific project or goal, not "I believe in your abilities," or "I believe in your talent." But "I believe in who you are. I believe in who you will become."

I tried to think of the last time someone had told me that. Then I tried to think of someone I could tell it to, and mean it.

In *The Edge of Heaven*, a young Turkish man recounts the story of Allah's command that Ibrahim sacrifice his son. The older German woman who is his audience immediately recognizes it as the Christian tale of Abraham.

"We have the same story," she says lightly, surprised and heartened. But it's not a political moment; the man ignores her.

"I was haunted by that tale as a boy," he says. "And I asked my father what he would do if the same were demanded of him." The man pauses. He has been failed in many ways by his father. "He said he would make even God himself his enemy in order to protect me."

In *The Joy Luck Club*, a daughter cleans up after a dinner party with her mother. Their time together quickly dissolves into accusations.

"You don't see me," the daughter says. She feels inferior to the children of her mother's friends, less pretty and less accomplished, and she believes her mother hates her for this.

The mother, shocked, replies, "Everyone at the table wanted the best crab. Waverly takes the best crab. But you? You take the worst crab. Because you have the best heart."

In these scenes, all the characters are crying. When I recall these moments, I feel like I could cry. How can it be that finding out we're loved fiercely is somehow more unbearable than believing we were barely loved at all?

One particularly client gets me incredibly hot. He's a little goofy-looking, young and earnest, tall. He recently found out his wife had been cheating on him with a work colleague (of his) for virtually their entire marriage. They have a toddler, a boy.

He had a cuckold fantasy before he found out about his wife's affair. Part of what hurts him is that he wasn't even able to enjoy it. He wonders how many times he fucked her after she'd been with the other man without knowing that she had. There's no enjoyment without knowing. And when he asks her about the other man now—"Was he better than me? Was he bigger?"—she says, "No, no," and won't talk about it more. But this isn't the answer he wants to hear.

He cautions each time that he may be too vulnerable to play the way we usually do, yet inevitably he asks me questions about how many men I've had sex with in a day, if I knew when I fucked the first that there'd be a second, the recounting gives way to the game. He asks me where I've been, why I'm late. I say I was at a bar and ended up flirting with two men until I finally let one screw me in his car in the alley.

"You didn't waste any time," he whispers.

"Well, I had to get to the second guy before coming home to you," I reply.

His cock is perfect: long, thick, pretty. Big enough to make it laughable when I talk about how other men do a better job of filling me.

"I was such a fool to think I could satisfy you," he murmurs, palm against my slit. Every touch is right. He makes me so wet he doesn't even need lube to finger my asshole—"See?" I say. "His come is still leaking out of me"—but no matter how much he begs me, I don't let him slide his amazing cock inside. I keep telling him he's not good enough, he's always bored me, the most he could hope for is to watch me with someone else someday—and then he comes shuddering under my hand, against my stomach, breathing: "Look at you. Of course you needed others. I'm such a fool. Of course."

I've yet to figure out—I'll never figure out—why men who like feet are so deeply ashamed. "This has been thirty years in the making," he told me. He'd never kissed a foot before. (I thought, *not even as a joke? Why not just grab a girlfriend's foot?* Like I don't know about shame, what it allows and what it denies.)

So now he kissed, licked, sucked for hours. The look on his face wasn't ecstasy. It was almost an expression of exhaustion. He came. We sat on his bed and listened to the sound of water running.

"You have a fountain?" I asked.

"Oh no, it's these classroom turtles," he said. He was looking after them for a friend, a teacher on vacation. "I don't know that I'm doing a good job of taking care of them. Am I supposed to let them out? I don't want one to get away."

"Classroom turtles!" I loved the phrase. "Can I see them? I can't remember the last time . . . "

In the next room, they bobbed in the water of their tank, scrambling back and forth against the glass, eager as dogs. I wanted to take them out and play but didn't ask. He gave me a generous tip. I walked down the road a bit, then sat on a slide in an empty elementary school playground and waited for a cab. It rained lightly and no one noticed me. The sky stayed resolutely gray, like it were trying to teach a lesson.

A man was walking his dog with a torso harness, a nylon hammock that the dog leaned into heavily. Even with the extra lift, the dog—a collie mix—sagged to the left as though being blown by a strong wind. There were crisps of blood on the fur of her front legs. She had that unique look of confusion that belongs to domesticated animals in pain: *I'm trying to do something hard. I want to trust you but I'm scared.* It was strange to see that happening in a sidewalk's shade on a sunny day, with so many small flowers and playing children nearby.

I'm always amazed by those who deny the inner life of other mammals. Of course we anthropomorphize extravagantly, concoct ridiculous stories about how they reason or what they think, give them the personality of an evil genius or a Southern belle. But if you spend any time around animals, you immediately realize what distinct personalities they possess, how capable they are of acting out of something beyond need or instinct, even if —especially if—their behavior is sometimes as inexplicable as our own.

My grandfather died this morning. We were told he had weeks but he really only had hours. It's hard for me only because it's hard for my mom, whom I love and worry for. He was my last living grandparent.

I worked anyway. I got my hair cut. I over-tipped one taxi driver and under-tipped another one. I thought about how terrifying it will be when my father dies because I'll either be full of regrets or feel nothing, and both are equally horrible.

The client I saw was someone new to me, a delicate elderly man with a face like an open sandwich. I don't know what that means, but it's what I kept thinking. He was incredibly gentle, and I had a long, perfect orgasm under his fingers while he held a glass dildo in me with his other hand. We talked about Buenos Aires and he told me he shared my aversion to leather and regularly reads *New York Times* obits because it's a great way to learn things you'd never otherwise know. He kept calling me a lovely girl and saying, "Charlotte, you've got to a put a picture of this smile on your website. That smile is just killer. A thousand watts."

When I'm working, I look in the mirror more times in one day than I do in a regular week. And every time I do, I make faces at myself. I puff my cheeks and flair my nostrils, like I'm signaling: *I know, Clown Face. I know that's not the normal you.* I don't just look at myself, I stare. I lean my weight on my wrists and rest my palms on the bathroom counter, and swing my body from side to side while I twist my lips. I talk to myself very quietly.

Today, I touched my first two fingers to the fine smiles lines at the left of my lips and thought, *You're not a baby anymore*. It was one of those hyper-self-conscious, affected moments in which you're not sure whether you're behaving in an authentic way or if you're just imitating something you think a movie character might do.

I get a lot of men who want me to dominate them. The new client mentioned this to me and said he didn't see me in that role because my touch was too tender.

"Well, rough is not my default mode," I said. I was sitting on his chest and twisting his nipples. He was looking into my eyes.

"I know what your default is," he said. "I can see it behind that smile."

It was an accident that I saw him again. He was one of my earliest clients when I was with the agency and he had terrified me. He'd pinned me to a wall, moved in weird, abrupt ways, made ugly sounds. I told my agent I didn't ever want to see him again but she pushed it. She set us up again, claiming it was a mistake. She told me he asked about me for months. And I know he did because he mentioned me to the other girls, talked about me on message boards. Not outwardly malicious but plaintive: *why won't she see me, what did I do wrong, give her this message, do you have her email address?*

If he recognized me this time, he didn't let on. I knew his face was familiar when I opened the door and there was an instant when I thought, it could even be—but I pushed it away. I told myself so many of these men look the same, I wasn't sure I'd ever even met him before. But it was him, and I had, almost four years ago.

It's easy now to ask why I didn't just end it as soon as I knew for sure. Why didn't I leave? I'm not sure if the truth is that I didn't trust myself to remember right, or if I wanted to see if he was different now or if I were different now. But all of that was a mistake.

I prayed for an orgasm, just one moment of escape, no matter how much I hated him or how vile I would feel, but it didn't come. I whimpered at one point and he said, "That's right, cry a little."

I went to dinner that night and sat across from my date, looking normal and feeling strange. He talked about Kabul, then about a court tennis pro, and as he spoke a dense spindle of pain shot up through the center of my chest like a lightening bolt. It faded, then flared back again. I felt the focus go out of my eyes.

I put my palm on my bare collarbone and held it there flat like I was bracing my whole body. He asked if I was ok. I blinked tears back. I said yes.

Sometimes my work is uncomplicated. There are no violations, no emotional entanglements, no struggle. So what am I supposed to write about? The myth of the suffering artist exists because ease seems silly, accidental, insubstantial. It's a state difficult to depict because it doesn't demand a description. There's no urgency to understanding or rendering pleasance. It just buoys you with lightness.

What should I say about sitting outside on a mellow warm night, listening to teenage tourists exclaim about the "really frickin' nice" hotel and scurrying around the sidewalk craning their heads for more secret service, before going upstairs to have a hyper millionaire suck my toes and tell me, after he's come, that I "have the prettiest face in the world?" It's fun. It's easy. It's ridiculous and sweet. I do not actually have the prettiest face in the world. I think he just liked my expression when I alternated between stroking his cock and snapping the clothespins on his scrotum.

It's strange to remember his influence and wealth while he's kneeling in front of me with his erection dripping pre-come on the carpet. He says regularly ranking as one of the country's most highly compensated CEOs is boring, and who am I to disagree? I'm not a CEO and never will be a CEO and yet my job is often an awful lot of excitement.

I keep a journal where I track what poses are irritating me or invigorating me and I try to write in a way that replicates my thought process when practicing that day. This means there are a lot of "fucking revolved triangle" and "fucking kukkutasana!!!" When I'm excited about something, the note is even dorkier. Today I wrote "headstand splits drop back to wheel—what a thrill!" That pretty much sums it up.

I'm at a retreat. This wasn't something planned in light of the pregnancy/abortion—I signed up for it weeks ago. One of the women assisting the instructor recently gave birth, and she's often ambling in the halls, holding her quiet baby. At the end of one session, she was pressing tissues over each breast because milk leaked through her bra and tank top.

I went to a class separate from the main schedule during which the teacher touched me lightly up and down my spine during child's pose. I'd been irritated with his style until that point, but once he did that I thought, *Oh, he's a nice person.* In savasana he said: "If there's anything you're holding on to, anything you're lingering on . . . just drop it. Be a good corpse and let it go."

The night I found out, I did yoga alone in an empty and dim gym studio. Everything felt "delicious," as they say, like my blood was thick with energy and I was aware of it circulating through every part of my body. When I'm having a deep yoga-love moment, I respond to nonexistent ultimatums: *I would have this baby if not having it meant I could never do yoga again.*

I didn't feel sentimental or suddenly in the company of another human being secreted around inside me. I felt powerful and singular, like there was more of myself to draw from. Later, I had a fit of being frustrated and angry with my body for betraying me, but it was short-lived. Conception is still fundamentally a pretty amazing thing. It's stupid to try to pretend it isn't special, to act like it's mundane and not miraculous to have this event trying to happen inside my body.

Mostly I just wanted to be around other women; I felt so close to my friends who have had abortions even though nothing had happened for me yet. When I called one and told her this, she said, "Welcome to the sisterhood."

The next morning I took a class that included a lot of instructors, so the woman leading let her impulses run wild. We chanted at the beginning, which is not something I'm particularly invested in, but I felt weightless and like my torso was very short, as though my head was sitting just above my pelvis and my spine had evaporated. She had us all make up a mantra. I imagined a glow in the center of my chest, then that same glow simultaneously in my low belly, like, *Ok, you too*. I thought for a moment I might cry, not because I was imagining some other person there but because it felt like agreeing to love some unlovable part of myself, like forgiving myself.

Then we whispered our own mantra to the person next to us, but in the second person. The woman to my right said, "You are peaceful." I whispered to the woman on my left, "You are strong."

I had the most amazing orgasm the other day. I know I recently disavowed my interest in orgasms, and it's still true that the idea of one, the goal of one, doesn't hold a lot of sway over me. But this was so lovely, so long, strong but gentle with no sharp edges or hard peaks. I used to think of this as a "sunny come," where there's no effort to make it happen, no straining or frantic fantasizing or any thought of any kind, just the swell of sensation. It's been a long time since I had one.

It's strange to be sentimental about one moment with no narrative to define it but at the same time it seems like the only thing worth being sentimental about, not the pleasure but the absence of everything, including the pleasure. The pleasure becomes the eraser, the means by which you're emptied—or not emptied but raised to a point beyond which anything can reach you and you dissolve. But then you come back reassembled and clean, and life seems so good.

"I want you to lick my armpits," I told him. Sometime this weekend after I've showered.

"Ok."

"It turns me on."

"Does a client do it to you?"

"No . . . I do it to myself."

"Liar. I'm going to do it right now."

"No. After a shower."

He pinned my arm over my head. We fought a bit but he won out.

"You taste good," he said as he pulled his mouth away. There was that brothy smell of saliva mixing with sweat—salt and sour—on my skin and on his lips. I kissed him like I was going to hide the taste, ingest my body's evidence, moving from the same impulse that has me suck a client's fingers immediately after they've finger me when I'm on my period.

We kissed for minutes but the smell was there like a gauze. Eventually I don't think either of us minded.

I met her for tea in public after an email correspondence. She had hummingbird energy, flightiness tempered by friendliness. She was looking at books on erectile dysfunction since so many of her clients are "mature."

This happened before the appointment, to calm her nerves; she'd never been with a woman before. Luckily, my client didn't require much of us. The bulk of our non-talking time was spent prancing and posing and admiring each others' bodies on his cue.

The only truly interesting moment of the whole morning occurred as she kneeled in front of me on the bed, legs spread, and I stroked her very gently with the long end of the Feeldoe. The client sidled up beside her and put two fingers on her clit. She closed her eyes and leaned her head against his, slowly lolling it there. Only seconds later, she barely whispered, "I'm coming" and then she did, quietly. Just before her very slight shudders, her labia swelled and bowed open like a flower unfurling in a time-elapse video.

I've never seen a more beautiful orgasm in my life. I wanted to tell her how sexy it was but I didn't want to make her self-conscious. We exchanged our real contact information and said goodbye in the lobby. Each of us reached out a tentative arm towards the other as though we would touch, but instead dropped our hands by our sides.

Every time I'm in an airport I practically quiver with the vision of the profits that could be generated. Restaurant after restaurant advertises vacant and rumpled men, alone and looking hollow, or sitting with coworkers at the bar and ordering 11am drinks. Travel at the right times, to and from the right places, and you'll see maybe one woman for every ten men. Ok, so an airport brothel is too much to ask. But what about an airport strip club? A peep show booth? Right between the Fox News store and the TGIFridays.

Rarely do these travelers look capable of genuine arousal or any type of interest in another human being. They live on sodas and snack food, shower with hard water and sleep on tight bleached sheets, see face after white middle-aged face that looks identical to their own. But trying for a turn-on would at least be familiar and distracting. My suspicion is that most would gladly pay to forget who they are, where they are and where they're going.

I finally watched *Unmistaken Child*. I wanted to see it around the time of my abortion but it had already left the theater—which was probably a kind coincidence. I assumed the Buddhist bereaved would be better internally prepared than any other human beings and that would translate to stoicism, even cheerfulness in spite of the absence. But Tenzin weeps in his master's retreat and I cried with him. His face is the clearest lake; you can see straight through to the bottom. His emotions are naked and whole.

And he is linguistically elegant. My favorite part of the whole movie, I think, was when he described his sense of being lost in the wake of Geshe-La's death as "almost like I want to give up many things." Yes. That is exactly how being lost inside yourself feels. And if that is what a dedicated, decades-long practitioner experiences, what hope do we amateurs have when it comes to our suffering?

"Please ask the High Lamas to search for him," another disciple says as one point, "so we can see him again." For the first time, I realized belief in reincarnation is a balm, a comfort for those scared raw not because they personally will experience life again (that, of course, is supposed to be almost a punishment) but because they will never be bodily parted from their spiritual peers while they are in this particular life. In other words, it's a version of impostor Anastasia coming home to Grandmother Romanov. Maybe the most revered, sedate Buddhists are strengthened not by making peace with the transitory nature of all things but rather endorsing the extraordinary promise that they will never be parted from their dear ones for long.

Once a child is recognized as a reincarnation, Tenzin asks the parents if they can bear to give him up for a life at the monastery, where he will be estranged from his family for years. The exquisite mother says "Yes, I can," and then she touches her fingertips to her lips—which people of almost all cultures do when they lie.

I had a dream that my old manager was trying to get me to take an appointment with a bear. She kept reassuring me that he was dorky and "loved strippers" I felt a look of horror freezing my face while she spoke. There was an alarm being sounded outside, a bear siren, warning people off the streets because he was free and on a rampage.

"Why are you making that expression?" she asked.

"Because he's a bear!" I said. But as the word flew from my mouth I understood he was just a man in a bear suit, living in a cave and playing a part. I was afraid of him nonetheless.

The turn of the year is a turbulent time for me. As winter burrows deeper into the city, I start getting riotous and wild, eager. Obstinate about getting what I want. Look at what happened early this year—I drowned myself in my own recklessness. I'm ready to do it again, in spite of the scare, in spite of the mellow moments, in spite of the grounding work I've been trying to do. *Lord, make me chaste, but not yet.* I day dream a lot. I stop reading in bed when I'm not yet at the edge of sleep, to leave a rim of time for fantasy before I fall away.

Sometimes I'm ready to delete everything here. Other times I upload a picture of my face and hover over the publish button and then close the window. I don't know what I'm doing or what I'm trying to do, here or in the world at large. All I know is that on some late nights, post-appointment, when I come home to my laptop and tea and ancient IKEA blanket, and I stay up typing and sifting and reading, figuring out what should appear here; the starving fire in my chest is quiet. So thank you for taking an interest in this, thank you for witnessing whatever it is. Though I feel like it shouldn't, your attention matters to me. Perhaps that is one thing I have in common with my clients.

When I was younger, my dad became a Mary Chapin Carpenter fan. He let me borrow his tape of *Come On Come On*. When I played it at home with my mom, she liked it so much she choreographed one of those late 80s aerobic dance routines to "Passionate Kisses." She had my brother and I come into our living room and sit on the carpet while she performed it for us in her pajamas. Even though she mothered with the intensity of a fierce feral cat, she was restless for larger things and always in a dance class or local tai chi group. She dropped out of grad school for the family that fell apart.

My mom dated very little and when she did, my father interfered in terrible ways. She lost her own mother when she was a child and played the role of single caretaker ever since. If she ever had a dream of finding a partner, she didn't show it. For years now, there is no man she would have. Sometimes when we are together I can feel the terrible matched love we have for one another, the unattained good life we each want for the other—desire so strong that it obscures reason, nearly eclipses sanity. She practically trembles from it. I keep things further from the surface.

What will I do when my mother is gone? In some way, I will be gone, the most sublime part of me left alone, huge and bereft. I worry I will become the maw rather than the thing around the maw, because the only person who held the other half of that part of me is no more.

I managed to be happy this week. My follow up HIV test was negative, given by the same nice guy who coached me through the murky results, and he remembered me. While I was sitting naked in a client's lap on the floor of his hotel room, hugging and stroking his back, he was breathing in my chest and biting my shoulder and losing himself in skin, and then "Passionate Kisses" came on his playlist.

We watched the last moments of the Super Bowl in a downtown art space wearing day-old yoga clothes, agog at the stupidity of the commercials, spotting small Ganeshas scattered in corners as we looped around the buffet and bar.

"It's a sign," Karyn said as we left.

"That we all have to get matching Ganesh tattoos," I confirmed.

"Right now," Mike added.

"Exactly. Because as [our teacher] says, life is short, and we could die tomorrow not having done it and then we'd have to come back because we had unfinished business. Still samsaric. Wah wah," I made the cartoon noise of failure.

That was the best part—making fun of our own clichéd earnestness with jokes about Dr. Bronner's and Sanskrit, essential oils and patchouli. We bent over laughing when Jacob began composing a letter to help Karyn overcome one of her habits. ("Dear Subconscious, I don't need to hear your shit right now.")

At one of the bars, Mike told me he used to strip, sometimes in my city. I'd gone to a male strip club for the first time only recently, a cavernous place where the dancers had impeccable bodies and large, Viagra-hard cocks windmill-ing with the continuous motion of their hips. (When I left, the doorman—a sweet, rather small young man wearing a necklace with a Buddha charm he'd acquired while stationed in Thailand—said, "Leaving so soon?"

"Yes," I said sadly, "but it was the coolest thing I've ever seen." And three giddy Asian men waiting in the line outside burst into cheers and gave me high fives.)

I thanked Mike for sharing that with me. He told me about some of the tough circumstances he'd been through around the same time he was working, and I told him that I knew I was a relative anomaly, very lucky because the lifestyle could be so difficult, and of how the girl I'd first befriended starting working when she was homeless and was now in rehab, how another was a former addict.

"But I learned a lot," he said. "I had moments where I was like, Wow, I'm seeing something no one ever gets to see. And some of my oldest clients are still my friends."

"That's how I feel!" I agreed. "Like I experience all sorts of situations most people don't even know exist. And that's a privilege."

I'd told Karyn what I did for work while she and I were crammed in the backseat of the car on our dark ride back, and the boys up front fell silent for a moment even though I'd spoken in a low voice.

"Suddenly they shut up," Karyn said.

"What's going on back there?" one of them asked.

"Nothing." I said. "Girl talk. You wouldn't be interested." And then loudly, "So I had my period, and I was like, 'Oh man, I'm bleeding all over the place *again*!'"

"Lalalala," Mike shouted, sticking his fingers in his ears.

And we drove on, near strangers with a common bond, potential friendships opening like seeds in the electric light of the city.

I've been thinking a lot about permanence and impermanence. Impermanence is the scary, tough idea, the one most people fear: losing money, a job, a friend, the love of a partner. We miss things we used to have and we pray to get them back.

But sometimes we pray for impermanence. We want to get over a cold, finish a long drive, be alleviated from our grief over a death. My understanding is that you remind yourself of this aspect in an effort to learn to love impermanence, and to see the grace in it. That's what I'm trying to do.

I had an awkward appointment with my favorite client. I don't know if you can trust me when I say that—he might seem more precious to me because of the newly precarious state of our relationship. He was having trouble staying hard with a condom on, and once he managed it, he came almost immediately inside me, from behind. He'd had a grueling week. He kept asking me if I was ok. The whole thing felt strange and I left not sure if we would see each other again.

So what did I want? I asked myself on the way home. *What did I think would happen? Would we stay in this perfect friendship forever? We'd keep enjoying each other's company and making each other laugh, never running out of things to talk about, getting each other off with our mouths, him always paying me and it never getting awkward, until one of us died?* I mean, that's honestly as good as it gets. That's the best scenario: one of us dies.

When I was back in my apartment, I checked my email. Often he writes me immediately after I leave. But this time he didn't.

Permanence is less scary. We don't have to deal with it because it doesn't exist.

In the middle of fucking me, a client asked, "What are we going to name our child?" I said "boy or girl?" He said both. I said Thomas and Charlotte, neither of which is a name I like very much. It was our first session. He asked me to sing him something so I sang "Eternal Flame" while next to him, nude and stretched out on my side, and he seemed overwhelmed. In response, he sang "O Sole Mio."

Wow, how special, right? How kooky and cool and unusual. And it is special. It's really special, and there were other elements that made it even more bizarre but I'll try to exercise a bit of discretion by keeping those to myself.

He also wanted me to snowball his massive load. He wanted to drink my pee straight from my cunt and he wanted me to kiss him afterward and when I didn't, he fell into a sour mood. Overall, I hated the whole ordeal.

I don't truly know what my point is. I think I want everyone to shut up about sex work because everything I hear seems thoughtless and shallow, or true, but repetitive and uninteresting. I know strippers, escorts, dommes—everyone—keep saying the same things because they feel like no one is listening but as someone who does listen and has been for a long time, I want all the chatter to stop. I'm fed up with it.

I still love people who are telling their truths in a matter-of-fact way, and their truth just happens to be about some type of sexual service for money. But I'm entirely over this "listen to my whacky sex work tale because I AM SO UNIQUE and it is SO INTERESTING." And I think I'm going to put a moratorium on telling any work stories for a while because the thought that I'm piling more garbage on this rhetorical heap makes me really disappointed in myself.

I finally realized: they want to fall in love. Once this intention is set, you would have to be actively unpleasant to deter it. There is nothing I'm doing to make it happen. I'm not calling love to me like it's a metal filament to my magnet. I can make my skin soft, smell clean, be kind, or do nothing. Either way, I will be loved.

So I don't matter. I truly don't matter. I just have to show up and be warm. The more non-existent my ego, the more fully I will be their refuge.

At the museum, we lingered in the gift shop over a 3-D puzzle from the children's section.

"I feel like I should be accomplishing something, but I don't understand what that is," I said, my fingertips pushing the primary-colored plastic.

"Is this in response to the toy or just . . . ?" He asked.

We both started laughing.

"That pretty much sums it up about my life in general," I said.

And I felt happy, like we were friends.

They tell me outrageous anecdotes that I scribble down later in the bathroom. They talk about their wives and both of us are uncomfortable. We trade books. We trade music. We trade massages

"You're not hot," one of them says.

"I know that," I say.

"You're stunningly beautiful, but it's not the same thing."

I let the hyperbole be, because it pleases them.

"You're my escourtesan," one says, and I laugh. "You're my time-share mistress. I want in a time-share in you. How does that make you feel?"

"Fine," I say.

We go shopping. I get close to coming but I don't. I come close again, over and over, but I try to save it so it happens just the way I want it to, which means it never happens, and eventually the urge fades away.

Sometimes they can't get very hard. Sometimes they can't come. Sometimes they come right away and then they get up to eat something and I'm allowed to leave. I feel proud if I make them laugh with surprise, particularly if it happens at dinner. Then I know good things will keep happening.

They touch me too much and I start to feel angry. I have to route my body's instincts into something else, convert what wanted to be a push into a pull or a stroke. I keep feeling angry and I remind myself that it will end soon and I won't even remember the offending sensations. When we're face-to-face and it's stopped, I think, *It's not his fault.* Then we go back to doing what we were doing, or else I get dressed and go.

If you're wondering what I have been doing, the answer is reading. It feels regressive and pure, like a triumph of myself over myself, like a glorious paring down. How good to choose to read instead of doing anything else.

Sometimes I come across a line that shovels a million memories into my brain. Even a few simple words like "brilliant, bracing sunlight" can reel me back to the summer-seeping-out-of-fall semester of grad school, wind rolling like water through and over my body, and the sidewalks' cold sunshine like the light of Heaven—it feels so long since I've felt that, how can it have been so long?

I remembered the other day that the older man used to tell me stories about he and I meeting while he was in college, daydreams of us the same age and him pursuing me ravenously, the two of us fucking in the library stacks and dancing at his favorite hang out. I'd prompt him to do it: tell me a story.

So many times we stayed in bed like tranquilized animals for the whole day, gazing out at the mountains, frying potatoes in his black pan and, at dark, chasing night spiders away. Now when he visits my dreams, I inevitably crawl into the sheets but then crawl out, thinking, "I don't have to have sex with you anymore."

You see how then, to fuck him, part of me fantasized he was my peer: his hair thick and black and perfect, his heart alert and tender. The boy of my dreams. The only picture I have of him, that I've ever had of him, was a reproduction of one taken while he was in college. I begged him for it, then framed it and kept it on my nightstand. But he was not my peer, he was more like my father, and he played the part by making up bedtime stories in which I was the star.

I had an exhausting night with a client who keeps intimating he's got some deep dark secret that he can't tell me until we start seeing each other on a non-paid basis. (I'm guessing it's a) a wife, b) kids, or c) both.) I fell asleep for about an hour but kept talking. That's a talent I perfected when I worked for the agency. The only real effort it requires is self-censorship—quashing the urge to say something related to the plate of squirming fish or the two mystery doors, or whatever else I'm seeing in my half dream.

I waffled between resolving to never see him again, or retiring, or both. Not really retiring, just retiring for a few weeks, which is what normal people call a vacation, right? Or being between jobs. He bought me a pile of books. It's all very oppressive.

I don't think my once-private parts can take anymore touching. If a person puts his hand on my breast, my impulse goes beyond violence. Anger's not complicated enough to convey what comes up. Maybe fatigue is closer? Imagine you've just landed from a fifteen hour flight in coach and now a stranger wants to paw your genitals, but it's like that all the time. At some point, even aggression starts seeming too dignified a response. Then the only available reaction is bawling.

The other day on the subway platform, a crazy man shouted at the ceiling. I took off my shirt and began folding it. "Move your hand," he yelled in my general direction. "You, move your hand!" There was a woman to my right and a young man to my left but their bodies were still. I ignored him and put the shirt away in my bag. "Yeah, show me them tits," he growled as I did, as if I were cowering, like my tits were my request for his mercy. I was wearing a tank top; I was on my way to teach yoga.

I think my life could easily be sectioned into stages that last several months to just under a year: the Pious period, the Deeply Depressed period, the Giddy period. Some of them are reoccurring. The Running Around period, the Popular period, the Sweet Like I'll Never Be Sweet Again period. This is not a time in my life when I feel sparkly. I'm worried I'm entering the Grind period. So the other impossible assignment right now is listening to someone talk about how beautiful I am, or how special.

I'm not beautiful or special. I just want my own bed, my own bathroom, and my own body.

The way you move your finger when fishing for a coin in a return slot—that was how he used his tongue. He came at me with his mouth open and that meaty tongue slashing side to side like a lizard's tail. After a certain point, you lose the privilege of calling it kissing. After a certain point, it is simply something terrible your mouth is doing to another person.

He tied his ropes like someone who had no idea what he was doing. He lashed my wrists together to the bed frame and I released myself when he wasn't paying attention, keeping the loose loops hidden in my fists. He asked me for my real name. He asked me where I went to school, all of them: elementary, high, college. He asked me where I live and what I did for work. I was evasive, then lied with a vocal eye roll.

It's been a very long time since I've been around someone as horrible as him. I thought about saying, "Get off of me. I'm leaving." I felt a mild tide of panic lapping me. I worried that was what he wanted me to say. So instead I said, "You've very unusual." It was mostly a wish. When he asked me to explain how so, I said, "We don't have the time."

"Sit on my cock," he told me, after he fucked me and took his condom off. He lay on his back propped on some pillows. His mouth had the odor of cigarettes and gin. Repulsive. I looked at his face and thought of how sad all of his sexual experiences must have been, and how sad they still are. It was not quite compassion but it was the best I could do.

"Spit on your cock?" I said, deliberately.

"Sit on it."

"No."

"Good girl." He closed his eyes.

"You have to come now," I told him, calling him by his name. He came. I don't know what any of it meant. I washed my hands. I went towards my clothes immediately.

"What were you doing all those times when you kept getting up?" I asked even though I knew what he was doing because there had been space to see through the terrycloth tie he'd wrapped around my eyes, and because I hear well.

"Going through your bag," he said.

"I can't believe it took you so long," I said. I carry almost nothing with me.

"I looked everywhere," he said. He replaced my work phone, which he'd scrolled through inconsequentially. There are only a slew of male first names. My real phone is password protected. "There's nothing about you in there."

I stared at him, my dress around my forearms. "You must think I'm incredibly stupid," I said.

"I don't think that at all," he said. "But you know everything about me."

"That's true," I said. "And none of it matters to me." What I meant was, You don't matter to me.

This is what I thought when I became afraid: *I'm the one bound naked. I'm the one under a blindfold. He had to drink before we met. His wrists and eyes are free but his heart is racing.*

Someone wrote me an email asking, "So what are the tricks to not being repulsed?" I don't know. I don't know any tricks. You just ignore it, I guess. You tell yourself it will be over soon and then it is. That's the best lesson to learn: it will always end. I find it harder to tolerate some of what they say more than what they do. Like, "You loved that, I could tell."

I've been lucky because I've seen so many men I'm attracted to. They wear nice suits. They're trim. They're tall. I like looking at them and being touched by them. Once upon a time the only type of guy who could turn my eye was a rail thin hipster with shaggy hair. Now my gaze settles solely on the buttoned down. I fantasize about military men. Osmotic fascism.

Maybe that's the trick: reprogramming.

I managed to track down a man from my past. It wasn't easy, because I couldn't remember his name. But with the internet, it is never particularly hard to find anyone. When I told him who I was, he said, "holy shit. I used to have such a crush on you." It was so good of him to say that. It means he remembers me like I remember him. He said, 'I can't believe how we flirted." Meaning, look how we're still flirting now.

When I was growing up, my father often said he loved us, but my mother didn't. She barely even whispers it now; she drags out phone conversations and then bulldozes it out at the end, almost comically, almost like she doesn't quite want me to hear it, like she's ashamed. I think she didn't hear it when she was growing up. So there only certain situations in which I can voice what someone means to me, because I've had very little practice. When I'm barely awake sometimes it comes over me like a wave and I cling against my boyfriend in our morning bed and breathe, "Oh, I love you," like he's going off to war. Only with animals can such sentiments be delivered soberly. "You're so special," I sometimes tell them when I am overwhelmed with gratitude. "You mean a lot to me."

Once I taught Pilates to an older woman who, at the end of it, hugged me for no apparent reason. I do not have trouble evincing warmth with strangers and evoking their effusive response.

But I spend a great deal of time alone, and I think I always will.

I have been sexually heedless with myself. I have been careful with the men who paid me and inexcusably careless with those who don't. Now I begin the project of changing that.

I want to visit R, the man whose name I forgot but whose impact I never will. I imagine there will be silk between us. It will be all sunshine, even if it rains, even during the night. I daydream myself finally nude in that pool, any pool, my hands on his head and my legs ringing his waist and we're kissing and it's the best kiss I've tasted in a long time, and it's so sweet because we waited. We waited years for this.

Tired of this absurd US Open tan. Tired of smelling men and smelling like a man. I look in the mirror at the pink halo over my collarbones and breasts where I didn't smooth on enough sunscreen at the rim of my shirt. I ask myself, *What now?*

How is this sex apathy not seeping through my skin and poisoning them? Am I very good? Or was there never any need to be good, only the need to be present?

I keep remembering or misremembering some passage from a Pema Chodron book to the effect of, "Wanting every experience to affirm and congratulate you is akin to wanting death." I feel like a victim of my own ego, like I am suffering from locked-in syndrome of the psyche: I can see the petty grasping that drives so many of my habits yet am powerless to stop it.

I planned to write about the realization that I sought out this job in part because it permitted and encouraged my physical insecurity, requiring as it does my being displayed and evoking pleasure through appearance.

I threw up scantly in the bathroom and remembered how hard I had to work when I was sixteen to teach myself to vomit. It never happened without coaxing, without deep digging on the fingers, due to the lack of a gag reflex that would later become a selling point. Although if you do it often enough with enough concentrated will, you can almost make it happen without any touch.

While with a particularly sentimental client, I thought, Your pain feels romantic to you but it only annoys other people. Of course I was addressing myself as well.

True/False:

Interesting things happen to all sorts of people, including the ones with boring personalities, but do not happen to me. At least not without a lot of effort on my part and sometimes drugs.

I have a poorly defined sense of "interesting."

All my fondest memories are losing their power, like masturbation fantasies used too many times.

I am only (romantically and platonically) compatible with a precise subset of human beings who present themselves on the rarest of occasions but instantly become beloved.

I make no effort to become friends with people who are not those mentioned above. (Those mentioned above require no effort.)

Recognizing that I am designed to spend most of my time alone is the result of successful self-inquiry.

Telling myself that I am designed to spend most of my time alone is a sign of self-indulgence.

Thinking, *I am supposed to spend most of my time alone, for the rest of my life, in order to function,* is grounds for entering therapy.

It is normal to find most human interaction shallow and predictable.

It is normal to be envious that such interaction comes easily to others but is quite hard for me.

Such interaction is actually not that hard for me, but I feel automated and false while engaging in it.

I am hurt by news of other people doing certain things (going to parties with celebrities) or possessing certain qualities ("sexy") that I feel are not accessible to me, even when I do not want to be or do those things, anyway, because they have never made me happy.

I believe everyone feels the same way I do.

I suspect no one else feels the way I do.

We went to his house after the opera and in the full lights of the bedroom I noticed my dress fuzzed white.

"Oh, there's lint all over me," I said, reaching behind myself to unzip.

"I know, sweetie. How did that happen?" He asked, already lying on top of the sheets.

"It—it was my wrap," I replied, suddenly disoriented. I stepped out of my heels.

I once mentioned to a different client that I had a better memory for voices than for faces. The faces of the few boys I've fallen deeply in love require mental assembly but their voices are there like books always open to the right page.

"That's special," he replied. "I can still remember the day I realized I'd forgotten the sound of my father's voice."

"You don't have any home videos? It's not on tape?" I asked.

"No," he said. And we sat quietly in the impossible sadness.

I kept hearing that line in my head the next day, not because of the words but because of the way they were spoken, like I was his wife of many years or his daughter. Walking in the sun, putting away laundry, sitting in front of my computer: "I know, sweetie. How did that happen?"

I can't understand where the horror comes from, what makes it rise up. In waking life, no one is so mean to me. That's an important point to make.

But in dreams, the man playing the part of my father faked his own death. I thought I saw him shot nearly point blank in front of me, but I realized he was still alive when he appeared behind me to put a hand over my mouth and drag my body underneath his—again and again urgently in strange ways, in water and in big open rooms. I thought it was over but I was wrong. Maybe every way only felt strange because it was with him.

I tried to tell my stepmother because I thought for some reason she would help me, but I wasn't discreet enough. Nothing I said was believed. Women I thought of as friends would look me in the eye and sneer and turn in disgust. No one would say my name. Then everything gave way. I was raped continuously, nonchalantly by my peers sometimes in front of other people.

One handsome young man told me he was going to feed me his shit while he fucked me in the ass. "No," I sobbed, hopeless. He grabbed me by my chin and held my ruined face still in front of his. "You're going to eat shit," he said, and he was right.

Near the end, I was so wretched no one normal could stand to be near me or even hear my voice. I couldn't blame them; I despised myself, always crying and crawling and begging for salvation in between the moments of being mounted. Outside in broad daylight, I tried to run away but the man with me caught me by my hair and neck and pulled me down to my knees. We were at the side of a country road. A short bus full of teenagers drove past.

"Help me!" I mouthed, exaggerated like a mime. I dared not say it aloud. Through the windows their faces registered concern and confusion. I put my hands in prayer at my naked chest, as if that would matter. I knew they would not stop no matter how creased their brows. I knew nothing would change for me.

I stayed up all night reading a book. Morning was still dark because this land is rushing toward winter. I trotted out into the street with wet hair and hailed a cab. I kept ending up on the wrong side of the places I needed to be. I wore a stupid outfit and felt proud. Soon I would be on a new continent in the first country I became fascinated with as a child. For me, the notion of travel was only alighted upon in service of seeing this place.

Earlier I was with a man who told me, "I want to understand you so I can understand an aspect of myself." And "I want to see you for the rest of my life. Even when you're sixty, you'll still look as beautiful to me. If you had come to me twenty years older, I would love you just as much. Even if your body weren't as pleasing, I would adore everything about you."

"What a Roxanne thing to say," I replied. "Climb, animal," is a line from Cyrano. Or maybe it's "climb then, animal" or "climb, you animal," but no, no words other than those two are needed. It was delivered to my brain a perfect phrase and stayed planted there like a gravestone.

I had an uncharacteristic outburst at dinner: "It's a framework to create a nation of indentured servants. You have to convince people that when a child is sick, it's more moral for the child to die than for the healthcare to be cheap. Tell them that life necessitates massive debt and not paying debts is the greatest evil."

In bed, he ducked beneath the covers saying, "I'm going to go under here and see what I can kiss." He said something perceptive about this arrangement negating the need for power games that most participants probably played regardless, too automated and too scared to give them up. He told me, "I never expected I'd feel this way in all my life."

He sent me an email saying that for once he felt entirely at peace. I prepared to live for a brief time in Africa.

From my seat in the felucca I swept my hand through the Nile. Children ran playing in the darkened green by the river's edge and cows plodded dutifully home in the dusk, single file up an incline. There is only one wish while traveling: *let me be changed.* Only one wish coming home. Still impossible.

It was my birthday and almost no one seemed to know. No friends sent messages, which is fitting because I am not the type of person who has friends. One client remembered, someone I'd not seen in a little while. The radio silence made me feel happy and right, as all familiar positions do.

In a different place on another night, a screaming neon riverboat reminded me of Vegas. I'd walked outside to get away from the acrid smoke of a sexy Japanese businessman who watched the belly dancer with a mix of sweet happiness and something inscrutable. I thought of all the immature energy I still have for "bad" things. I could not imagine myself not being with men for money, and that was ok.

The ancient Egyptians believed there would be a judgment after dying that involved weighing the deceased's heart against a feather. If the heart was too heavy, it was fed to a she-demon.

Almost always in the distance lies the Sahara's squalid profundity. At a ruined rest stop, a little girl sat on the steps lamenting as two men walked away, holding out her hands. Too young to be in a burqa. One driver, unprompted, declared that if a woman was not a virgin when married, her family would kill her. This was, he implied, appropriate. His wife was made a mother at thirteen. I couldn't decide if it was a good or bad thing that all of his four children were boys.

I had another bad dream, so similar to the last one. My boyfriend and I sat on our couch with a man between us. My lazy legs were splayed over the man's lap and the sensation of my boyfriend stroking my calves and thighs was suddenly crowded out by the feeling of his cock pushing inside me. I excused myself as calmly as I could and walked into the bedroom.

He followed me and I yelled at him, "I'm not going to have sex with you in front of my father! I mean, I'm not going to have sex with you *on* my father!" I was horny and wanted to masturbate instead of having sex, a luxury I doubted I'd be afforded. Before I could, a different man swept me up and away to another room.

I understood this holding me man had rented me for sex and it was as though I'd never been so used in my life. The idea was like ice water on my brain. Yet when he was pressed to me on the floor, I rolled over and flipped open a record book, and saw that I'd been doing this for a long time, usually seeing several men a day for hours at a time. I had a momentary impression that it was my father who arranged this. Everyone was broken down into strange categories of fetishes and tastes, most of which made no sense. Categories like "bra+talk+feet."

The young man was tall and kept his body welded to mine, his arms wrapped around me wherever we moved. I was pre or past verbal, mostly only whimpering and crying without many tears, saying, "No, no." My own arms were behind me or bent against my chest, dormant. He wore jeans and his absurdly large erection filled them. It was a cock so huge it only belongs in a dream. He kept kissing my murmuring lips almost chastely, with tenderness.

He put his hand against my cunt and it was wet, I felt his fingers through the netting. "I'm going to fuck you very hard in the ass, for a long time," he told me. "No, no," I shook my head. "Like this then," he offered, and trapped a buzzing vibrator between us. "No, no," I cried again, because I didn't want to come without his cock inside of me. It was the most beautiful day. Sunlight seeped into every pocket of the house. I swear I could even hear birds.

In awake life, a client sent me an email from his phone. It was unintentionally cut short but I stared at it for some time for before I realized this. "Charlotte," it read. "Many thanks for your mess"

He sometimes says our first date was a month in Europe, which is not quite true. There were periods of melancholy and bitterness between us in that long time, probably because I had no business doing anything other than recovering from a break up that would become even uglier in the coming weeks. Our sex was strange and endless. I had my first vaginal orgasm in Geneva, after masturbating alone with a showerhead, after an even earlier bout of long fucking, and immediately after or rather, during, what felt like two hours of being glued together, and the orgasm was probably as much a confused cry for mercy as it was any sign of pleasure.

When I think about how in love he must have been, I don't feel guilty as much as I feel humbled and regretful that he'll never be that in love with me again. It was a love that required a good deal of unfamiliarity, but he still loves me in familiarity. He laughs when I'm being obnoxious; I notice that. I am capable of gratitude even though it does not come naturally to me. Mostly I am increasingly disinterested in being loved and instead yearn for some situation in which I am compelled to love greatly.

Still the dreams: the revolting face of a young man who seems to be my romantic partner, tiny infants crawling on the floor of a grotesque supermarket, stepped upon by male customers who don't see them there amid the refuse and damaged produce.

There is a scene in *The Last Unicorn*, a film I watched many times when I was young in spite of the fact that it must be one of the darker, more adult movies ever made, in which the unicorn frees a caged harpy. The harpy is hideous and menacing, an uglier version of a vulture, and it's understood that she will most likely kill any creature nearby once freed. But the unicorn releases her because, as the harpy tells her, "We are sisters, you and I." So there is no choice.

I will also confess that when I see older clients whose health problems render them erection-less but who still like me to stroke their cocks, I often think of the skeleton drinking his empty bottle of wine and moaning, "But I *remember* . . ."

"You look smaller than usual. I mean, don't get me wrong, you were always small but you look . . . bonier."

"Thank you for corroborating my experience!" I said. "I've been feeling bonier ever since I got back from Egypt." And I have. I even used that exact descriptor.

Moments later, when I was sitting on my heels in front of him, naked, he put his hands on the tops of my thighs and said, "See, bones? You look good! But—"

"Those aren't bones, that's muscle!"

"Let's not be kidding ourselves," he said, and we kissed.

I made him laugh harder than I'd ever seen him laugh by describing something stupid from an old *Adbusters* magazine. And the sex felt good and it felt almost new, like something special, and that was miraculous.

Good things are happening in other parts of my life. I think if I could tell you about all this clearly, you would be proud of me.

"This is getting better, isn't it?" my teacher asked, positioning herself against my leg. I laughed a little, made a face.

"But it is, isn't it?" she pressed.

"Yes," I admitted.

"I know, sometimes it's still discouraging," she said, looking down, moving her hands, kneading release and length. "But be not discouraged."

Date in the morning, date overnight, date the next night. Two thousand dollars worth of lingerie, which does not translate into as much lingerie as one would hope. This Is Retirement.

Minor panic attack during a blowjob. I made a fist with my left hand between his legs and watched my knuckles blue white like baby teeth, then curled up in a fetal position afterward and thought of a contemplation I like, about what it would be like to live with perfect energy. Sometimes it's good for an attitude adjustment but this time I pushed the thought away angrily and told myself instead: *I just need to calm down right now.*

My favorite quote, Heraclitus: No man steps in the same river twice, for it is not the same river and he is not the same man. On graduation weekend, what feels like ages ago, the class I taught had a river theme. The river is always there, the river of—whatever. Love, serenity, wholeness, perfect energy. You can dip into it when you need it, when you remember it. Maybe, with practice, you find a chance to be happy.

I didn't wash my hair for three days after and it was not only to save his scent. Normally I want my own smell back. If there is any chance he feels the way I do, I may never hear from him again. He is too good,

I think, to play with that fire. I, of course, cannot refuse. During one moment after he tried to articulate the conflux of emotions from the wake of our sex, he asked if he was making any sense.

"You don't want to hurt anyone," I said. Because if there is one thing I recognize, it is earnest, useless intention.

Maybe he feels no connection beyond the physical. Just before he came for the third time, he moaned, "You're so hot," and if I was not hurt I was at least disappointed. I don't even want to be attractive to men anymore, and lately base attention seems even more ubiquitous than usual.

During what should have been a period of resolution and resignation, the universe presents me with one beautiful man after another, with envelopes full of wettish worn cash, as in, *why on earth would you give this up?* It's rare for me, in person, to be approached by men as good-looking and sexy as the ones who pay me. I suppose it's because so many sexy ones are married.

I heard a song lyric—"it's all been forgiven"—that struck me as the most profoundly kind concept any human mind could believe. In a more new age-y construct, one might say there's nothing that needs to be forgiven. But that's plainly not true. If you're an honest person, you know the list of deeds for which you must beg forgiveness only gets longer. Because as you fine-tune your radar for pain in the world, you fine-tune your memory for every moment when you created it.

A new client told me he has two sons, and I said, "I bet you're a good father."

"I try," he said. "It's not easy for me." And I knew he was right. As soon as the platitude had left my mouth, I knew I was wrong. For a moment I'd believed that because he is a good person, he would be a good father, but no, I could see he wasn't. He is usually cold, he won't tell them he loves them, he will be silent on many topics when they need his voice. Not out of cruelty but because of who he is. He will fail them by being himself, and even trying harder will not change that.

A puddle so deep it was a pond, full of rocks. I almost fell in. We practiced asana near it, in the scrubby, ugly space around with people of all ages and colors and dress. A man in front of me dug in the sand with his bald head, diving forward over his crossed legs and then rolling back up.

"What's this pose called?" The two people with me joked as we sat in ardha matsyendrasana. "Prasa? Prasa? Prasarita padottanasana?" And in my head, I heard my Sanskrit teacher's slurred, flat honk of "prasareeta," her pronunciation mocking the way Americans usually attempt the word.

An impeccably dressed Mexican man led us through a chant. He kept making us repeat the word "dharinam" but added an extra bounce on the end, so it was "dharinam-nam." Then he silenced us and shouted "Cuál está adentro aquí?" smacking his sternum with his hand.

"Tú corazón," someone said but then—"La liberación," someone else yelled out, correcting him. "La última liberación!" Many people nodded and made rolling motions with their body. "It's like a cult," I thought. But I still believed it was right.

Earlier I'd ridden a schoolroom lifted into the air by a giant wave. The male teacher came to me after we hit ground and started handing me pamphlets. He was panicking, I realized. We thought we'd all die soon because the ocean wanted to swallow us. "Come here," I'd told him, and opened my arms so I could hold him against me. He laid on top of me and it was bliss.

Do you feel it too, with this new year? My bones keep whispering to me "it's time, it's time, it's time." There's only horizon.

It'd been so long since I saw a face that excited me. Then I saw his, with its wide lips and strong bones, and his mouth's slow way of unraveling words. After I met him—I made him laugh and we had mutual friends, so there was a sense of relaxation between us—I had a dream in which he excoriated me. He yelled about what a bad person I was, how I had nothing in common with him and would never be allowed to taint his life, but a smile was building in me as I listened because I knew this all meant he realized what we meant to each other, and he was scared. And I knew I only had to deliver myself to him and he could scream or cry or even beat me but we would be tied together forever and he would not be able to resist fucking me. In this sleep reality, I knew where he lived and in my certainty I went to him, and when he opened the door he was speechless and bereft of escape. The thing between us was not love because it was more powerful and more terrifying, prehistoric, primordial.

I have dreams (you know I have dreams) but it's rare for there to be that much intensity around someone who exists in my waking life. I thought about finding him the next morning and asking him simply if he too had had a vision. Not about me specifically. I would just ask, "Did you have a dream?" I felt like there was not much I couldn't ask him or tell him. Like "You have a beautiful face," without it being a come on.

But I didn't. I wasn't scared, I was wary. There are a lot of pointless connections I bring back to the morning after: I dream I'm smoking a cigar and loving it, having never smoked a cigar, and then that day there's no one else at the nail salon but a middle aged white man with an unlit cigar trapped in his mouth throughout his manicure and pedicure. I get signals that are not much use, like a flash in the middle of my college retail job, wondering what would happen if my brother were in a car accident, and then two hours later I meet my parents at the hospital. I believe what I see, because what I see often becomes my living truth, but it's like looking down into a clear lake. There might be some visible network of roots, but you don't have to plunge your hand in and tear at them with your fist.

After a few more encounters, I gathered he's in some type of a relationship with a woman who seems radically wrong for him, which I suppose will be revealed to each of them soon enough.

"We're moving into your building!" she told me the last time I saw her. And so it goes, this laughably tenacious universe. "We'll be your neighbors!"

I'd gotten it wrong in the dream. In reality, the door would come to me.

Before we met, I read his Wikipedia page and laughed. I wondered if there was any way to tease him about it without seeming like I was making fun.

But there was barely any way to talk to him at all. Soon I could no longer bear to look into the emotional maw of his face. He probably didn't want me looking there.

He left me alone in his bedroom briefly and I looked out through his windows, past my own nude reflection to the New York City skyline. I felt the entirety of an expansive absence that had no space to contain any emotion other than itself. It reached beyond any language I knew.

I'll be alright, I told myself as I crouched over his body, facing the brilliant panes of glass once again. *Even if I'm alone for a long time, I'll be ok*. I like being alone. I may even like this work mostly because it drives me further into myself.

He was moving the next day. His apartment was empty of everything except the bed and boxes.

"You have such a beautiful view," I said.

"But you don't notice the view after a while," he replied, barely glancing over his shoulder.

My boyfriend says I'm not trustworthy because I have so many names. I can't conceive of living without them. I can't see why it makes me dishonest, although I was having tea with a client/friend recently and I said I wondered how much the internet will spur the fragmentation of our personalities. It seems to me the worthier mission is to live like who you are all the time, completely, everywhere, to wear your singular name like a skin.

A client asked me to sign *Coming and Crying* and I asked under which name, and he said I didn't have to if I didn't want to. I signed Charlotte Shane and I somehow misspelled it. I'd never written the name by hand before.

I'm earning wrinkles, the finest feathering of lines below each eye. I only notice them during work appointments because the makeup makes them more noticeable. I feel a mix of pride and horror. I like the way they look but I know no one else will and one day soon when the rest of me begins looking old, too, I'll hate them.

I took a class with my new neighbor and tried to be only in myself but I did look at his bare arms as he sat behind the desk, and at his legs as the fabric of his shorts slid slowly away when he was inverted. I wondered if I'd lost any chance of having sex with him by thinking about it so much. I didn't try to make myself attractive before coming. I was unshowered. I shook out my morning hair and folded over my legs.

"You were a philosophy major," one man asked me. "No," I lied, confused. I made something up. I can't remember what I write on my ads or in emails or on my website.

I saw a young man who reminded me of my brother. No no no, oh no, I thought, as soon as I met him. No no, you should have a girlfriend. I can't take your money. I can't spend the night. I cataloged all the features of his face that were like my brother's, and therefore like mine, and also those that were not.

Sometimes, in the winter, it's so dark and the train moves so slowly that it seems as though we've fallen away from the world.

I had a dream that my father found my blog and knew it was mine, that he sent me emails I (barely) skimmed on my phone asking why I'm with so many men, had I really been pregnant? He wrote, "Why so many men?" or possibly, "Your parade of men," neither of which are phrases he would ever use. I felt the power of his revulsion and also the baffled pain underneath his ignorance. The emails frightened me but simultaneously reminded me how little he knew me. I felt, as I did in high school, that I owed him nothing.

But I did not wake up feeling well.

In retrospect, my recent disclosure to a client was horrible. I gave so much away because I felt like—what? He was listening? I told him dozens of honest things about me but why. It seems so shameful now. Now I am ashamed.

Yet I liked him.

"You're so cute," I said.

"Why?" He asked.

I didn't understand the question. "Your face. It just is."

I couldn't tell if my being truthful was a tactic, or if it was cavalier, or what any of it meant. What any of it means. Everyone ends up alone, sometimes I think I am trying very hard to emphasize how many times

I will end up alone. He had one of those thick cocks with the heft of butchered meat. He was gentle and held my hips still against him. He apologized for being hairy and I asked him if he didn't like it. He said, considering, "I'm conscious of it."

At some point I came. At some point I went away.